ILLUSTRATED LIBRARY OF WONDERS,

CHARLES SCRIBNER & CO. NEW-YORK.

THE

WONDERS OF WATER

FROM THE FRENCH OF

GASTON TISSANDIER.

EDITED,

WITH NUMEROUS ADDITIONS,

BY SCHELE DE VERE, D.D. L.L.D.,

OF THE UNIVERSITY OF VIRGINIA, AUTHOR OF "STUDIES IN ENGLISH,"
"AMERICANISMS," ETC.

With Sixty-four Illustrations.

NEW YORK:
CHARLES SCRIBNER AND COMPANY,
1872.

Entered according to act of Congress in the year 1871, by
CHARLES SCRIBNER AND COMPANY,
In the office of the Librarian of Congress at Washington.

RIVERSIDE, CAMBRIDGE:
PRINTED BY H. O. HOUGHTON AND COMPANY.

WATER.

CONTENTS.

I.—THE OCEAN.

II.—THE SYSTEM OF CIRCULATION.

V.—THE USES OF WATER.

LIST OF ILLUSTRATIONS.

I.

THE OCEAN.

"The element which we term fluid, mobile and capricious, does not really change, but is regularity itself."—MICHELET.

"It is science which has discovered within less than a century the true poetry of the sea. The mariner sounding the depths of the abyss, and the meteorologist studying his atmospheric chart and investigating the causes of tempests, have greatly contributed to dissipate vain and superstitious terrors, and in proportion as we cease to fear this mighty mass of moving water, we admire its sublimity."—A. ESQUIROS.

"Whether as solid, liquid or gas, water is one of the most admirable substances in nature."—TYNDALL.

CHAPTER I.

A GLANCE AT THE OCEAN.

"A SAILOR placed in the midst of the ocean experiences sentiments analogous to those of the astronomer, when he views the stars and interrogates with his eyes the blue vault of heaven." MAURY.

There is no more imposing spectacle than that afforded by the sea when our view is limited by no shore. "Whilst contemplating the Ocean," says Humboldt, "he who delights in creating a world of his own, where the spontaneous activity of his mind can exercise itself unshackled, can feel himself penetrated with the sense of infinitude." In watching the ceaseless march of the waves, which creep gently upon the shore, the flying foam which alternately appears and disappears, and the restless undulation of the billows chasing one another with a plaintive measure, one can well understand how the inventive imagination of man should have personified this mass of inert matter, and one feels no surprise at Schleider's words, "Its vast surface rises and falls as if it had been gifted with the power of a gentle respiration." The observer looks everywhere for some distant horizon, but the liquid circle with which he is surrounded melts so insensibly into a vaporous outline, that earth and sky blend intc each other and become one. He tries to measure the depth and immensity of the abyss, but is arrested in his calculations by an overwhelming sense of the mysteries which he feels instinctively lie concealed under the veil with which they are covered by nature. He remembers the solemn words: "His way is in the seas: His path is in the great waters."

EXTENT.

"An immense mass of water covers the larger portion of the globe."

BUFFON.

"On the globe," says Michelet, "water prevails, land is the exception," notwithstanding which, it is by no means easy to estimate the superficial extent of the sea. The slow changes of the firm land, which rises or sinks, the waves, which are incessantly at work diminishing the rocky shores, the banks of madrepores and polypes, which daily rise higher and higher from the bosom of the sea—all these causes constantly modify the slope of continents and cause perpetual alterations in the form of our globe. It has been, however, clearly ascertained that the sea covers two thirds of the surface of the globe, hence more than 52,000,000 square miles are under water. The sea is, moreover, very unequally distributed, the Southern hemisphere being more abundantly provided with water than the Northern, so that the terrestrial globe may be roughly divided into two parts, one being looked upon as the world of the sea and the other of the dry land.

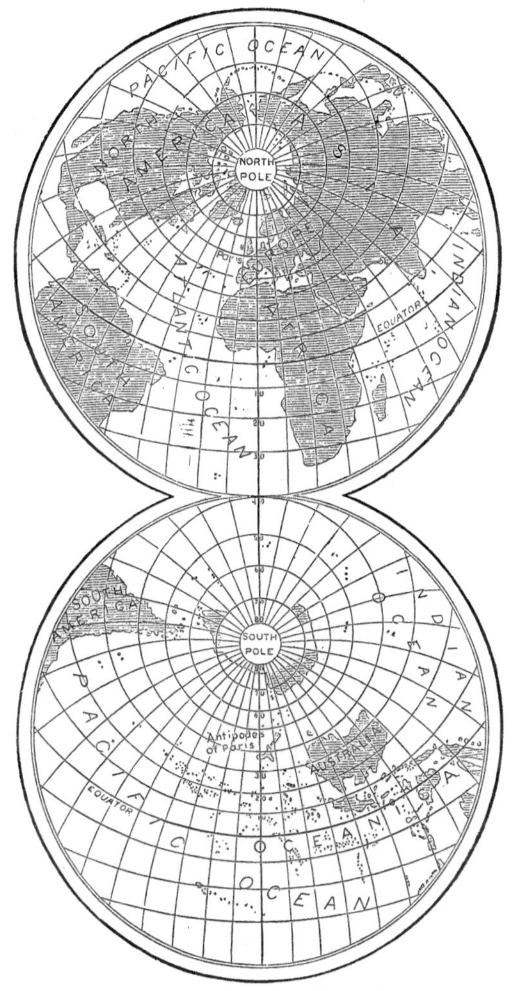

LAND AND WATER HEMISPHERES.

In our day, at least, the liquid element covers nearly three fourths of the surface, the solid soil only a little more than a fourth. The largest mass of continental land lies on the northeastern part of the globe, while the ocean prevails on the south-western portion. The former is, of course, the principal stage of the history of our race ; here alone the surface of the earth shines forth in all its beauty and usefulness. The miniature part of the globe, where only the smallest of continents and an innumerable host of islands lie scattered like the stars in heaven, it consists almost exclusively in the uniform monotonous element of water ; incapable of supporting large groups of races, or of developing them according to great and distinct types, its inhabitants are mostly in a state of primitive barbarism, in which they have remained perhaps for thousands of years. It is not quite a century since they also have been admitted into the great brotherhood of nations by the enormous development of navigation and colonization. In the very centre of this aquatic half of our globe lies New Zealand, and not far from it New Holland, islands which, on account of their peculiar and exceptional position, cannot fail to have a grand future.

Even where the waters still cover the earth, as during the Deluge, life is present, and beyond measure abundant. For this vast surface of waters is not quiet and inanimate ; far from it ; for in its dark bosom new myriads of beings are born incessantly, day after day. There live and breathe and move in its mysterious depths vast hosts of animals and plants, which surpass those of the firm land, if not in beauty of form and perfection of shapes, certainly in numbers and in variety. Charles Darwin has stated that our forests did not shelter as many animals as the lower forest regions of the ocean, where seaweeds and fuci unfold their soft foliage; and even at the very bottom of the great deep, the soundings made last year (1870) have proved that a fullness of life is pervading the faint twilight. Hence it was not the immeasurable mass of water only, but its teeming, boundless fertility also, which made the Greek philosophers look upon the sea as "the house and mother of life," which caused Indians, sages and Egyptian priests to kneel down on the banks of sacred streams and adore them as visible images of the Deity.

DEPTH.

"We perceive as many inequalities on the bottom of the sea as on the surface of the earth."
BUFFON.

During many centuries the most erroneous ideas prevailed on the subject of the depth of the sea, and the early nations beheld in this vast liquid waste an impassable barrier, a terrible gulf without bottom and without shore. The fathom line seems to have been thrown at random into unknown space, and the ocean appeared to repel the efforts of those navigators who sought to penetrate its secrets. The operation of sounding the sea is one attended with great difficulties. The fathom line, continually

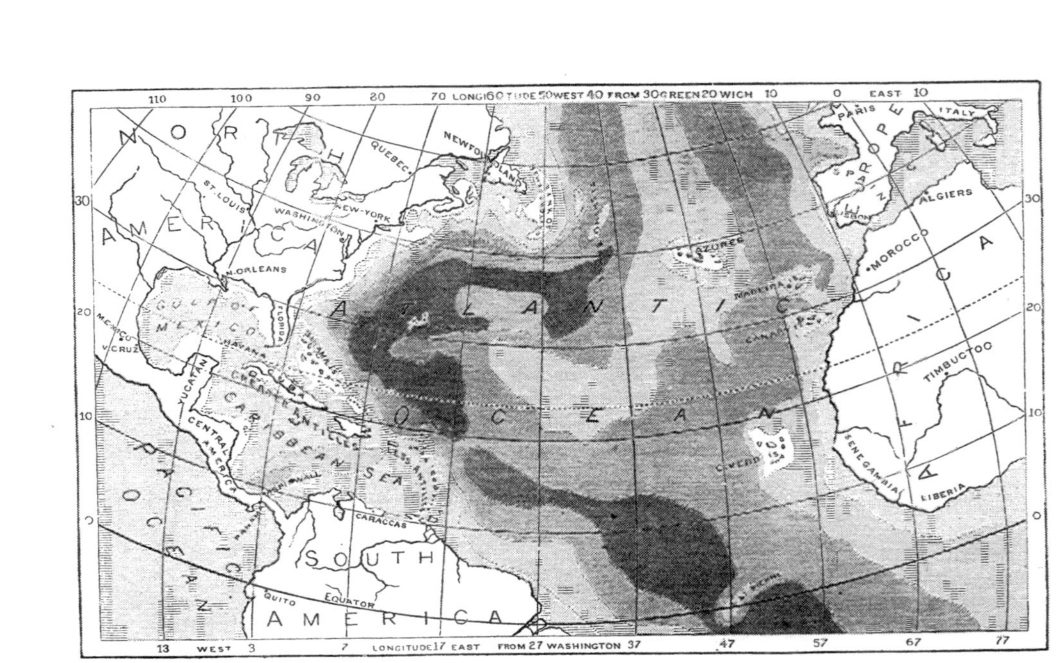

CHART OF THE DEPTH OF THE ATLANTIC OCEAN.

drawn aside by the currents of the sea, is apt to take an oblique direction instead of sinking down in a vertical line. It continues to run out even after it has reached the bottom.

Notwithstanding this, ingenious contrivances have been invented capable of remedying these inconveniences, and reliable measurements have been arrived at by Maury and other navigators. Brooke's line has given the most satisfactory results; after having touched the bottom of the sea, it brings back specimens of great value to science.* A ball of between six and seven pounds weight is pierced, and through the whole is passed a loose iron rod, terminated at its lower end by a cylindrical cavity As soon as the rod reaches the bottom the ball is set free by the action of a lever, and remains beneath the water, while the rod is easily brought up again to the surface. The figure shows on the left the line before it has reached the bottom, and on the right the ball falling in consequence of the shock into the water. The mean depth of the ocean, according to Humboldt, is nearly 10,000 feet; according to Young, that of the Atlantic Ocean

---

* It is in a plateau of the Atlantic that Brooke's invention brought the first specimens from the bottom of the sea. Though in appearance earthy, the matter extracted from the depth of the sea was composed of microscopic shells, in perfect preservation, belonging to the family of the foraminifera. In the Indian Ocean, on the contrary, spiculæ of sponge, incrusted with flint, have been found at the depth of 12,800 feet. It is evident, therefore, that in the depth of the sea are to be found soils of various kinds, calcareous and siliceous.

must be nearly 3,300 feet, and that of the Pacific, 13,000 feet. Dupetit Thouars has taken two celebrated soundings, one in the great southern ocean, where he found bottom at 13,000 feet—the other in

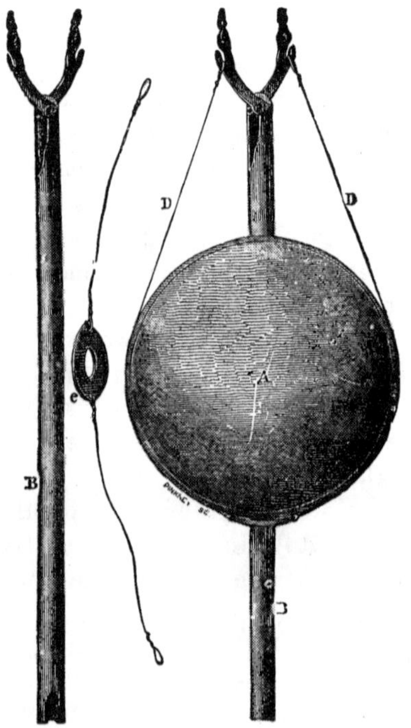

Brooke's Sounding Rod and Ball.

the great equinoctial ocean, of which the depth is 11,500 feet. Not far from the shores of the United States, Lieutenant Walsh, U.S.N., paid out a vertical sounding line nearly 33,000 feet, which fact contradicts the calculations of M. Laplace, who, founding his opinion on the influence exercised upon our planet by the sun and moon, declared it to be impossible for the depth of the sea to exceed 25,000 feet. However this may be, it has been shown by demonstrative evidence that the ocean does reach immense depths, which, however, does not appear to surpass in any case the height of some of the loftier mountains of India and America. Sometimes, again, it covers the earthy crust only with a thin sheet of water. At the mouth of the Po the depth of the sea does not much exceed 150

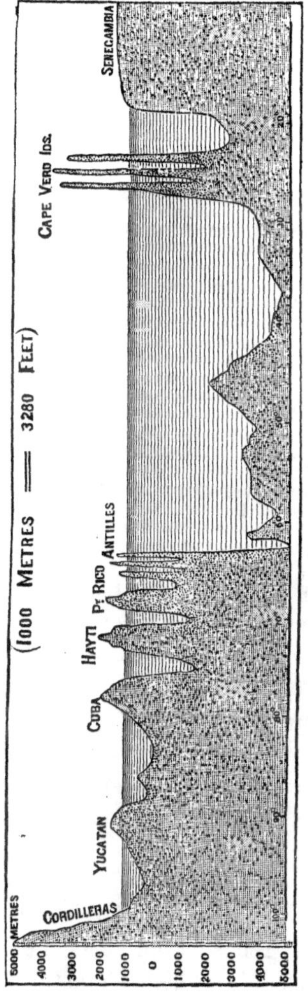

Profile of the Depths of the Atlantic Ocean.

feet; while the bottom of the Baltic never sinks beyond 650 feet, and certain parts of the ocean would not entirely cover some of our public buildings. The dome of the Pantheon at Paris would rise above the level of the Straits of Dover, and this shallowness of the straits which separate France from Great Britain encourages the hope that the two countries may be united ere long by a submarine tunnel. It will not be long before science gives us yet more intimate and accurate information on the subject of the depth of the ocean, and Maury, when still Director of the Observatory at Washington already constructed an admirable Orographic chart of the basin of the Atlantic. On this chart, which we here reproduce, the dark shades represent the depths, averaging 23,000 feet, and the lighter ones those of from 5,900 to 6,500 feet.

These same variations of depth, seen in outline, show more fully their irregularities, and the vertical aspect of the immense trench which separates the Old World from the New World, exhibits the hilly uneven character of the ground which lies beneath the waste of waters.

If the sea were to retreat from this gigantic furrow, leaving bare the terrestrial epidermis, what vestiges of shipwrecks would be disclosed amid the ripples of the shallow water? "Then," says Maury, in his Physical Geography of the Sea, "would doubtless come to light that terrible combination of human bones, relics of all sorts, heavy anchors, precious pearls, out of which fantastic imagination has woven so many troubled dreams." Thus, the bottom of the sea is formed of mountains and valleys, elevations and table-lands, ravines, and slopes, and hills, and plains. Our continents are, in point of fact, nothing more than non-submerged summits of these mountains, and the dry portions of the globe appear more or less according as the sea reveals them; while the waters, in obedience to the laws of gravity, collect by reason of their mobility in the vast basins below, and spread themselves over the lower parts of the terrestrial covering. If the surface of the globe, instead of being ruffled and uneven, were as smooth and uniform as a ball of ivory, the sea would cover it entirely with a liquid of about 650 feet in thickness.

Assuming a mean average of 13,000 feet for the depth of the sea, it has been calculated that the ocean constitutes a volume 150,095,456,500 cubic feet of water. In order to contain this liquid mass it would require a spherical bottle of from 50 to 60 leagues in diameter! The sheet of water which covers almost entirely the surface of the globe is considerable, relatively to the dry portions, which are termed *terra firma*, but it is very little, compared with the whole mass of our planet. If we divide the entire globe into 1,786 parts of equal weight, one of those portions will give the total weight of the waters of the sea!

COLOR.

"Cæruleum Mare."—Virgil.

The water of the sea, if enclosed in a bottle, appears colorless, but seen from the shore, it appears generally of a beautiful green, and when viewed from a greater distance it assumes an azure hue. The Polar Seas are, according to Scoresby, of an ultramarine blue, the Mediterranean is sky blue, (Costaz) and the poets themselves would find it difficult to describe the exquisite effects of color in the Bay of Naples, when the rays of the sun cause the waves to sparkle with a thousand fires like the sapphire and the emerald. The Black Sea owes its name to its frequent tempests; the White Sea to its masses of floating ice.

The natural hue of the waters is frequently modified by the presence of animal and vegetable life; it is thus that the polar regions are at times streaked with millions of medusæ, the yellow shade of which, in combination with the blue of the water, produces green. Certain parts of the sea become at times suddenly white as milk, while at others they present the color of blood. These singular phenomena, which were observed and noted by ancient authors, are due to vast quantities of sea-weed which float upon the waves and disguise its true color.

The Red Sea has frequently presented the appearance of a sea of blood. In July, 1843, for two days the natural color of the waves disappeared beneath a pellicle of carmine. Analogous facts have come at various times under the observation of *savants* in the Gulf of Oman, and not far from the mouth of the Tagus, where the sailors of the ship "Oreole" saw, in 1845, the waters of the Atlantic covered with a purple mantle, which rapidly spread over a surface of over six square miles. These accidental colorations were for many centuries a source of terror to the superstitious; but man has now ceased to behold in the fortuitous apparition of microscopic algæ floating on the surface of the water, signs of the anger of heaven, or presages of coming calamities.

The black mud and the yellow sand which carpet the bottom of the sea modify the color of transparent, shallow waters, and produce the most diverse effects, owing to the refraction and play of light. The state of the sky is also a cause of variations, and the sea may be looked upon as a vast mirror, changing its aspect according to the images which are reflected upon it. Black and sombre when thick clouds hide the rays of the sun, it attires itself in a thousand sparkling fires, when the vault of the firmament is transparent and azure. Nature has, says the poet—

> "Made the skies to gleam o'er the ocean,
> And the ocean to reflect the skies."

In some places, as in the neighborhood of the West India Islands, the sea is so perfectly transparent, that a ship traversing those waters seems to hang suspended in the air, and the inexperienced traveller is seized with vertigo as he looks down into the vast deep, and beholds there, for the first time, a whole world of plants and animals full of life and action.

In the polar regions, on the other hand, it is greenish, in the Gulf of Guinea white, near the Maldives black, on the coast of California red as cinnabar, in the Persian Sea green,—and as with every rolling wave and every fleeting cloud the colors change—as in the day, sunlight and reflected light weave strange fantastic images on the dark green surface, and by the aid of the wind a thousand beautiful patterns, while at night countless mollusks light it up in red, yellow and green hues, the ocean may well be called the fairy kingdom of Light.

It is probable, however, that the water has a color of its own, which appears to be either blue or green. In this respect it resembles the air, colorless to a certain thickness, and blue when our eyes can sound its depths. As we descend into the ocean, the emerald shades gradually disappear, the light of day fades away, and we penetrate little by little into a gloomy twilight, and are at length hurried beneath thick darkness.

During the night the sea becomes radiant with a strange lustre. The white foam is replaced by fiery streamers, which continue to unroll themselves until lost to sight; each wave turning upon itself shines with a mysterious brilliancy; each billow sheds luminous rays. These phenomena are the the effect of an infinitude of animalculæ, which illumine the undulations of the waves, while the stars are lighting up the broad expanse of the heavens. Nothing is more striking than this spectacle, which appears in all its splendor and under the most varied aspects on the surface of southern seas. Sailors talk of enormous balls of fire, which appear to roll over the waves, of cones of light pirouetting over themselves, shining garlands, glittering serpents, and of bright clouds which wander over the waves in the midst of the darkness. The phenomenon is in such cases complicated by a mirage, and the nocturnal dance of phosphorescent animals explains all

The Phosphorescent Sea.

these marvels. The sea is not a vast liquid desert; there is not a single drop of water inaccessible to the manifestations of life, and in which the prodigious fecundity of nature does not bring into play the activity of a whole animate world.

TEMPERATURE.

The ocean consists of three immense thermic basins, the two first being situated at the poles, while the third, lying midway between the two others, is situated near the equator. The temperature of the sea, heated by the action of the solar rays, under the equator, is tolerably high; but at a depth of 1,200 fathoms it sinks down to 40°. The further we go from the equator, so much nearer to the surface do we find this temperature of 40°; and on reaching a latitude of 45° it appears as near as 600 fathoms. At this distance from the equator there appears to exist all round the globe a zone, in which the temperature of the ocean is constant and uniform in all depths. In proportion as we recede from this limit and approach either of the poles, we find a lowering of the level of uniform temperature, and it is only found at a depth of 750 fathoms, in the latitude of 70°. Near the poles themselves the surface of the water is frozen, and formidable glaciers float over it during the whole year. Immense mountains of ice are constantly being drifted along by the waves; and the light, as it plays over these transparent masses, produces one of the finest spectacles given to man to contemplate on earth.

Scenes really magical break the monotony of these arctic regions, where lofty structures of ice

FLOATING MOUNTAIN OF ICE.

present themselves to the dazzled gaze of the voyager. Light gusts of wind appear to impart a gentle, quivering motion to the transparent shafts and the floating colonnades, when lo! the whole disappears as if beneath an enchanter's wand, to reappear at a distance under new forms; and though not an atom of vegetation bears witness to the vitality of the earth or charms the eye, the sky produces pictures of the most thrilling beauty. But at what cost does the voyager behold all this strange loveliness? In order to see it he must endure the long nights of an arctic winter, and live in the midst of frightful solitudes; hidden under a pall of thick darkness, everything around him is mysterious and terrible; and the strange sounds made by the icebergs, as they dash against one another and crumble into fragments, fill the mind with the most mournful presentiments. Terrible indeed is it when the luminary from which we derive both heat and life is no longer to be seen above the horizon.

CHAPTER II.

THE MOTION OF THE SEA—SUPERFICIAL AGITATION.

"Wave follows wave; billow doth billow chase."—DELILLE.

THE water of the sea is in ceaseless agitation; its surface obeys the impulses of the wind, and its waves dash themselves madly and forever against the rocky shore. To look upon this incessant struggle between land and water, this irreconcilable strife betwixt solid and liquid, it might seem as though inert matter, jealous of organic being, strove to imitate the activity of life. Whilst gazing upon the waves which dash against the cliffs, one feels inclined to question whether this heaving mass be only a thing—only an inorganic element; one feels tempted to believe that a breath of life causes this movement in these never-resting waves, animating a being which has its moments of anger and of calmness, whose voice, at times sweet and harmonious, can anon become menacing as the cries that escape from an oppressed bosom.

Nevertheless the agitation is only superficial, and amounts to amazingly little when compared with the vast mass of the ocean. The fiercest tempest that ever lashes the waves of the Atlantic produces but a faint ripple on the surface; its waves never rise above twenty feet. When wave meets wave, of course a fierce contest arises; and as the two terrible combatants grapple with each other, the spray rises aloft, and is, at times, tossed a hundred or a hundred and twenty feet high. But even such a distance counts but a trifle when the sea has a depth of thousands of fathoms.

> "Far, far beneath, the noise of tempests dieth,
> And silver waves chime ever peacefully;
> And no rude storm, how fierce so e'er it flieth,
> Disturbs the Sabbath of that deeper sea."

It is a very different thing, however, with the tidal waves. These affect the whole mass, and the entire ocean seems to arise in a gigantic effort to follow the moon, which it adores, and finding all endeavors vain, to fall despairing back into its place again. They produce sudden and fearful effects where they appear regularly; but far greater, and sometimes truly awful phenomena, when, as spring tides, they overleap all bounds, or unexpectedly rise where they were never seen before. Of old, these fearful, sudden visitations were ascribed by the superstitious to the wrath of some offended dignity; and it is well known that Aristotle was reported to have drowned himself because he was unable to fathom the mystery of these irregular tides. Even inland lakes are not always exempt from such catastrophes. As late as the summer of 1871 the town of Duluth, in Minnesota, was thus inundated by a considerable tide rising from Lake Superior, and making repeated assaults upon the apparently doomed city.

Storm Scene.

Such gigantic waves, while they are to be met with in almost all seas, have different effects: near the coasts they give birth to breakers, which are a just object of dread to mariners; at the mouth of rivers they produce solid bars, and this phenomenon assumes enormous proportions on our own shores, where the largest fluvial arteries in the world fall into the ocean. At the period of the high tides nothing is more terrible than the struggle between the waves of the sea and the current of the Amazon. Instead of requiring six hours for the rising tide, the sea rises in three minutes. The whole breadth of the river is overrun by one tremendous wave 15 feet deep, and by a legion of waves which follow one another, and, rushing up the stream, cause the air to echo with a fearful thunder. All obstacles are overthrown or destroyed; trees are uprooted or snapped in two; entire plains, lifted from their level, are drifted away, and everything swept out to a distance of 600 feet from the coast.

It is to tidal waves, coming from opposite directions and meeting, that the not less formidable phenomena of whirlpools are due, once famous in song and story. Among these the most celebrated used to be the Maelstrom. It was represented as a gulf perpetually roaring, always yawning to swallow up any ship that might venture too near its formidable jaws; an everlasting waterspout, which was believed to make the effects of its violence felt in the district of Lofoden in Norway, and indeed more or less over the whole North Sea. Waves of a prodigious height, liquid mountains, animated by a hurried and giddy movement, really rush from all points of the compass towards the same point, pursuing each other with fury, and at length suddenly disappearing as if swallowed up in a deep abyss. But its size and its power have alike been exaggerated; and recent explorations have proved its comparative insignificance.

In like manner, all the romance that once clustered around the far-famed Scylla and Charybdis has long since given way to sober fact and thorough knowledge. Where Ulysses once trembled, and Phœnician sailors brought rich offerings to appease the pagan deities, Sicilian fishermen now sail boldly, and at best utter a thoughtless Ave, in honor of the great queen of the seas. Their terrors have passed away with ignorance and superstition; and like the Maelstrom they are avoided only when continued winds or fierce tempests have made them peculiarly violent.

THE TIDES.

"If the waters offer matter of wonderment to our sight, it is mainly in the spectacle of the ebb and flow of the sea."—PLINY.

The waves are the caprices of the sea; they vary according to localities, following the impetus of the wind, and are not governed by any force which is constant in its effects. The sea is, however, agitated by other more regular movements, which may be looked upon as the most admirable wheels in the great mechanism of Nature. Our globe is isolated in the immensity of the universe, but it is not solitary. Ever subject to the influence of those stars which people space, it yields to their attraction; it is in close relations with the skies. Even as the flower looks up to the sun, turning its face towards the great source of light, so twice a day the ocean swells her bosom and raises herself up under the powerful attraction of sun and moon. The combined action of the two luminaries sweeps daily around the globe two immense waves, which rise

Equinoctial Tidal Wave.

to their utmost heights at the new and the full moon. During six months of the year the high tides occur in the day time, and during the other six months at night. At that period they encroach upon the shore in order to bathe those parts which have heretofore been sheltered from contact with the waters. The most considerable tides rise in the open sea to a height of about 20 feet; but as they approach the seaboard of the continents, which appear to oppose barriers to their invasion, they sweep rapidly in, clear all obstacles, and sometimes even rise 60 feet above their mean level.

All seas are more or less subject to this marvellous influence of the tides; everywhere, beneath the empire of the waves, ebb and flow depress and elevate the liquid surface. Incessantly opposed and modified by the shape of the coasts, by headlands, by currents, and by the force of the winds, the action of the tides is most felt in straits and in gulfs. Some of the highest are met with in the gulf of St. Malo, in the British Channel, and in the Pentland Frith. Their vertical height is nearly 50 feet off Ushant, 45 between Jersey and St. Malo, and from 60 to 75 near the south coast of the Bay of Fundy. In the polar regions Franklin has proved that the tide never rises above 20 inches, and sometimes only three; and in the centre of the German Ocean it is absolutely imperceptible.

It has often been affirmed that the waters of the Mediterranean were not subject to the oscillations of the tide; this assertion has been disproved by observations made at Toulon, at Venice, and at Algiers, in which places the existence of ebb and flow have been observed. In all seas of small extent, and in general in all lakes, the tide has but slight perceptible influence. This fact is very easily explained. When the tide is high in one part of the ocean it is low at a distance of 90°, and the liquid promontory is formed at the expense of the surrounding waters. In lakes of small extent this species of compensation is impossible; and the flow of the tide cannot raise the surface of the water. These facts were often presented as an objection to the Newtonian theory of the tides, but are, on the contrary, a complete confirmation.

The tides purify and wash the shores, cleaning and sweeping our ports; the currents, which result therefrom, disencumber our roadsteads of the masses of mud which load them, clear the mouths of rivers, and produce a pure and wholesome freshness. These undulations of the ocean, these powerful pulsations of the water, are influenced by stars which are separated from our planet by millions of leagues; nor have they less mathematical regularity than that which directs those planetary bodies themselves. At a fixed hour the formidable masses of water, raised by an invisible power, rise and approach the shore. They rise, they precipitate themselves with resistless power, but only to stop gently at a precise moment, without ever passing the boundary which Nature has traced. It is surely an honor to the human race to have succeeded in calculating the very hour, nay, the exact minute, in which the oscillations of the sea begin and end in every part of our globe.

Nevertheless, as yet unknown combinations will, at times, produce terrible disasters that cannot be avoided by any foresight or precaution. Thus, occasionally, a powerful wind happens to blow in the same direction with the tide, and gives it incredible force and fury. No lofty embankment reared by the hand of man, no rocky rampart raised by Nature herself, can then withstand its power; and towns are swept away in an instant, and thousands of persons lose their lives. In some parts of the globe the tide produces remarkable effects from the peculiar formation of the coast which it strikes. The most striking instance is that of the island of Mauritius, where a long, rocky promontory runs far out into the sea, and has been worn by the waves into numerous caves and grottoes of marvellous beauty and grotesqueness. The waters have forced for themselves an outlet through the roof of one of these caves, and when the tidal wave reaches the coast it fills the cave, and then, with indescribable grandeur, flies through the opening to a height of sixty feet, accompanied by a thundering roar which is heard for miles out at sea.

THE CURRENTS.

"We observe in the sea rapid currents, the limits of which appear to be as invariable as those which control the powers of rivers."—BUFFON.

There exist in the sea immense currents which may be regarded as veritable rivers in the bosom of the ocean; veins of a great arterial system, they play a highly important part in the harmonies of the globe. They establish a kind of equilibrium between the extreme temperatures of different climates, transporting toward the poles the warmer waters of the tropics, and carrying the cold waters of the glacial regions towards the torrid countries of the world.

Christopher Columbus was one of the first to record observations on the sea currents. He recognized, after his second voyage, that the waters of certain parts of the Atlantic followed the apparent motion of the stars. "The waters," says the great navigator, "move with the sky."

The physical geography of the ocean is a science which is still in its infancy, the initiative having been taken by an able and fruitful mind, that of Commodore Maury, and it is only lately that the route taken by any of the marine currents has been accurately determined. It is now, however, distinctly known that the march of the waves of the ocean is as regular as that of the heavenly bodies.

Two great powers cause these mysterious movements in the ocean. One is heat, the other, the revolution of the earth around its axis.

With regard to the former we must bear it in mind that near the equator the water of the sea is heated to a high temperature on the surface, while at a certain depth it retains an icy coldness. The cold polar water, heavier than the heated water of the tropics, continually rushes up from the two poles, and as it is gradually warmed up in its progress toward the equator, the colder water flows naturally below, the warmer, much lighter, above. The latter is in this manner driven toward the poles, and meets on its way the polar water coming in the opposite direction; this forms currents above and below each other, or where islands, capes and continents make this impossible, side by side.

In like manner the rotation of the earth differs at the equator and at the poles: at the equator the earth moves with a velocity of 1,400 feet a second, in our latitude with only half the velocity. The polar current can, therefore, not go straight to the equator, but is apparently checked and flows from east to west; hence the north polar current follows the coast of North America and the south polar current the coast of Chili. In the tropics both are affected by the trade winds, follow their impulse, and thus form an equatorial current nearly 250 miles wide, which encircles the earth.

The most powerful and best known of all these currents is the Gulf Stream.

It is the prolongation of the equatorial current of the Atlantic, which, after having followed Western Africa, makes a bend westward, and, widening as it goes on, veers toward America. At some distance from the coast one branch of it becomes detached, descends toward the south, and forms the Brazilian current. The main artery, on the contrary, goes northward to the coast of Guiana, receives in its bosom the waters of the Amazon and the Orinoco, penetrating at last into the Gulf of Mexico, along the coast of which it travels.

It is from this storehouse that the equatorial current escapes, and hence it bears the name of the Gulf Stream. It precipitates itself across the straits of Florida, and produces an impetuous flood of 900 feet in depth and 14 leagues in breadth. It travels with the speed of nearly six miles an hour, and its waters, warm and salt, are of an indigo blue, unlike their green shores, formed by the waves of the sea. This formidable mass of warm water causes great external agitation during its passage, and pursues its course without mingling with the ocean. Compressed between two liquid walls, the waters of the Gulf Stream form a moving body, which glides over the empire of the sea, pushing far away anything which may be cast adrift upon its bosom. "In the greatest droughts," says Maury, "it never becomes dry, and in the highest floods it never overflows its boundaries. Its bed and shores are alike layers of cold water. In no part of the world does there exist so majestic a current. It is more rapid than the Amazon, more impetuous than the Mississippi, and the united waters of these two rivers do not represent a thousandth part of the mass which it displaces."

With the aid of the thermometer the navigator can follow this great liquid artery; plunged alternately in its edges or in its centre, it indicates temperatures which differ 15 degrees. Powerful and rapid, the Gulf Stream pursues its way in a northerly direction, following the shores of the United States as far as the banks of Newfoundland. It then has to sustain a terrible shock from a polar current, which drifts along immense icebergs, absolute mountains of ice, so immense that one of them weighing more than twenty billions of tons swept the vessel of Lieutenant de Haven 300 leagues toward the south. The Gulf Stream, with its warm waters, dissolves the floating ice; the icebergs break up the soil; gravel, and even small fragments of rock, which they have carried along with them, are swallowed up by the sea. The myriads of infusoria and other animalculæ which swarm in the Gulf Stream collect upon these fragments, whilst rocks, earthy matter, *débris* of every description, are piled up and heaped up pell mell, till they rise to the surface, and will one day appear above the ocean level, promising islands, and, perhaps, continents, for it is thus that the banks of Newfoundland have already been formed.

But in this fierce contest the Gulf Stream is vanquished. It is broken by the impetuous shock and becomes subdivided into several currents. One of these flows northward and melts the ices of Norway, softening its rigorous climate. It still preserves sufficient impulse to advance as far as Iceland, and occasionally to cast upon the coast of that island trunks of trees or fragments of wood which it has torn from the shores of the New World. It is the only fuel which the Icelanders, half frozen as they are at the foot of a volcano, are able to obtain.

The right arm of the Gulf Stream tends eastward and directs its course to the British Islands, which it surrounds with what may be termed a mild and genial liquid girdle. It softens the climate of Scotland and endows it with emerald prairies.

Its left arm enters the British channel and causes the fig-tree to flourish in Brittany, while it forces into early maturity those fruits of the earth which so richly abound in Cornwall and Devonshire, and supply the markets of London itself. Without this genial current, which dispenses so widely the blessings of life and heat, Scotland would have the climate of Siberia, which, situated beneath the same latitude, has to endure almost intolerable cold; and without its soft influence the winters of Brittany would be no longer mild as they are.*

During the winter, landing on the shores of the United States is difficult and dangerous; the poor sailor is exposed to storms of snow and gales of cutting wind which severely try his courage and his power of endurance. Masses of ice surround his ship, a freezing mist benumbs the crew, the rudder becomes fixed and frozen, and its management is a hard and perilous task. Disaster seems imminent.

But the Gulf Stream is at hand to help the voyager in his need.

If he makes haste to steer his vessel into the stream, he will see as if by enchantment summer succeed to winter; the melting ice falls gradually off and the sailor takes heart under the reviving warmth. Like a new Antæus he regains strength, and, thanks to the generous current, he reaches his desired haven and once more beholds his native land.

The Gulf Stream exercises an important influence upon meteorology. Violent storms and squalls usually follow in its track. The waves of this mighty current are frequently agitated by tempests

* The temperature of the Gulf Stream varies in its widest part. The principal current is composed of lesser ones running parallel with each other, but having various degrees of temperature. At its entrance into the Caribbean Sea it has a maximum temperature of about 96 degrees.

excited by gales, which blow in a circular course; terrible cyclones; vast columns of air in every direction, revolve upon themselves and give birth to tremendous whirlpools. The sea is still more formidable when the wind blows in a direction contrary to that of the Gulf Stream, and it often happens that the atmospheric currents traverse from one end to the other, the curve described by this body of warm water.

Another gulf stream, less known, but by no means less important in the economy of our globe, is that of the Pacific Ocean, which, sweeping along the coasts of Japan and Asia to the northeast, crosses the Pacific and washes our northwest coast as far down as the Bay of Panama, where it again diverges to the westward and forms the great equatorial current of the Pacific. Its average temperature is only about 85°, and on its heat depends the extraordinary productiveness of Japan. Another effect of this singular current is the absence of all icebergs in the Northern Ocean, south of Behring Straits: a branch of this gulf stream, after striking the Aleutian Islands, sweeps the Behring Straits into the Northern Ocean, and thus relieves whalers of a formidable danger. Another peril, however, even more fatal, they cannot escape, for the contact of the warm waters of this current with the cold waters of the Japanese seas produces constant and dense fogs, precisely as the Atlantic gulf stream gives rise to similar fogs on our northeast coast. Our new possessions in Alaska benefit largely by this Pacific stream, enjoying, at least on the coast, a wonderfully soft and mild climate, the temperature in winter corresponding to that of Washington city.

In the vast liquid triangle formed by the Azores, the Canaries, and the Cape Verd islands, in the centre of the great oceanic circle, of which the Gulf Stream forms a part, are to be found, on a tract extending over many thousand leagues, such a quantity of marine plants that the progress of ships is frequently obstructed. The companions of Columbus, alarmed at this obstacle, and astonished at the sight of such abundant vegetation, and all these fuci, with their close-growing stalks, imagined themselves to have reached the extreme limits of the navigable world.

This accumulation of algæ is also due to the currents of the sea. The Atlantic is an immense basin in the midst of which the weeds torn from its shores form what is called the Sargasso Sea. It can be shown by a simple experiment how nature, with her powerful resources, accomplished this phenomenon. Place some light substances, such as pieces of cork, in a basin full of water, propel it into circular motion and they will immediately collect in the centre. The Sargasso Sea is not indeed a phenomenon peculiar to the Atlantic; it is to be found, on the contrary, in all great oceans. The Pacific Ocean, also, has its gulf stream and its Sea of Sargasso.

In the South Sea the currents are far less known, and are in fact much less perfectly developed. It is probable, also, that these maritime rivers are not mere isolated currents, but parts of a great network—individual veins of a vast system of circulation. They form thus an extended circuit, indicated by corked bottles which have been caused to float on their surface. Several of these little floating buoys, left in the water off the coast of Africa, have been found again after many years, near the shores of Scotland, they having followed regular routes traced on the surface of the ocean. The cocoanuts of the Seychelles are in the same way carried along by the marine current. After having borne them for a voyage of 400 leagues, the waves cast them on the shores of Malabar, where they take root, and thus thrive far away from the country which gave them birth. The Hindoos believe that the ocean nourishes in its depths the marvellous trees which produce that enormous fruit.

The great current which takes its rise off the eastern coast of South America, has carried from Guiana and Brazil no less than thirteen species of plants, as far as Congo. Certain other seeds, provided with a covering impervious to water, are also tossed by the waves and rocked by the storm during their voyage from India to Brazil.

The fruit of the cocoanut-tree and the pods of the mimosa are snatched from the soil of equatorial America by these rivers of the sea, to be afterwards cast upon the rocks of Scandinavia, where the want of heat alone prevents their further development.

These highways of the sea render, besides, signal service to navigation, and, thanks to the facilities which they give, we can accomplish certain voyages in as many days as it required months before their direction was well understood.

Thus a vessel coming from Europe to this country, follows the coast of the Old World till it falls into the equatorial current, which carries it swiftly across to the West India Islands; while our vessels, going to Europe, are similarly aided by the Gulf Stream. Ships sailing along the coasts of Peru and Chili northward, require only as many days as they require weeks when sailing southward, aided, as they are, by the Pacific current in that locality.

The main purpose of these currents, however, seems to be the equalization of the temperature of our globe. The Antarctic current thus tempers the heat on the coast of South America, while the warm Gulf Stream endows Ireland, England, and Norway with mild winters, and checks the polar ice, which does not extend half as near to Northern Europe as it does to our continent. Hence in the Old World trees grow ten degrees farther north than with us, and when Labrador is buried under snow and ice, Norway, under the same latitude, produces rye, potatoes and buckwheat, oaks reach Drontheim, beeches Christiania, chestnuts the northern part of Scotland, and myrtles and camellias—here rarely surviving a winter north of the Carolinas—thrive in Ireland and southern England.

Hence agriculture and navigation, with all their beneficent influences, can be carried on in Europe at a latitude at which, in our country, life is impossible to all except the hunter and trapper. Large portions of the Old World depend literally for their existence, as for all their civilization, on the Gulf Stream—a year's interruption, and northern Europe would have long, cold winters, short hot summers, frozen lakes, and snow-covered plains, stunted trees, and a few berries instead of abundant cereals.

The discovery of these currents, so long unknown, is one of the proudest conquests of science, a fruitful victory which offers to the thinking mind a vast field for study and meditation—a discovery invaluable to the navigator, who, lost in the immensity of ocean, can now find tracks already formed, threads which can guide him through the vast labyrinth.

Duperrey, Berghaus, Petermann, and more recent ly Maury, have prepared admirable charts of the ocean. The circulation of these currents, which furrow, as it were, the fluid portion of the globe, is represented with the direction of their course, and the various temperatures are also indicated. The seaman, furnished with this atlas, is armed with new resources which permit him to risk more hopefully the fortune which he confides to the uncertain waves. The fisherman also has gained thereby much useful information, and can now find his way in all seasons to the quarters most favorable to his craft, in following the indications afforded by the temperature of the water.

He must never, for instance, enter into the currents of warmer water, if he wishes to invade the territories of the whale, for that huge animal only exists in cold regions; the torrid zone arrests his march like a wall of flame.

Besides these great ocean currents, there are several smaller currents well known, most of which, however, are not permanent but periodical. Thus the Persian Gulf discharges a part of its waters from September to May, which returns to it during the other months of the year. The Baltic, also, has a continuous current into the North Sea through the Sound and the two Belts, probably because it does not evaporate all the water with which its numerous tributaries supply it during the summer. The Mediterranean, on the contrary, aided by the burning winds of Africa, evaporates so actively, that currents of new supplies enter it periodically from the Black Sea through the Dardanelles, and from the Atlantic through the Straits of Gibraltar. A current in the opposite direction has often been suspected, but is improbable, since the Mediterranean has both a higher temperature and a larger admixture of salt than the Atlantic. A still smaller current sweeps along the coast of Syria southward, and has been the cause of filling up the ancient ports of Phœnicia, and thus almost destroying the commerce of Syria.

In all these oceans, however, the great circulation is not merely superficial, but submarine under-currents traverse from side to side the empire of Neptune, in the bosom of which immense hidden arteries extend themselves in unknown directions.

In the middle of the Atlantic, Lieutenants Walsh and Lee, of the U. S. Navy, having fastened to a fishing line a block of wood charged with lead, dropped it into the sea to a depth of from 2,500 to 3,000 feet. The apparatus was fastened to a float in order to prevent its sinking to the bottom, and then left to the mercy of the waves. "It was a truly singular spectacle to see the float advancing against wind and sea and current, at its usual rate. The crew could not suppress their astonishment; it seemed as if some marine monster must be bearing the block along."

An English officer was crossing the Danish Sound in an open boat. He found himself carried away by a current. He threw into the water a pail furnished with a cannon ball which he allowed to sink to a great depth, holding, at the same time, this novel species of anchor by a long cord. It was not long before the boat began to be carried along in an entirely different direction, exactly the reverse of that of the surface current. A submarine stream carried into its own course the craft to which the ball had been attached, and rivalled the surface current in its force.

What enigmas lie still buried in that ever-moving mass! What problems to solve—what observations to follow up—what experiments to try in order to unveil all the forces which set in motion the mechanism of the waves!

Astronomy has found a Newton to pierce with his eyes the profound mysteries of the heavens; but the army of waves, continually at war with daring man, who braves the combat, holds concealed many more mysteries which a future Galileo may reveal to us.

What sets in motion this mighty marine circulation? Is it due, as Romme affirms, to the impetus of the wind, and the action of tides?

The agitation of the air produces the superficial

agitation of the waves, but that solution only gives rise to another question, viz., how the *submarine* streams are set in motion?

The vast wave produced under sidereal influence occasions a vertical motion, but it is impossible that it should cause the movement of the Gulf Stream. The prime mover of the great oceanic machine, is to be sought elsewhere. Where then is the secret spring hidden. Whence comes the first impetus? Heat is the most obvious cause of the marine circulation, but even heat, to use an expression of Maury's, would prove insufficient here. There is another force at work, stranger and not less important, and that force is salt. Salt is one of the chief causes in producing the circulation of the sea. "So abundant is it in the sea, that were all the salt in the ocean collected and placed upon America, it would form a mountain 4,500 feet in thickness."

We perceive that evaporation carries daily from the equatorial seas enormous quantities of water, which rise into the air in the form of clouds.

But this water is all fresh. Its withdrawal consequently only tends to increase the saltness of the sea. The surface layers, rendered more saline by the action of heat, descend and become replaced by lower and lighter strata. Thus a double vertical current is produced. In the deep layers, meanwhile, is produced at the same time a movement toward the poles, of the denser waters of the equatorial regions. The ocean is thus more or less movable, denser or lighter, in proportion as it is fresh or salt. Its waters move and become agitated under the influence of their variable specific gravity. The veins of the sea, which streak only the surface of the waves and not the depth of the ocean, have a higher temperature than the adjacent waves, which more than counterbalances the difference in their degrees of saltness. At the same time, in naming salt as one of the causes of marine circulation, we have not thereby entirely accounted for the latter. Other causes combine with the saline property of the sea. Maury ingeniously suggests that the motive power of the currents resides, to a large extent, in the infinitesimally small beings which people the ocean. The madreporic zoöphytes are invisible creatures, mere atoms in the kingdom of nature, and yet of indispensable utility to her machinery.

These microscopic animals form and create gigantic polypæ. Each joins its own minute work to the work of others—they secrete calcareous atoms, which become welded together, and increase so as to form archipelagoes, and in time to fashion new empires and continents.

Each one of these little creatures has its nourishment. It extracts from a drop of water the salt necessary for its subsistence. It draws from the sea the calcareous matter which it requires; it snatches from the waves solid matter which they hold in solution. It changes thus the weight of the water, causing its specific gravity to vary. The water, which thus becomes lighter, is then set in motion by the pressure of the molecules that surround it. Each tiny being, a mere atom, gives individually but a very feeble impetus; but the force of animalculæ is rendered irresistible by their formidable union. "Combined action," says St. Simon, "multiplies the product an hundred fold." And these zoöphytes prove the truth of the remark by the enormous results which they achieve.

"How are we to set down in figures," says Maury, "the quantity of solid matter thus daily extracted from the sea? Does it amount to tens of thousands, or thousands of millions of tons? This is a question impossible to answer, but whatever the amount may be, the effect produced on the motion of the water is immediate, and we see that a species of animal, devoid of locomotion, the life of which is scarcely distinguishable from that of a plant, seems more or less to be endowed with the power of shaking the entire mass of the ocean from the poles to the equator."

Thus these streams of the sea, whose track is followed by navigators in the midst of the vast Pacific, these currents whose source is still largely involved in as much mystery as their final issue—these hidden arteries within the bosom of Ocean—this circulation, so irresistible, so vast, so terrible in its immensity, is set in motion by the heat of the sun, which evaporates the upper waves of the sea—by the excess of salt which is the result of that evaporation—and by these imperceptible beings which are incessantly at work in the ocean's depths—these living atoms, which, adjusting the balance of the universe, may be termed the compensators of the ocean.

CHAPTER III.

DESTRUCTION AND CREATION.

"The ocean is at once the coffin and the cradle of the earth."—BERNARDIN DE ST. PIERRE.

THE STRUGGLE OF WATER WITH LAND.

The waves undermine rocky shores, cut, hew and shape stones, waste and wear away continents; they dash against the feet of lofty cliffs, and daily encroach upon their bosom by the landslips which they cause. Sometimes they divide and excavate rocks, thus giving birth to fantastic constructions, bearing the impress of a style altogether indescribable, a grotesque order of architecture, which creates bluffs, capes, breakers and reefs. Let us quote a passage from a great poet who paints in magic colors the spectacle offered by this sea-built architecture.

"These structures," says Victor Hugo, "possess the entangled forms of the polyp, the sublimity of the cathedral, the extravagance of the pagoda, the massiveness of the mountain, the delicacy of the gem and the horror of the sepulchre. An extraordinary system of dynamics here presents problems happily solved. Frightful cliffs tottle over our heads, but they do not fall. It is impossible to say what sustains

ROCKS WORN BY WATER.

these giddy structures. Everywhere are seen overhanging masses which seem top-heavy, enormous gaps, structures which appear suspended in mid-air contrary to every principle of mechanics. This Tower of Babel seems to have escaped from the dominion of law; rocks heaped together pell-mell compose a monster monument. There is no logic, and yet a vast equilibrium. It is more than solidity; it is eternity. Nothing thrills the mind more than the contemplation of this strange architecture, always ready to totter and yet always standing. Everything assists in its erection and everything opposes it. It is a combat of lines, which results in an edifice. Nothing is comprehensible here but the fact that all this is the result of an antagonism of two forces: the ocean and the hurricane."

The traditions of maritime countries present to us numberless examples of the ravages and sudden changes to which their shores have been subject by the action of the sea. We find striking proofs of this in the formation of the Zuyder Zee, the Bies-Boch, etc., in the exceptional tides which have altogether altered the aspect of the islands lying between the Texel and the mouths of the Elbe, and have indented the winding shores of the Cattegat, and fashioned the recesses of the Lymfiord. Bays, gulfs, and capes have been at different times produced under the potent influence of the tempest, and are still produced by the play of the waves, which are now heaping up banks of sand and pebbles on the sea shore, and now destroying their own creations, causing the dykes and the rampart to disappear, to which they themselves have given birth.

The action of the waves is not merely exerted over a shifting soil, but is felt by the hardest and most solid rocks. The more abrupt and resistant the shore, the more it suffers from the irresistible element. Nothing is sufficiently strong to resist the army of waves, and the land always succumbs in its contests with the sea. It only triumphs when it avoids a battle, as Fabius did with Hannibal. If it offers to the sea a flat and uniform seaboard, the waves advance gently up to the shore and their wrath is appeased. Before an enemy who attempts no resistance they lose their impetuous force and quietly deposit on the shingle round stones and fine sand—creating more than they destroy.

The natural configuration of coasts is favorable to the action of the waves, when the stratifications of the soil offer to the sea layers and leaflets, the lowest of which, continually attacked by the liquid element, everlastingly shaken by the reiterated shocks of the waves, are hollowed out all the quicker the more easily the material can be disintegrated. The upper layers advance menacingly and form frowning prominences, but it is not long before they also disappear and precipitate themselves into the ocean.

Of all the shores beaten by the tempest there are none which present a more imposing appearance or give a more vivid idea of the power of the waves than the fiords of Northern Europe and of America. These fiords are deep bays, long and narrow, leaving between them vast rocky peninsulas. One might call them an enormous fringe, of which every thread is a peninsula denticulated and opening into miniature bays, canals, and straits. So lofty is the es-

Action of Waves on Rocks.

carpment of these coasts, that Mount Thorsnuten, situated to the south of Bergen, attains at a mile's distance from the shore a height of nearly 5,000 feet. In a great number of these bays, cascades and waterfalls descend from the summits of the cliffs and rush into space, forming on their way parabolas, beneath which barks and fishing-boats have free room to pass.

During seven centuries the waters of the English Channel have advanced over 4,000 feet over the land, and the cliffs upon its shores have consequently moved more than a quarter of a league since the time when Peter the Hermit preached the first crusade. The Straits of Dover enlarge day by day, and according to Mr. Thomé de Gamond, the sea gains on the cliffs of Gris-Nez at the rate of 75 feet a year! If in years gone by the encroachments have not been more rapid, it must have been 60,000 years since France and England were separated by the piercing of the isthmus which once united them.

Many coasts and whole islands are surrounded by a wall of gigantic blocks of stone, the remains of former masses of rock which the waters have undermined and destroyed; in other places colossal rocks, shaped like huge pyramids or immense mile-posts, stand solitary in the midst of foaming water, or the waves have forced a passage through lofty rock-walls and formed gates fit for giants. Like causes have produced the far-famed caves of Ireland and Scotland in volcanic basalt, and those of Syracuse in Sicily. England, especially, is still the scene of the fierce destructive power of the ocean. On the coast of Scotland, submarine forests are seen beneath the waves, and boats are now floating where a generation ago large herds of cattle were grazing peacefully; a vast lake, the Zuyder-Zee, was suddenly formed by a single effort of the sea in 1225, and recovered from its tyrannical grasp only a few years ago; Heligoland and the islands on the coast of Schleswig disappear inch by inch, but without a day's respite, and who knows how few ages may have passed since the Channel was land and England a peninsula of France?

We have already remarked that the dip of the rocks opposed or assisted the action of the waves; but the hardness of the rocks and their chemical composition also control the changes which they are made to undergo. The friction of the waves is occasionally strong enough to cause a rise in the temperature sufficient to produce absolute combustion, and it has often been observed at Valencia, that the cliffs appear to smoke, like a streak of incandescent lava, consumed by slow combustion. The cliffs do not resist the efforts of the ocean merely by the hardness of their material, they often take the precaution of clothing their bases in armor by way of defence against the repeated attacks of their enemy. An abundance of vegetation of algæ and seaweeds carpet every fissure of the rocks like a fantastic suit of hair; these plants divide the waves into thin threads of water, into filaments of foam. Elsewhere heaps of mollusks and other shells form a more solid coat of mail, a thick and impervious buckler against which the tides beat in vain.

Other coasts are not thus protected, and consequently wear away without offering any resistance. Enormous blocks are detached from the upper portions; they are broken by the shock of their fall and are soon swept away by the waves, which retire, as if wishing to take a new start before recommencing the attack. They break up into small fragments and divide into pebbles, and the heaps thus raised afterwards protect the rocks to which they once belonged, and produce the shelving banks which put a stop to the conquests of the sea. One might look upon them as so many corpses heaped pell-mell round the fortress, whence the enemy has succeeded in tearing them.

Upon the shores of the Mediterranean, near Vintimille, and also upon the coast of Brittany, there are everywhere masses of ruins of this description to be seen, which resist the efforts of the waves.

In one word, everywhere we find the sea busy levelling the coast; it breaks down the haughty promontories which encroach upon its limits and deposits their dust at the bottom of its vast empire.

REPRODUCTIVE EFFECTS.

Nothing is lost, nothing is created anew. If the labor of the waves was merely destructive, it would be followed by a complete annihilation of continents; but the sea repairs the ravages which it has caused, and lessens the disasters to which it has given birth. The waves hammer and pound the rocks on the sea shore, but the ruins thus made are not lost; they are carried to other places where they form sediments upon sediments. The quantity of solid matter held in solution by the currents of the tide is so

MASS OF DEBRIS OPPOSING THE WAVES.

considerable, that in order to raise the level of the soil in certain districts, the water carried up by the tide is kept there for some time. Thus, by frequently repeating this operation, the vast estates which border on the Delta of the Humber have been raised nearly six feet. The tides fill up in the same way the cavities and hollow places which corrugate the bottom of the ocean, by means of the sediment which they discharge into them age after age.

At the upper end of the Red Sea, it has been remarked that the Isthmus of Suez has increased in size with extraordinary rapidity, owing to oceanic deposits. This Isthmus, as we are told by Sir Charles Lyell, has doubled in width since the time of Herodotus. At that period the town of Hieropolis stood on the seashore; in our days it is as far from the Red Sea as from the Mediterranean, being situated exactly in the middle of the Isthmus. In 1541 Soliman II. found in the port of Suez a valuable harbor of refuge, capable of giving shelter to his entire fleet; now an immense bank of sand has replaced the canals which sheltered his vessels. During 1800 years the territory of Tehama, situated on the Arabian Gulf, has received from the sea a tribute of two leagues of soil in sediment, which has gradually accumulated during this time. If we penetrate further from the shore into the land, we find at a certain distance from the existing sea ports the ruins of ancient towns which flourished long ago under the same names, and the remains of their walls, once washed by the sea, present now an obstacle to the encroachments of the desert sands.

One part of the Delta of the Nile is day by day diminished in size by a powerful current of the Mediterranean, and the waves, which follow one another in unceasing assaults, carry to a considerable distance the valuable sediment brought down by the earthy stream. They transport this solid matter as far as the shores of Syria.

Mr. Girard, one of the most illustrious scientific men, who, at the time of the French expedition into Egypt, was commissioned to investigate the remains of the Canal of Amron, is of opinion that the whole Isthmus of Suez is of oceanic formation, and considers it as a vast dam constructed by marine currents. Although this opinion is open to objections, it is none the less certain that that Isthmus, now world-famous from the works which have been so successfully achieved there by one of the ablest intellects of modern times, constantly increases in width in consequence of the continual augmentation of the deposits, which are forever accumulating on the shores of the Mediterranean.

Examples of this description abound. The shores of Guiana increase and gain upon the dominion of Ocean, as in other parts of the world the sea inundates and invades the land. It is, as Lockhead informs us in the "Edinburgh Transactions," the Gulf Stream which brings to those countries the sediment borne away from the Delta of the Amazon.

The transport of these earthy materials to far distant countries by the waters need be no matter of astonishment to us, for it can be easily explained by the state of extreme subdivision to which the solid substance becomes reduced. Fine emery powder will remain for a long time in suspension in water, and takes more than an hour to settle in a moderate sized vessel. It is inferred from this that if the marine currents carry with great velocity to the surface of the ocean an extremely fine earthy dust, and if this dust sinks very slowly to the bottom of the fluid, it may be carried to a very great distance before reaching the bottom of the ocean. If a sediment as fine as emery powder can be carried along by the Gulf Stream, which travels at the rate of a league an hour, this sediment will have drifted 2,200 feet in 28 hours, whereas during the period it will only have sunk into the bosom of the current to the depth of 224 fathoms.

Thus the sea which wears away our continents with so much violence does not merely carry on a a work of destruction, but, after having tormented the land with its ruthless blows, after having invaded its shores, it transports the sediment to other coasts, thus compensating for the wounds which it has inflicted, closing them with the same hands which had caused them. But the land itself is, by some strange power of its own, capable of opposing a vigorous defence to the action of the waves, by a mysterious, gentle motion with which it is endowed. The subterranean fires which have corrugated the terrestrial epidermis are far from being extinct, and every day earthquakes and other convulsions spread terror over some country. But these abrupt movements, these tempests in the realms of Pluto, are the exceptions, even as the hurricane is exception to the rule which directs the movements of the ocean. During an earthquake the sea loses all at once its surface equilibrium; it becomes subject to terrible oscillations, and its waters invade the continents, where they produce formidable eruptions, and often remain in the countries which they have inundated. The history of the Greek Archipelagoes and the Islands of Japan are replete with such disasters. But subterranean fires seldom work in a manner so violent; they usually lift up the earth gently and raise it insensibly. The hand of a clock appears immovable, yet it travels in one hour sixty divisions of the dial; it is the same with the shores of many continents; under the influence of an invisible spring they slowly perform an upward and regular movement, and thus drive back the waters of the ocean.

Numerous writers explain certain phenomena of the sea by saying that the water has retired, that it has abandoned its bed, that the immovable shores have seen their empire extended through the flight of the liquid elements, whereas exactly the contrary has really happened. The level of the sea is immovable, but we are deceived by its appearance. The water, always agitated on its surface, seems the very image of instability, whereas it is endowed with remarkable permanency, and the earth, according to Pliny the emblem of immobility, is, on the contrary, endowed with motion. The ocean never retreats from the shore. It is chased thence by the shore, which is itself continually rising.

The ocean does not slowly invade certain coasts; it arrives there by a forcible advance, to which it is compelled by the slow lowering of its shores beneath its own level. Let us take care not to rely too much on the testimony of our senses, but to view facts with the eye of reason, and we shall then find that many ideas are not less real and incontestable, because they are contrary to generally received opinions. The laws of hydrostatics teach us that what we term *the sea level* is nothing else than a surface of equilibrium determined by the forces of attraction exercised by the solid over the liquid portions of the globe. It is impossible for any part of this surface to occupy a fixed and invariable position, unless all the other points preserve theirs as well; it is equally impossible for the waters to rise or to fall in any place in a continued manner, unless all the other parts rise or fall in their turn and become subject to corresponding changes of levels.

Now we are acquainted with a great number of places in which the sea has not been subject to the slightest change since the commencement of our history. Its general surface has not changed the stability of the liquid level, which covers almost entirely the surface of the globe, appears a positive fact, the most incontestable that can be brought forward, because it has sustained the ordeal of a long succession of ages.

How otherwise can it be accounted for that from 1822 to 1837 the sea has abandoned the shores of Chili (as it appeared to the inhabitants of these countries) and that no variations should have been felt on the neighboring coasts of Peru and California? These apparently contradictory facts would furnish a complete reputation to the most certain laws of hydrostatics. How is it conceivable that the sea should have risen in the lower part of the Arabian Gulf, in the Straits of Messina, and on the coast of Portugal, while it remained immovable in the adjacent parts of the ocean? Instead of praising the immutability of the earth, it would be more correct to speak of that of the sea, and we must learn to understand that the level of the ocean is unchangable, while the solid surface of our planet is susceptible of elevation, of depression, and of every kind of modification.

An error existed here, very similar to that which during so many centuries fostered the idea of the immutability of the earth. Our eyes still show us the sun revolving round our planet, but science has taught us that our own microscopically small globe performs its daily journey around the central fire which warms it and describes an ellipsis which it never ceases tracing.

Like all truths, that which we announce here remained long unsuspected, and the sinking of the level of the sea was the opinion of all the older naturalists. In 1731 the Academy of Upsala resolved to verify the important fact, and to try carefully all the experiments which could solve the problem. Notches were cut at high water mark on rocks washed by the Baltic Sea, and some years after, it was ascertained that these marks had risen several centimetres above the surface of the sea. Thus it was proved that the level of the Baltic had considerably sunk, but these conclusions met with strong opposition, and fresh experiments were tried. The ultimate result arrived at from all these experiments was that on various parts of the same sea the level of the water was subject to an apparent depression more or less sensible on different shores, and that in other parts (the coast of Scania) it rose, on the contrary, very perceptibly, because the notches cut on the rocks at high water mark were here found to have disappeared beneath the surface of the sea.

It is impossible to reconcile these enormous differences at so little distance from each other, because it cannot be supposed that the level of the ocean, far from being entirely on the same horizontal plane, should form an undulating surface. It is evident from these experiments that the level of the Baltic has not varied more than the level of all other seas; but that in Finland and some parts of Sweden the soil of the earth has risen little by little, and is gradually elevating itself without having received any perceptible shock, while the southern coast of the same peninsula sustains corresponding depressions.

The shores of Greenland have been gradually sinking during the last four centuries, over a space of nearly 600 feet. They become thus gradually submerged by the ocean, and some ancient nautical erections are already swallowed up in this manner.

The Temple of Serapis, on the slope of Puteoli, is another striking instance of the movement of the soil. The Temple, built in a florid style of architecture, was certainly not originally erected upon the margin of the sea, where its columns would have been incessantly washed by the waves, and yet it is now found standing on the very edge of the shore. The three columns, which alone remain, present, at a height of nine feet above their base, a zone perforated by shell-fish, which attacked the stone when it was sunk in the depths of the sea. Thus this temple, built upon a site completely sheltered from the waves, was afterwards plunged nine feet below the water, and has again been raised above the level of the sea by the oscillations of the soil.

Many are the islands of the Indian Ocean which have risen up from the seas, and which are now slowly returning thither by means of a gradual depression, whilst other volcanic islands rise above the surface of the waste of ocean like the immense back of some gigantic sea monster.

In our own days the unexpected apparition of the volcanic islands, which surged out of the waves in the midst of the Greek Archipelago, seems to warn us that the forces of nature allow themselves no prolonged repose, and that the subterranean fires which long ago corrugated the terrestrial pellicle and furrowed it with scars and wrinkles, are still active beneath our feet.

This strife of the elements, this combat between fire and water, materially alters day by day the appearance of this, our earth.

II.

THE SYSTEM OF CIRCULATION.

"An incessant evaporation carries water from the seas to the surface of continents. Pure when it came from the sea, the rain returns it charged with saline matter derived from the soil."—H. MARIE-DAVY.

CHAPTER I.

WATER ON ITS TRAVELS.

"What can be more admirable than to see the waters traversing the skies (migrare per cœlum), and return to the earth in the form of rain to quicken and revive the plants, give birth to fruits and grains, and nourish trees and vegetables."—PLINY.

THE navigator who leaves Europe in order to cross the Atlantic, sees an entire change in all the aspects of Nature as he approaches the equator. Thick clouds obscure the sky; continued rains darken the air. The sombre atmosphere of these strange regions inspires him with feelings of melancholy and of fear; but without this curtain of vapor to oppose a barrier against the burning rays of the sun he would be overpowered by the intolerable heat. A mass of similar clouds surrounds our whole globe, forming a dusky ring, which may appear to the inhabitants of other planets like the rings of Saturn. The stormy seas on the line were formerly the terror of sailors, and these masses of vapor caused a sense of dread in the minds of those who ventured into these remote regions. And yet the thick cloud which thus hangs forever over the waves is really the safety of the earth, and that which, in other countries, procures for us the charm of an azure sky and the delight of a beautiful sun. This band of clouds is the great regulator of temperature over our globe; it is the real source of the rivers which water our fields, the floating reservoir from which comes all the water that refreshes and revives our continents.

By a physical law, obscure in theory but clear and precise in its results, every mass of water surrounded by air perpetually exhales into that air a quantity of vapor, the volume of which is always in proportion to the height of the temperature of the water. It may be conceived, therefore, how, under the influence of the burning tropical sun and the heat its rays produce, the seas of the torrid zone continually give out an enormous amount of vapor; a thin mist ascends incessantly from the liquid surface, and, lighter than the air, it rises and gives birth to the black and sombre streamers which obscure the equatorial atmosphere. As soon as these clouds have reached the highest regions of the air, where the temperature is sufficiently low, they return in part to their liquid state and again fall into the sea in the shape of rain; but the uncondensed vapor, in consequence of its lightness, produces in the higher strata of the atmosphere, currents which flow towards the poles.

These currents transport it to our own regions, where it dissolves in rain, or condenses in the form of snow, as it meets the ice-covered summits of lofty mountains.

Thus a great distillation is at work all over the

surface of the globe, the burning rays of the tropical sun acting as the furnace which heats this gigantic alembic. The equatorial ocean is the boiler of this immense engine, the higher regions of the air furnish its cap; the cold atmosphere, the icy summits of the mountains of the north, the frozen seas of the poles form the refrigerators; the streams, the water courses, the rivers, and the lakes are the receivers, incessantly filled with enormous volumes of water which they return to the sea. This distillation is forever beginning anew; the water of the receiver being always sent back again into the boiler to be submitted to a new process of distillation.

This majestic stream which pours into the sea has received its transparent fluid from the ocean itself. The pure and beneficent water from the crystal spring is none other than the salt water of the sea purified in this great laboratory of nature. It came, no doubt, originally, from tropical regions, accomplishing its journey under the form of light vapor; but after its metamorphosis into rain it came down again to the earth and dwelt there for a time. It quenches the thirst of all who live near it; it causes the grass to grow that carpets its margin; and when its mission is accomplished it will flow off on the current of a stream and return to its birthplace—the great ocean.

The sea has been aptly compared to a miser incessantly bent upon adding to his hoard. It does not restore what it has stolen during shipwrecks, and if it lends to the earth the water on which depends the development of all life, it is only to exact afterwards a fuller payment of the loan. Every drop returns to the vast reservoir; the very breath which escapes from our mouth only rises into the air to condense into a drop of water, which the sea will ultimately absorb.

In thus travelling across the earth and through space, water is also commissioned to distribute heat over the globe, and to modify the temperature of different climates. When it escapes first from the equatorial seas it has been heated in the furnace of a burning sun; it stores up the heat, it carries it along with it and distributes it over colder countries. Under the form of rain it softens the climate of northern regions, and gives to every animated being that vital warmth of which the sun is so lavish under the tropics, and of which he shows himself such a miser in countries nearer to the poles.

Before it passes off again in the form of large streams, water traverses continents, penetrates into the tiny channels which are formed for it by fissures in the soil, percolates into porous ground, glides through cracks in stones, sucks its way through interstices of flints and pebbles, creeps between the roots of plants and rises up in the stems, insinuates itself into the cellular system, dissolves and takes away from the soil the mineral materials which it meets with on its course, and conveys them to living beings who assimilate them to their own substance. At times it unites itself to minerals and makes its abode in substances, in combination with which is forms hydrates; at other times it rests immovable in marshes, laboring hard in decomposing organic matter, presiding over the putrifaction and decomposition of reeds, weeds, and trees, which form peat and turf.

It seldom remains stationary long; and after having, in a liquid state, traversed the bodies of animals, or the stalks of vegetables, it is exhaled again and rises as vapor; thus it escapes once more and returns to the atmosphere, which it will again quit in the form of rain, hail, or snow, to commence anew its everlasting round.

Like a tender, ever watchful mother, water incessantly bestows its benefit upon every part of man's vast domain. Beneath his feet, in the dark bosom of the earth, unseen and unheard, it flows through countless veins and arteries, or gathers its tribute from a thousand sources in gigantic basins and lakes,—the "sealed fountains of the deep," as Holy Writ graphically calls them. Or it greets the bright light of day, and flows, a beneficent stream, through the lands and cities of man, joyously going to meet the great ocean; or, modestly hiding its gifts, it opens a tiny spring on Alpine heights, to slake the chamois' thirst and to refresh the tiny moss.

And wherever this omnipresent element appears it assumes new shapes and new forms of beauty. A marvellous Proteus, it evaporates under a warm breath into mist and vapor, and weaves faint blue images on the horizon; or it rises on high to decorate the skies with their varied panoply of clouds, if cruel cold does not force it to harden into hail or ice, or to divide into stars of matchless beauty, as virgin snow. But whatever its shape, the deep poetry of water is never lost. If clouds and mists lead our imagination astray to weave a thousand fancies out of their ever-changing, fantastic forms, snow, with its chaste whiteness, its gentle, dream-like fall, and its sudden disappearance, suggests to us dreams of perfect peace and fairy bliss. How terrible, on the contrary, and yet how imposing, the hail storm that suddenly rises, dark and dismal, on the clear blue sky, and mercilessly destroys the rich harvests on golden fields, not sparing even the giant trees of the forest. Ice, again, chills us by more than physical cold; and yet the mystery charms us irresistibly as we glide over the cracking, thundering surface of lake or river, and think of the mighty spirit under our feet, held captive by fierce frost, but ready to awaken at the first gleam of sunshine, and with irresistible wrath to cast off its hateful fetters.

Hence it was no mere idle dream of the ancients, when they represented the hoary god of waters under the ever-changing form of Proteus, who appeared to the weak and the ignorant in a thousand lying shapes, and only to the wise and the strong—for knowledge then already was power—revealed both his real nature and his most valuable secrets. For, a true Proteus, water is still, even to the mind of our day, omnipresent in appearance and yet ever escaping—to-day a sweet image of calm peace, to-morrow raging in wild fury and swallowing goods not only, and gigantic vessels, the triumph of human skill, but covering provinces with its terrible waves, and hiding forever whole cities and blooming lands in its dark, unfathomable bosom. The traveller moves with marvellous speed by the aid of water, compelled to labor as steam; he greets it with joyful gratitude under the dark shade of the orange-tree or the palm in the Orient, and amazes the credulous son of the East by accounts of the huge icebergs of the Pole, and the bridges built by the frozen fluid from country to country. Ever within reach, it ever eludes our grasp; and without rest, and without ceasing, it races onward in its eternal course around the globe. The merry spring rushes with youthful haste through the narrow valley into the broad plain; a mighty stream, it rolls its gigantic waves into the great ocean, and with it rushes daily around the whole of the earth. As fairy vapor it rises high up to heaven, and in sportive play, chasing cloud after cloud, it repeats its course, until it returns once more to the earth as gentle rain or grateful dew, filling every spring and every goblet held up by a thousand tender leaves and beauteous flowers.

Solid, liquid, and gaseous, these are the three forms under which it appears. Water, vapor, and ice—these are the three appearances which it assumes. It never leaves one but to take the other. It quits the ocean to irrigate the dry land. It deserts the continents to return to the realms of the waves; it flies through space, creeps upon the ground, and flows within the sea. Trusting itself to the light breeze, or to the gentle slope which it happens to find, it obeys whatever agents may command it. It penetrates into the crevices of the earth, warms itself in their depths, and bursts out again from them, boiling and impetuous. It wears away and polishes the rocks over which it falls; it transports from one country to another the minute seed of a plant and the egg of an insect; it carries away trees and stones along the bed of the torrent; it heaps up sand and pebbles on the shore, and undermines the earth which it oftentimes causes to cave in all of a sudden.

The poets have often looked upon water as the emblem of inconstancy and mobility. The fluid part of the globe is indeed subject to constant agitation; if it be on a declivity its weight carries it along with a speed commensurate with the incline of the ground on which it happens to flow; and thus originates the torrent, the stream, the river. If it is in a basin, closed in on all sides like the sea or a lake, it is rocked by the action of the wind, and thus originates the wave and the current. The assault of the waves, which rush up to the shore to die away there; the miniature cataracts formed by a brook which ripples between stones, present to us the appearance of free and independent motion; and yet in this liquid element, so capricious in appearance, there dwells the most admirable regularity. The circulation of the water around and over the earth obeys a mechanism as regular as that of the circulation of the blood in our bodies. Its passage through stream and river resembles that of the blood in our veins; and the transformation of salt into fresh water may be compared to the constant changes of our arterial and venous blood. What can be grander, and at the same time simpler, than the journey of a drop of water, which, exhaled from the ocean, traverses the atmosphere and falls back again to the earth in a raindrop? After having drawn, both from the air and the soil, the food required by all living creatures, after having given life to all on its way, it returns to the sea and at once commences anew its beneficent round.

If we cast our eyes on the immense forests of the New World, we see hovering above the green branches a thin floating mist. That cloud is the messenger of life, which traverses the air, clears space, and hastens to water and refresh the flowers and fruits of Europe.

Marvellous and sublime harmony! The earth borrows from the sea the materials to form its streams and its rivers, and the continents fraternally interchange forever the source of all life and fertility: "Verily, all the rivers run into the sea; yet the sea is not full: unto the places from whence the rivers come, thither they return again."

CHAPTER II.

THE WATER IN THE ATMOSRHERE.

"A portion of the heat of the tropics is carried towards the poles by an aerial messenger, and it is thus ever equalizing the earth's heat."

TYNDALL.

THE VAPOR OF WATER.

THE air, even when it is pure, transparent and azure, is nothing but an immense reservoir of vapor, it is a vast gaseous sea without limit or shore, which covers the earth on all sides to a certain distance, and beneath its benign shelter live mankind, animals and plants.

The surface of the sea, as we have already remarked, emits constantly into the air a vapor indispensable to the needs of life: a drier air we should not be able to inhale; it would parch up the lungs, injure plants and animals, and produce the bad effects which we know to result from the Simoom of the Desert. But a too damp air also has its disadvantages, and every one has heard of the *malaria* of certain warm and ill-drained localities.

Visible clouds and fogs are frequently confounded with the vapor of water, but that is a grave error.

This vapor is an impalpable gas which the atmosphere, in combination with the waters of the sea, is constantly generating. Its presence in the air is constant, but it is to be met with in greater or lesser proportions. It exists, moreover, usually in almost infinitesimal quantities, seldom forming more than one half of one per cent. of the whole mass, and yet it is incredible how much this slight admixture of watery vapor affects the meteorological phenomena of the globe. It exercises an enormous influence on terrestrial revolutions, and, to use the words of Tyndall, "if we were to say that in England on a day of ordinary moisture the atmospheric vapors exercised an activity an hundred times greater than that of the air itself, we should speak within the truth."

It is the faculty of absorption which secures such power to this vapor. The surface of the earth is apt to lose by radiation the heat which it has absorbed; but the aqueous vapors contained in the air take up that heat, warm themselves by it, and cover the earth with a warmth, securing it against a cold which would be fatal to every living creature. Wherever the air is very dry, (it is never completely so,) we are subject to great extremes of temperature. In the day time the rays of the sun reach the surface of the earth without meeting any great obstacle on their way, warm it, and produce a high degree of heat. In the night the earth radiates this heat back again to the sky, and the result is an extreme low temparature. In the steppes of India, on the table lands of Himalaya, on the plains of Australia, in every country where the climate is very dry, excessive heat during the day alternates with a bitter cold at night. In the midst of the Sahara the rays of the sun so raise the temperature of the ground that it is unpleasant to place the hand upon it, while at midnight the cold is so intense, that water, if it could be found in so varied a climate, would freeze. This difference of the temperature arises from the fact that the air, deprived of vapor, cannot retain its caloric. The vapor of water is a genuine transparent covering, which may be compared to the burnous of the Arab; it partially intercepts the rays of the sun and prevents their acting with too great force upon the globe, while, on the other hand, after the sun has set it does not permit the heat absorbed by the soil to be lost again by radiation and thus preserves all animated nature from cold.

It may be objected that this vapory mantle which preserves us from cold must at the same time prevent the solar rays from reaching us. This is not altogether true. The vapor of water is a screen which arrests the earth's own heat, but allows the heat of the sun to pass; for the dark rays emanting from the earth differ from the luminous rays derived from the sun, and hence, it absorbs the former in much greater abundance than the latter. Thus a pane of glass permits the light to pass freely, but it partly arrests the heat which accompanies it—in the same manner the vapor of water interrupts the dark rays, whilst it gives free passage to the luminous rays, and its absorbent power is especially exercised on the heat which is emitted by the sun. In consequence of this admirable and marvellous arrangement, the average temperature of our globe is higher than would be the case if we depended solely upon the sun without the protection of watery vapors.

FOGS.

Nothing is easier than to deprive the air of the water which it contains; it is only necessary to cool it in order to condense its vapor as in the refrigerator of a distilling apparatus. A decanter of cold water placed in a warm room will become covered with beads of vapor, a cloud of dew which settles upon it. So it is in nature. When the temperature of a body of air sinks rapidly in consequence of the disappearance of the sun below the horizon, a moment arrives in which the air becomes condensed into drops of extreme minuteness called vesicles. Our breath produces in cold weather a visible cloud, the steam which escapes from a railway engine gives birth to a series of similar globular vesicles. It is in this manner that, from an infinity of small invisible spheres, which resemble miniature soap-bubbles, fogs and clouds are formed. Naturalists are not agreed as to the nature of these vesicles. Some see in them little balloons inflated by watery vapor. While, according to others, they are little spheres of watery vapor without any interior cavities.

Fogs have often been looked upon as the cause of certain maladies and as exercising an influence inimical to health; it is certainly evident that mist is the indication of a superabundance of moisture in the atmosphere, and that it is usually formed in the midst of a stagnant body of air, in which the smoke and impurities arising from below are readily accumulated. Great evil sometimes result from this, and in marshy countries it is by no means unusual to see frequent fogs accompanied by fever among those exposed to their influence.

CLOUDS.

Clouds are fogs situated at a certain distance above the earth; between cloud and mist the chief difference is that of position. There are, however, clouds consisting, not of vesicles but of small needles of ice. The clouds have a perfect mobility, and their classification is almost impossible, though Howard and other meteorologists have tried to discover certain leading types among the forms which they most frequently assume. Thus four kinds of clouds have been classified. The *cirrus*, the *cumulus*, the *stratus* and the *nimbus*. We do not insist upon these classifications, which are of no importance, for every cloud has its particular form, and a fragment of vapor which detaches itself upon a blue sky is subject to all the caprices of the wind; it fashions and modifies itself into an infinite variety of shapes.

CONDENSATION OF VAPOR—RAIN, SNOW AND DEW.

To make the water, held in the air in the form of vapor, leave it, it is sufficient to cool the air; the well known experiment of the iced decanter must be carried out on a large scale. Of all the means by which the air may be cooled or heated, there is none more efficacious than to compress or expand it. Every one has seen the air tinder-box. By means of a piston we strongly compress the air in a stout tube, and thus the air becomes sufficiently heated to light a piece of tinder; if we then cautiously let the air escape, it expands and grows cold again. The air which escapes from the lips when we whistle gives us a sensation of coolness. How is that? Simply because it has been compressed in the chest. The air exhaled by the open mouth has not been compressed, consequently it does not produce the same sensation.

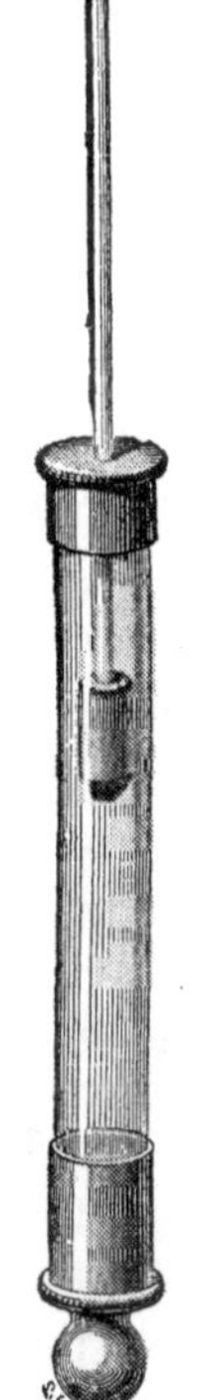
Air tinder-box.

How does nature compress the air to cool it and cause it to abandon the water in the state of rain by the condensation of vapor? Probably by carrying it into the higher regions of the atmosphere, where there is less pressure. The dilated air becomes cold and precipitates the vapor in the form of hail, or if the cooling process be violent, of snow. If we imagine a wind to blow regularly in the direction of a mountain or forest, the damp air meeting with an obstacle does not the less pursue its course. It surmounts the obstacle and rises into those regions where the pressure is less, thus producing rain. It has been frequently remarked that when a current of air is directed against a forest, the vapor it contains will condense in rain; if the obstacle is in a higher stratum, such as a mountain, the fall of temperature is more considerable, and the water solidifies instead, and forms snow or hail. Out at sea the same effect may be produced by atmospheric currents which meet on their way and displace considerable volumes of air. The primary condition of the production of rain is, therefore, a displacing of the air; it varies according to the direction of the wind and the changing level of the ground. This collapsed mist—for such rain at first really is—would of course fall directly back into the ocean in a continuous drizzle but for a curious and beautiful provision of nature. When examined through a microscope the clouds are found to consist of congeries of little bubbles, resembling soap-bubbles, so that De Saussure once, when caught in an Alpine fog, saw these bubbles floating past him as large as peas. Drifting along under the influence of the wind, they finally collapse into compact drops, to be drawn down, by the earth's attraction, in showers to the ground, whence, after having discharged their important functions, they are again raised into the fresh water ocean overhead.

We may conclude our remarks upon rain by adding that the true causes of its production and variations in different countries are at present quite unknown. We do not intend any disrespect to the late

Mr. Mathieu and his successors, but the science of meteorology and of predicting the weather, will, no doubt, one of these days, reach a point when it will discover by close investigation, and numerous experiments, the laws which regulate the movements of air and the distribution of rain.

It is well known that efforts are made in almost all civilized countries to measure the quantity of rain falling in a given time. Rain gauges, simple tin boxes of a certain capacity, with a funnel-shaped opening to receive the rain and lead it into a lower box, enable us to judge the amount fairly, while dew is measured by bundles of wood, the weight of which, when perfectly dry, compared with their weight when saturated with dew, gives the quantity of dew fallen in a given time. There is added to these instruments a third vessel, open or porous, filled with a certain quantity of water, carefully weighed; after being exposed to the air for a number of hours, the vessel and its contents are weighed once more and the difference indicates the amount of evaporation.

By these means it has been found possible to measure accurately the amount of rain which falls in any place during the year—in other words, how many inches of rain would cover the ground if the whole quantity had fallen at one and the same time. It has thus been found that the temperate zones receive annually about 30 inches, the tropics 90, and a few exceptionable regions even 200 inches. While it hardly ever rains in Persia, Arabia, Central Africa, and on the coast of Peru; Aracan, Chiloe and our own American northwest coast can boast of almost daily rains, while the Falkland Islands, like the polar regions and the eastern coast of China, are almost continually wrapt in fogs and mists. In certain places, as in Lombardy, at Viviers and Lund, the amount of rain seems to have diminished, but at Marseilles, Copenhagen and Stockholm, it has increased. The next question arising is : How large a proportion of this rain evaporates, how much is taken up by plants, and how much remains for rivers and water-courses? These calculations have not yet been brought to a satisfactory result; so much only is known that a third of of the whole amount suffices to feed the rivers of the earth. These led also to the remarkable discovery that rain does not penetrate loam beyond six inches, but pierces and filters through rocks to an unfathomable depth.

This latter portion is, of course, the origin of many springs, some of which are hence periodical, when they depend exclusively upon the supply furnished by rains. In Germany such springs are called May springs, because they do not begin to flow till the sun of spring has thawed sufficient water in the upper mountains to fill them once more after the long frosts of winter. Some springs, in the neighborhood of glaciers, flow only by day, others only by night, because the sun alone melts enough ice for their support, and the supply has often so long and so hard a road to travel, that it does not reach the outlet till the next morning. On the banks of the Lake of Como, a spring near the Villa Pliniana flows periodically, now fully and now feebly, as the wind affects the melting of the ice above.

The condensation of watery vapor does not always take place in the great body of air itself ; it may be produced on the surface of bodies and on the surface of the soil. This phenomenon takes the name of dew when the vapor condenses into water, or *rime* or *hoar frost*, when it is deposited in a solid state.

It is to Dr. Wells that we owe the true explanation of these curious phenomena. During the night bodies become cold in consequence of radiation and the vapor of water condenses in proportion as the air is moist and the sky clear.

CHAPTER III.

THE ARTERIAL SYSTEM OF CONTINENTS.

"What beauties, stern or gentle, with soft delight,
Brooks, streams and rivers, bring before our sight!"—DELILLE.

RIVERS.

WE have followed the drop of water which we saw escaping from the ocean in the form of vapor, abandon itself to the breeze, allow itself to be rocked on the ever-moving air, and finally to be condensed into water, or ice, in the higher regions above the earth's surface. Let us now come and watch the melting of those eternal snows which crown the mountain top, and the formation of those thousand brooks, those countless torrents which descend from the slopes and wind their way, serpent-like, through valley and plain. Let us follow these liquid veins to the rivers with which they at last mingle their waters. Let us watch the rain as it penetrates here and there into clay or flint soils, and gathers in other localities in the cavities of the earth. Let us be present at the birth of the springs, where we see a miniature stream, flowing between herbs and flowers, a crystal thread, the embryo of the great river. Let us walk along its banks and listen to its murmur, and we shall not long doubt the possibility of the little brook, now so modest and so slender, becoming one day an immense body of water:

> "A thirsty giant at one draught could drink it,
> The green dwarf Oberon 'mid his play could leap
> From bank to bank nor wet his garment's hem."

So sings Hegesippus Moreau. But as we follow its course we see tributary streams appear, swelling its waters and increasing its volume. Its banks widen little by little, its volume increases, and ere long a majestic water-course fertilizes rich and populous kingdoms.

What can be more charming in its perfect purity and simplicity than the first origin of one of these rivers! High on the branches of lofty trees hang dense mists; under the cooling influence of their grateful shade pearl after pearl drops down, till every leaf, every blade has its precious, glittering jewel; and drop after drop it steals, and slips, and glides into the thirsty soil, and meets others and joins them in great glee. No eye sees the marvel; the earth guards her mysteries jealously; but yonder, where the rock leaves a tiny opening, a little bed of moss has formed, and in its centre rises the diminutive spring. Indefatigably it works its way upward, and yet so gently that no ear ever yet heard its first coming. Rich grasses spring up to shelter it from the burning sun, bushes and trees rise in statelier form to mark the birthplace, and soon gaththering strength the tiny rill runs off, out into the forest, down into the valley, off to new, distant lands.

And as it runs, it grows, and ere we can say, here it begins or there it begins, the river is at our feet, peaceful herds are reflected in its pure mirror, golden harvests mimic its gentle waves, trees creep up to its banks and place their sentinels on many a bluff and cliff, and yonder, in a sheltered bay, a little mill moves merrily under the new impulse, or a rich city rises on its banks, with lofty houses and stately cathedrals.

For the sources of many of the greatest rivers on earth are of most modest dimensions; the rivers Apurimac and Camisia, in Peru, and the Rhone in the Alps, are striking examples. In other cases, however, and especially in limestone regions, rivers start, as it were, fullgrown from the place of their birth. Of these the Sorgue, which has its origin in the famous spring of Vaucluse, is perhaps the most interesting. The source forms a square pool, 150 feet long and 90 feet wide, deep sunk in a limestone rock, so that the walls rise bare and perpendicular like a huge fortress. The basin below is filled with pure crystal water, supplied by snowy-white, foaming springs on the right and the left hand; one of these measures a foot in diameter where it breaks out of the live rock. A rocky path leads on the left down to the level of the water; half way stands on a little ledge a fig-tree, which overshadows the romantic spring. From here you perceive in the right corner of the basin a gigantic vaulted passage, which forms the entrance to an unfathomable well, and in the background opens a vaulted door with a view on a second lake. At low

SOURCE OF THE APURIMAC.

water the basin is but half filled, scarcely three feet deep, but when the water rises, new springs, some of which foam up at the bottom of the basin, enormous floods, fill it up to overflowing, till the waters boil up furiously and pour like a huge avalanche into the front basin, where they soon cover the path, and in violent upheavings reach, twenty feet high, to the roots of the fig-tree. Thus the Sorgue presents the rare spectacle of a river which is navigable a few feet from the spot where its source first breaks forth from the bosom of the earth.

All limestone regions, rich with caves, present similar, though less striking instances, of such springs, coming forth like Pallas Athene, fully armed. The Valley of Virginia is rich in such rivers, and one, Lincoln's Spring, turns a large mill not ten feet from its origin, and would bear boats of considerable size.

The chains of mountains trace for the rivers the routes which they must take. The higher mountains of the world collect the waters of the ocean and pour them down their sides back again towards the sea. Our mountains are not elevations cast up at hap-hazard on the earth's crust; on the contrary, they form a network symmetrically designed according to a regular pattern, so that the lines follow one another with a certain degree of precision, and the whole framework is systematically arranged. The rivers which water the great plains of continents are, in like manner, distributed with the same harmony which presides over all the creations of nature.

In the continents of the Old World, the lower chains of mountains take a direction from west to east,—those which extend from north to south being only secondary branches. The largest rivers flow in the direction prescribed to them by the elevations and depressions of the ground. The Euphrates, the Persian Gulf, the Yellow River, the Blue River, all the great water systems of China, travel from west to east, and the same holds good with regard to the chief arteries of all our continents; the larger water-courses of Africa and Asia, —the lakes, the Mediterranean Sea—all extend from west to east, the Nile and some rivers of Barbary forming the only exceptions.

Our own continent presents the same regularity in the distribution of its great liquid arteries. An enormous chain of mountains divides America into two great water sheds; and all the waters which glide down these immense slopes direct their course towards the sea, in accordance with the general law.

Such is the general view, as seen from a distance. In examining this great system of irrigation more closely, we perceive that the rivers pursue their winding courses with singular irregularity, alternately widening and contracting, following now a straight and now a circuitous path, describing a thousand sinuosities, meandering leisurely through valleys, and then being hemmed in between rocks and narrow channels, gliding rapidly down sudden slopes or remaining almost stationary in level lowlands, rushing down in rapids, leaping in cataracts, or reposing in lakes.

The mere force of the current of a river is able to modify the aspect of its route. Below is shown a curve traced by a course of water; the current winds back as if to retrace its steps, and the isthmus, *a*, constantly worn away by two opposing currents,

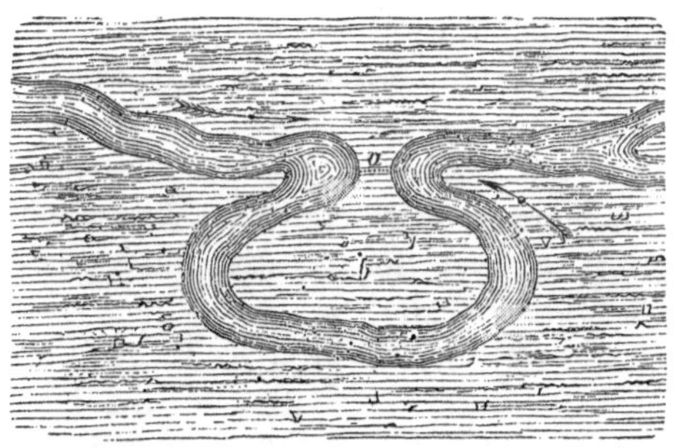

Curve described by a Stream of Water.

will no longer exist before many years are past, while the peninsula, *b*, will one day become an island.

LENGTH AND DEPTH OF RIVERS.

The greatest rivers of Europe are, the Volga, which has a course of 2,500 miles; the Danube, 2,423; the Don, 995; the Dnieper, 1,230; and the Vistula 530 miles.

In Asia, the river Yang-tse-kiang travels over a distance of 3,000 miles; the Cambodia, or Mekong, describes a course of over 2,000 miles; and the river Amoor 2,200; while the waters of the Ganges pass over a length of 1,960 miles, and the Euphrates nearly 1,780.

The Senegal, in Africa, accomplishes a journey of 3,000 miles, if we include the Niger, which is only a continuation of the same great river. The Nile has a course of about 1,300 miles in extent.

America has the largest arterial system of any part of the world. The Mississippi fertilizes the country which it traverses to a distance of about 4,350 miles, and the superficial extent of its basin, counting in its tributaries, is about 1,400,000 square miles, or more than seven times that of the whole of France. The width of the great American river varies from 80 feet to 1,200 yards, from the fall of St. Anthony to its confluence with the Illinois; it measures over a mile at its confluence with the Missouri, and even more at New Orleans, where it joins the Arkansas. Its depth is from 90 to 120 feet at its confluence with the Ohio, and from 100 to 110 feet between New Orleans and the Gulf of Mexico. It travels at the rate of two feet per second, or about 33 miles per day, and during the flood, in June, offers many difficulties to vessels ascending its course. The river Orinoco describes a course of 575 leagues in length, and the river De la Plata of 800.

But far more powerful yet is the vast stream of the Amazon, which falls into the waters of the Atlantic through an immense estuary, nearly 150 miles in width. Everything is colossal about this

SOURCE OF THE CAMISIA.

river, which restores to the sea all the rain and snow deposited in a basin of 2,000,000 square miles. So deep is it, that a plummet of 312 feet in length cannot always fathom its abysses; and so wide is it as to offer unobstructed navigation to vessels for three thousand miles of its course, whilst the horizon, touching its surface, hides its shores from view. It is, in point of fact, a fresh water sea, which at flood times discharges 732,000 cubic feet of water, moving 24,000 feet, each hour; that is to say, a volume sufficient to supply 3,000 such rivers as the Seine, in France.

At the time when the snow melts in the upper mountains, or when the tropical rains begin to fall, some of these gigantic rivers increase still further the immense volume of their waters, and overflow vast territories. Others, again, dry up altogether during the summer heat, as is the case with the wadis of Arabia, Africa, and Persia, and some rivers of New Holland. Still others are so undecided in their course—the water-shed being too low—that they branch off and connect with tributaries of other great streams; the Amazon is thus united, by bifurcation, with the Orinoco, and several great streams in Upper India form, by the same means, a perfect network. Such a division is, of course, highly favorable to navigation and the building of canals, as has already been shown in South America in the vast plains watered by La Plata and the Amazon.

The most rapid rivers are the Tigris, the Danube, and the Indus, etc. All the great water-courses receive into their channels a number of rivers, which form more or less extensive ramifications of the main artery. The Danube receives into its bosom about 200 rivers or brooks, the Volga 33.

If the sea were to become dry, it would take the rivers of the world 40,000 years to fill its basin once more.

SHORES AND FLOATING ISLANDS.

What a variety of aspects, what a diversity of features is represented by the course of all these rivers! The blue or vermilion colored water of some glide along over a bed of silicon, others, on the contrary, flow in yellowish waves over a slimy or muddy bed; some meander over a fertile soil and traverse hills enamelled with every description of plants, while others again dash over sharp rocks, or languish amidst the sands of the desert. In temperate zones it is the fresh and flowery turf, poplars and willows which seek the waterside and sink their roots deep in the moist soil. In Africa, the graceful foliage of the palm trees overshadows the surface of the rivers, as in the immense valley of the Nile; while the gigantic baobab darkens the waters of the Zambesi and other rivers. In tropical regions a luxuriant and entangled vegetation covers the banks of rivers, and dense copses of trees raise their lofty tops from amidst a confused mass of vegetable growths, their foliage towering high above the thick reeds and the water-plants with their gigantic leaves, while lianas and other creep-

TABLE OF COMPARATIVE LENGTH OF PRINCIPAL RIVERS.

Note: *The lengths are indicated in kilometres.* 10 " " 6.2 miles.

EUROPE AND ASIA

English Chan.l — Seine 630 — Côte d'Or
B. of Biscay — Loire 990 — Mt. Gerbier (Cévennes)
Mediterranean — Rhone 1050 — Mt. Furka (Alps)
Adriatic — Po 650 — Mt. Viso
Atlantic — Tagus 840
North Sea — Rhine 1100 — Mt. S. Bernard (Alps)
Elbe 1270
Oder 890 — Sudetic Mts.
Baltic Sea — Vistula 960 — Mt. Skalza (Silesia)
Don 1780 — L. Ivan
Black Sea — Dnieper 2000 — Hills of Wolkonski
Danube 2730 — Mts. of the Black Forest
Caspian Sea — Volga 3340 — Plateau of Waldai
Arctic — Obi 4300 — Altai Mts.
Lena 4440 — Werkholeniens Mts.
Yenissei 3180 — Mt. Sayansk
Japan Sea — Amoor 4380 — Kentei Mts.
Yellow Sea — Hoang-ho 4220 — Kuen-lun Mts.
China Sea — Yang-tse-kiang 5330 — Mts. of Thibet
B. of Bengal — Cambodia 3890
Brahmaputra 3000 — Mts. of Thibet
Ganges 3110 — Himalaya Mts.
G. of Oman — Indus 3630
Persian G. — Euphrates 2760

AFRICA

Mediterranean — Nile — L. Tzana — Blue — White 5100? — L. Nyanza — L. Louta Nzigho
Atlantic — Senegal 1550
G. of Guinea — Niger 3200 — Mt. Loma

AMERICA

Arctic — Mackenzie 3030 — L. Athabasca — Rocky Mts.
Pacific — Columbia 2500 — Rocky Mts.
G. of Mexico — Mississippi 6690 — Missouri — Mt. Sabine (Rocky Mts.) — Mississippi — L. Itasca
G. of California — Colorado 1470 — Cordillera of the Andes
St. Lawrence — L. Erie — L. Ontario — L. Huron — L. Michigan — L. Superior
Atlantic — Orinoco 2500
Amazon 7700
Pacific — Parana 3650 — Sn. Parana (Brazil)

OCEANICA

Murray (Australia) 1500 — Mt. Tambo (Australian Alps)

TABLE OF COMPARATIVE LENGTH OF RIVERS.

ing plants weave in the midst of this living labyrinth a thousand graceful garlands. The decayed trunks sink down between the living, but so dense is the vegetation that they cannot reach the ground, but are suspended in the air by a thousand stems and tendrils, forming a thick undergrowth, upheld by a thousand bands which entwine the living with the dead. The fecundity of nature appears here in its full power in the midst of this exuberant vegetation, which overflows in all directions. This overabundance of vegetation causes in American rivers a remarkable phenomenon, produced by the accumulation of huge trees. Native trees uprooted by the force of the wind or by land-slips, are swept off by the current, arrested in their course by islands, shoals and other obstacles, and form new islands, which, stretching across the river, become soon formidable impediments to navigation. Among the largest rafts, as they are called, of this kind we may mention those of a branch of the Mississippi, the Atchefalaya or Red River, which constantly bears along with the current a large quantity of wood brought from the North. During the last forty years this river has amassed such a quantity of floating débris in one spot that an enormous island has been formed. In 1816 this mass sank and rose as the river fell or rose; but this did not at all prevent the growth of vegetation from covering it, as with a mantle of verdure, and in every autumn it was gay with flowers. In 1838 the trees of the floating island had attained a height of sixty feet, and at last measures were taken, first by the State of

Louisiana, and then by the Federal Government, for the destruction of this immense raft, which formed an insurmountable obstacle to navigation. On the banks of the Red River, the Mississippi and the Missouri, the traveller often encounters accumulations of the same kind, and the courses of these rivers are, like that of the Atchefalaya, encumbered with masses of uprooted trees, and the too abundant remains of wrecked vessels. "United by the creeping plants," says Malte Brun, "and cemented by the mud of the river, this débris forms in time floating islands—young shrubs take root on them, the pistia and the water-lily display their yellow leaves; serpents, caymans and birds come to make their homes in the midst of these green and gay rafts, which sometimes are floated down to the sea. But here and there a larger tree is caught in a sand bank and becomes stationary; it extends its branches like so many hooks, from the grasp of which the floating islands cannot always disengage themselves. A single tree is thus often sufficient to impede the progress of a thousand others, and in the course of years these spoils from far-off shores accumulate and give birth to islands, promontories and capes, which at length change the entire course of the river."

THE COLORING OF RIVER WATER.

Nature seems to take a delight in tinging the waters of the Orinoco and other American rivers with shades of every hue. Some are blue, some green,

SNAGS IN THE MISSOURI.

some yellow; some are brown as coffee, some black as ink. The waters of the Atabapo, the banks of which are carpeted with carolineas, arborescent melastomes, those of the Temi, Tuamini and Guainia are of the color of chocolate; under the shade of the palm-trees, Humboldt says, they assume a black tint, and when imprisoned in a transparent vessel they appear of a golden yellow. These varieties of color, due, no doubt, to the dissolving of organic matter, converts the water into a complete mirror, and when the sun has disappeared below the horizon, the Orinoco forms an opaque mass and reflects with admirable clearness the rays of the moon and the constellations of the South.

The waters of the Orinoco, like those of the Nile and many other rivers of Africa and Asia, transfer their black color to their banks and the granite rocks which they have washed for so many centuries. Hence the discoloration of rocks and cliffs, which rise amphitheatrically above their shores, becomes an unfailing evidence of their former level. On the banks of the Orinoco, and in the rocks of Keri, at the mouth of the Iao, cavities may be seen painted black by the action of the river, and yet these cavities are more than 150 feet above the present level of the waters. Their existence demonstrates a fact already proved by other analogous evidence on the beds of European rivers—that those rivers, which strike us now-a-days by their vastness, are, after all, nothing more than the remains of gigantic bodies of water, which traversed our continent in the geological era before the birthday of mankind.

SUBTERRANEAN CIRCULATION.

The torrents of rain which the clouds pour down upon the surface of our globe, do not all return to the sea, following the tracks worked out for them by trenches, furrows, and the beds of rivers. Enormous quantities of water penetrate into the bosom of the earth, percolate into stone, sand and clay, absorbed by porous rocks, and descend by their gravity till at last they find their subterrauean voyage stopped by layers of impermeable substances. A natural drainage is thus constantly at work under the thin crust of the earth, and the waters are to be found accumulated beneath in vast unknown reservoirs. Streams, water-courses, and even large rivers sometimes disappear suddenly into a bottomless gulf; swallowed up by yawning mouths they penetrate into mysterious ravines and escape into deep and unexplored abysses. The Guardiana is thus lost in a flat country, in the centre of an immense prairie, but reappears on the surface of the earth after having traversed the subterranean arch of a natural bridge, under which, to use the Spanish phrase, a hundred thousand horned cattle could find "pasture." The Meuse loses itself at Basoilles, and the Drôme in Normandy disappears suddenly in the midst of a plain, in a hole over thirty feet in diameter. These examples might be easily multiplied, and numberless instances might be cited in which rivers are partially lost, as is the case with the Rhone. According to Pliny, the Alphano, in the Peloponnesus, the Tigris in Mesopotamia, and the Timavius, in the territory of Aquilega, accomplished the most mysterious journeys after burying themselves under ground.

Besides these local infiltrations there exist within the bowels of the earth liquid masses of another nature, real currents and veritable subterranean rivers. The action of subterranean fires drives into the cavities of volcanic rocks, currents of water which are kept in motion by the igneous force.

Hot springs suddenly spring out of the ground, and then again disappear as suddenly by the way they came; lakes cover square miles with their limpid waters and then leave them dry once more; masses of water run off through unexpected openings and fill the ground beneath with liquid streams in all directions.

The most remarkable instance of such a mass of water varying in its level, is to be seen in a lake at Zirknitz, in Carniola, which extends in winter over a surface of six miles long and three miles wide. Toward the middle of summer, when the sun pierces the earth with his burning rays, its level sinks rapidly, and in less than three or four weeks its bed is frequently completely dry. The water escapes by means of numberless clefts and fissures in the limestone rock, which forms the bottom and which at that time may be distinctly seen. It goes to supply the neighboring streams by subterraneous channels and caverns, and the peasants do not hesitate to sow millet and buckwheat where the water was just now 50 feet deep, or, to reap the luxuriant herbage which springs up spontaneously, they use the sickle where they previously employed a fishing net. When the hay has been got in and the soil of the lake has rewarded the husbandman's toil by a rich and abundant crop, the water returns by the same opening and inundates the valley, bringing back with it the fish that have followed it in its subterranean wanderings. Zirknitz is in fact a true subterranean lake, as migratory as a swallow, which in summer buries itself in the bowels of the earth and in winter comes forth again to fill its basin. Intermittent lakes of the same nature are to be found in France and various other countries. "Near Sable, in Anjou," says Arago, "there existed in 1741, a spring, or to speak more correctly a gulf, 18 to 24 feet in diameter, usually known by the name of the bottomless fountain. It frequently overflows, bringing with it a prodigious quantity of fish, such as pike and trout; there is ground, therefore, for supposing that this spot formed the vault of a subterranean lake." The upper layers of stratified gravel are often found to alternate with layers of water at various depths. It is thus at St. Nicholas d'Alimont, near Dieppe, where as many as seven sheets of water have been counted, placed one upon another and separated one from the other by solid layers of earth. In 1831, while an artesian well was being dug at Tours, the workmen brought up from the depth of the earth clear water, which contained branches of briars, marsh plants and seeds in a state of perfect preservation, proving decisively that they could not have been any length of time beneath the water. That these reservoirs are not merely the result of infiltrations, is abundantly proved by the fact that they frequently carry along with them bits of wood and shells which could not have passed through the pores of the natural filters. The celebrated fountain of Nismes, which discharges on an average 1,000 quarts of water a second, has often been seen pouring forth ten times as much after one of the violent rains common to that region. Moreover, it has been observed that such an exceptional overflow often occurred after heavy rains had fallen at a considerable distance, a fact which proves that water can rapidly traverse great distances, making its way through subterranean passages.

While thus penetrating into the fissures of the soil the water becomes heated in its passage through the solid crust of the earth; it attains often quite a high temperature, and reappears on the surface of the earth in a boiling condition. The thermal springs of every description owe their heat to such an increase of temperature by long subterranean wanderings. On their way they dissolve the rocks which obstruct their passage, the component parts of which, being united with the water, form mineral springs endowed with more or less valuable medicinal qualities. It is thus, also, that Iceland produces those marvellous fountains of boiling water which are known by the name of Geysers. Every half hour a heavy rumbling sound announces the bubbling up of the boiling liquid. It bursts from the ground with a loud noise, and rises in an immense column 18 feet in diameter, and 150 feet high. Presently the column of water vibrates, it falls back upon itself and disappears in the mysterious underground opening from which it arose. But again it appears and rises up on high before the astonished gaze of the traveller who penetrates into those wild regions. "The enormous quantity of water raised," says Lord Dufferin, "its violence, its latent power, the vast masses of luminous vapor, bursting forth with inexhaustible profusion, all combine in rendering this phenomenon one of the most remarkable freaks of nature." New Zealand in the same manner presents very striking instances of boiling springs. "All round Lake Roto Mahana," says a recent traveller—Hochstetter, "there rise from every foot of ground dense volumes of vapor, and there are more than 200 geysers issuing from the east side of the boiling lake. The most remarkable of these burning mouths is the Te-Ta-Rata, the principal outlet of that mass of water which has become heated by contact with the central flames of our globe. The enormous column of water rises up in a boiling state to the summit of an eminence from 90 to 100 feet, and fills with one jet an oval basin 200 feet in circumference, bordered round its edges by a snow-white drapery of stalactites."

Nor must it be forgotten that we have geysers quite as remarkable in size and beauty in our own country. The valley of the Yellowstone, we are told by Governor Langford, is full of cascades, craters and boiling springs, there being probably no other region

FAN GEYSER.

on the globe where nature has crowded so much of grandeur and majesty with so much of novelty and wonder. A few miles above the union of the Fire Hole and the Burnt Hole River, there is a large basin filled with magnificent geysers, twelve of which were found by the intrepid traveller in full action. Six of these, from vents varying from three to five feet in diameter, threw water to the height of 25 feet, while others threw columns of boiling water from 90 to 120 feet at each discharge, which lasted from 15 to 20 minutes. But others were still more magnificent. Thus, on a gentle, incrusted slope, a large oval aperture was suddenly observed, the sides corrugated and covered with a greyish-white silicious deposit, which was distinctly visible at the depth of 100 feet below the surface. "No water could be discovered," says Governor Langford, "but we could distinctly hear it gurgling and boiling at a great distance below. Suddenly it began to rise, boiling and spluttering, and sending out huge masses of steam, causing a general stampede of our company, driving us some distance from our point of observation. When within about forty feet of the surface it became stationary, and we returned to look down upon it. It was foaming and surging at a terrible rate, occasionally emitting small jets of hot water nearly to the mouth of the orifice. All at once it seemed seized with a fearful spasm, and rose with incredible rapidity, hardly affording us time to flee to a safe distance, when it burst from the orifice with terrific momentum, rising in a column the full size of this immense aperture to the height of sixty feet and out of the apex of this vast aqueous mass, five or six lesser jets or round columns of water, varying in size from six to fifteen inches in diameter, were projected to the marvellous height of two hundred and fifty feet. These lesser jets, so much higher than the main column, and shooting through it, doubtless proceed from auxiliary pipes leading into the principal orifice near the bottom, where the explosive force is greater. If the theory that water by constant boiling becomes explosive when freed from air be true, this theory rationally accounts for all irregularities in the eruptions of the geysers.

"This grand eruption continued for twenty minutes, and was the most magnificent sight we ever witnessed. We were standing on the side of the geyser nearest the sun, the gleams of which filled the sparkling column of water and spray with myriads of rainbows, whose arches were constantly changing,—dipping and fluttering hither and thither, and disappearing only to be succeeded by others, again and again, amid the aqueous column, while the minute globules into which the spent jets were diffused, when falling sparkled like a shower of diamonds, and around every shadow which the denser clouds of vapor, interrupting the sun's rays, cast upon the column, could be seen a luminous circle radiant with all the colors of the prism, and resembling the halo of glory represented in paintings as encircling the head of Divinity. All that we had previously witnessed seemed tame in comparison

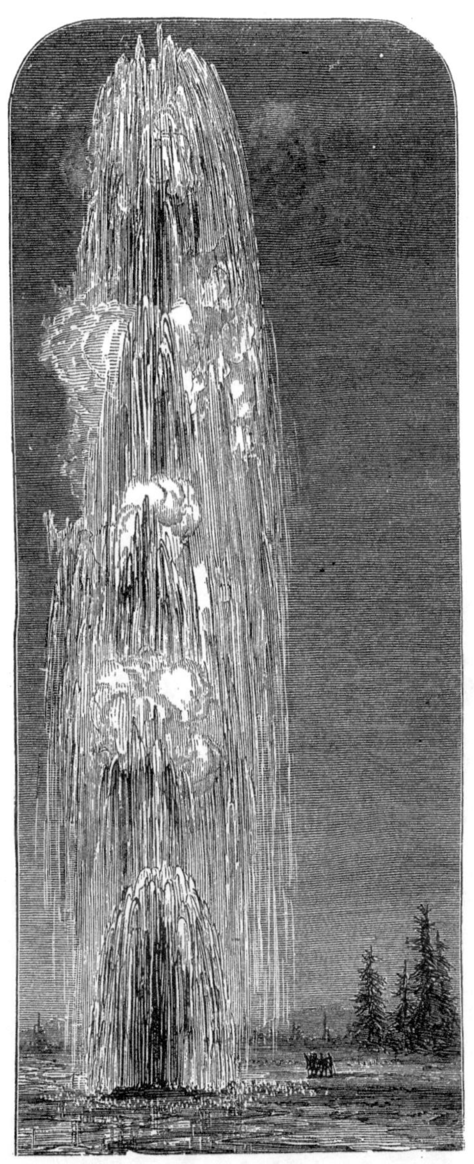

THE GIANTESS.

with the perfect grandeur and beauty of this display. Two of these wonderful eruptions occurred during the twenty-two hours we remained in the valley. This geyser we named 'The Giantess.'"

"*Wonders of the Yellowstone;*" *Scribner for June*, 1871.

III.

THE ACTION OF WATER ON CONTINENTS.

"The waters seem incessantly laboring to level the inequalities of the globe."—SIR CHARLES LYELL.

CHAPTER I.

MECHANICAL AND PHYSICAL ACTION.

"The waters play a very important part in the changes which are made upon the surface of the globe, especially by the movement by which they may be animated."—BEUDANT.

WHILST travelling over the earth by way of river beds, lakes and basins, and subterranean canals, water is forever accomplishing works important and innumerable. Its destructive power is mainly shown in the peculiarity it possesses of expanding by congelation. Penetrating into the fissures of the hardest and most compact rocks, it succeeds in breaking them by the mechanical force which it develops in solidifying; enormous blocks of stone are thus detached from the mountain-sides, as if a powerful and irresistible lever had raised them for the purpose of precipitating them into the valley beneath.

The solvent power of water plays also a great part in the constant changes which our earth undergoes; the water eats away the soil with which it comes in contact, by gently diluting the earthy matter; it penetrates through all fissures, deprives the earthy particles of the natural cement which binds them together, and in that way produces landslips, which are often followed by the most formidable convulsions. Its powers of transportation are still more important; earthy matter being incessantly washed away and carried along by the running water; stones, even rocks, being sometimes carried to a great distance. The friction of the fragments, finally, borne along by torrents, operates like a steel file, capable of polishing granite and other hard substances, and of producing enormous excavations in the mountains.

These multiform effects, these various works, are often accomplished simultaneously, but in order to study profitably these different actions of water, it is necessary to pass them in review one after another. We will therefore enter on the subject methodically, keeping sure hold of the thread which is to guide us, so that we need not be afraid of losing ourselves in a labyrinth of facts.

THE CURRENTS—TRANSPORTATION.

We may well find matter of astonishment in the facility with which currents, far from rapid in their course, transport heavy sand and gravel. But it must be remembered that the weight of a rock in water is not the same as in the air, for every one has noticed how much lighter he feels when the body is in the water. Archimedes made the same curious observation long before us, and it led him to the

RAVINE OF OCCOCAMBA.

discovery of one of the most important principles in hydrostatics.

Whenever any substance is plunged in water it loses part of its weight, equal to the weight of the volume of water which it displaces, and as the density of a great number of stones is not more than double that of water, it follows that substances drifted along by a current generally lose half of what we term their weight. The waters of the majority of rivers do not flow with any great rapidity, and yet the quantity of mud which they carry along with them is enormous. It has been ascertained that the waters of the Po hold in solution $\frac{1}{160}$ of their own weight in solid matter, those of the Rhine $\frac{1}{100}$, those of the Yellow River $\frac{1}{200}$. A current which flows at the rate of two feet per second, will carry along with it a large quantity of fine sand; with a speed of thirty inches, fine gravel; and if it has a speed of three feet per second it will sweep along stones the size of an egg.

From the calculations of Major Rennel it has been ascertained that the Ganges pours into the sea, at the time when it is at the highest flood, a mass of water weighing 2,850 tons a second. Taking into account all the fine sand and sediment which it carries along, it has been calculated that this river must cast into the ocean 1,300,000,000 cubic yards of solid matter every ten days. In ordinary times, when the river is not swollen, this mass of solid matter requires three weeks for its discharge. The total mass of deposit drifted down by the Ganges into the sea during the space of one year would, according to Sir Charles Lyell, exceed in weight 42 of the great pyramids of Egypt; and that carried down during four months of the flood season would be equal to 40 pyramids. The mind has no faculties adequate to the conception of the grand scale on which the river Ganges carries on its vast transportation. Looking on the slow course of this powerful body of water, watching it traverse majestically the alluvial plain through which it flows, it would be difficult to realize the mighty work it accomplishes. What efforts would be necessary on the part of man before he could hope to effect the same end? It would require from eighty to one hundred vessels of the East India Company, each loaded with 1,400 tons of sand and mud, to transport from the upper basin of the Ganges to its mouth, a mass of material equal to what the great river so easily carries during the four months when it is flooded. If to these labors of the Ganges be added those of all the other rivers, we arrive at prodigious results, and see in water a Titanic laborer that never ceases to tear from our continents the earthy materials of which they are formed, and to bear them far away into the realms of the ocean. But rivers do not only drift away mud; they carry in their waters various mineral substances held in solution. The water which falls upon the earth dissolves the rocks and stones which it meets in its course, and confines in its liquid prison-house the carbonate of lime, gypsum, salts of magnesia, rock salt, silica, and oxide of iron, which it takes from the surface of the earth.

ROCKS TORN AWAY BY A TORRENT.

JUNCTION OF YANATILI AND QUILLABAMBA RIVERS, PERU.

The pure water of the clouds returns charged with salts to the sea. The result is, apparently, a constant accumulation of soluble materials in the sea, and an augmentation of saltness, which might be supposed to arrest the development of life in the marine world. But all the plants which grow upon the seaside, all the seaweeds which are reached by the tide, all the forests growing at the bottom of the ocean, are supported by absorbing the mineral elements of the sea, and by assimilating with themselves the salts which they meet with there, a circumstance which greatly tends to equalize the action of rivers. The zoöphites and mollusks are, in like manner, nourished by the carbonate of lime which the fresh water in its course has drifted into their domains, and thus they change into corals, madrepores, and shells, the chalk cliffs which formerly covered our continents. "Is not that spectacle a grand one," says Dumas, "which is offered to us by Nature, in the sublime simplicity of the means which she employs? The water of the clouds, charged with the carbonic acid of the air, falls upon our limestone hills; it becomes charged there with the carbonate of lime, which it pours into the bosom of rivers. Carried onwards into the ocean, it is soon drawn into regular currents, and, seized by microscopic animals, it adds one more stone to the new structures, which are gradually prepared there for the future empire of mankind."

TORRENTS AND RAPIDS.

When water glides down a steep declivity, its velocity and powers of transportation are wonderfully augmented, and enormous rocks, thus borne away, follow the rapid march of rivers down the sides of steep mountains; streams precipitate themselves with extreme violence, chasing before them blocks of stone, which frequently weigh a ton and more; at times they poise them at hap-hazard upon other rocks, and do not carry them away until after a stoppage of longer or shorter duration. Thus it happens that rocks, whose first home was on the summit of mountains, are carried down into the valley, and thence into adjacent plains. There the river breaks them up into fragments and rolls them on to the sea. Amidst the downs which characterize Northern shores, among the millions of broken and polished shingle, there is, perhaps, many a pebble which has come down all the way from the summit of the Alps.

In the New World, large rivers often precipitate themselves down the slopes with astonishing rapidity. These rapids do not always prevent navigation, and the American Indians used to venture in their light canoes along such rapids, defying the formidable obstacle. The rapids of Montmorency, in Canada, thus formerly suffered the canoes of the natives occasionally to glide down upon their bosom.

In a great number of localities, such rivers appear as torrents of mud, when clay and turf gradually sink to the bottom and produce terrible ravages in their course.

The peat bogs of certain parts of Ireland, being situated on an incline, thus sometimes become swollen after long, heavy rains, and gradually begin to move as soon as they have changed into a sort of soft and viscid paste. Then they glide and slide down rapidly, notwithstanding their muddy consistency; their rapidity increases visibly, and soon they are able to overcome every obstacle. In 1835, after the landslip of the Dent du Midi, in the Alps, an enormous mass of earthy *débris* formed a black and compact mud, which did not contain one tenth part of water; notwithstanding which, it flowed down into the Rhone, carrying huge blocks of stone into the bosom of the river, causing the latter to overflow the opposite bank.

The celebrated mud torrents of Peru and Java have often been described by travellers; they slip down declivities, and cover entire fields with an immense mantle of clay.

FLOATING ICE.

In those countries in which the cold of winter is sufficiently intense to convert the surfaces of rivers into ice, the power of transportation possessed, as we have shown, by all running water, is considerably augmented. In 1821, M. Larivière being present at the breaking up of the ice at Niemen, on the Baltic, saw a floating block of ice nearly 30 feet long, carried down by the current of the river, and run aground on the bank. In the centre of this mass of solid water, a block of granite, more than three feet in diameter, was discovered. This stone, resembling the red granite of Finland, had thus been transported on a raft of ice.

All floating ice contains numbers of pebbles and fragments of stone, which, imprisoned in a frozen envelope at the moment when the latter is formed, are carried along until the day when a higher temperature releases them by melting the mold in which they are contained. It is possible that the loosening of rocks which are frozen on to blocks of ice, may take place even under water; for the weight of the mass thus formed may become sufficient to cause it to sink, as has often been seen in the rivers of Siberia.

WATERFALLS AND CASCADES.

The numerous cascades which we meet in the rivers of Europe and Asia, and, indeed, of all countries, afford us, beyond any other work of nature, striking evidence of the effects of water in modifying by its inroads the shape of continents.

In our own country, the Niagara escapes from Lake Erie, cuts its way through the soil with great rapidity, and after a course of 34 miles, precipitates itself into an immense abyss in order to reach Lake Ontario. An island, situated on the edge of the Falls, divides it into two distinct sheets of water, one producing the Horse-shoe, and the other the American Fall. The mass of water precipitates itself into the abyss, while its waves roll over a bed

FALLS OF NIAGARA.

of hard limestone, overlying, in horizontal strata, a bank of soft clay. The limestone rock juts out nearly 40 feet into open space, and forms a threatening projection, an enormous protuberance, which appears every instant on the point of tumbling into the gulf beneath.

The lower bed of clay is incessantly undermined by the clouds of vapor and foam which continually rise from the basin into which the cascade falls, and strike the earthy wall with the violence of shot. The limestone bed, thus deprived of its support, becomes disintegrated and crumbles into pieces, which fall into the lower basin, causing by their fall a shock which is sometimes felt at a great distance, and echoes through the air like a clap of distant thunder.

When the river has passed the falls and reached the foot of the gigantic declivity, it rolls its hoarsely roaring waves down the bottom of a valley which it has scooped out for itself in its fury—a valley, the walls of which it is perpetually raising from the bottom. On the bed of the river are heaped, pell-mell, rocks, tossed promiscuously one upon another; its shores bristle with jagged cliffs, which prevent the traveller from looking down into the bottom of the ravine, unless he approaches close to the threatening precipice. These vast heaps of fragments, these rocks, which came perhaps originally from some far distant country, form a marvellous combination of all that is wild and grand, and prove that all these materials have been torn, dragged, swept away from the soil which gave them birth, by a force which is none other than that of water—a power no obstacle can resist.

The destruction of the rocky layers through which this short but terrible river flows, the modified form of the limestone rocks through which it hurries on its course, have caused the falls to move backwards and still force them to take a retrograde course. In 1829 Mr. Bakewell ascertained that the Canadian Fall was situated at a distance of 120 to 150 feet from the spot which it occupied 50 years before. If the retrograde movement of the falls had been going on always with the same velocity, the ravine into which they precipitate themselves would have been dug out in 10,000 years. To render such calculations exact, it would, however, be necessary to know and understand the topography of the country before the formation of the falls. The action which takes place under our own eyes, may be widely different from that which took place centuries ago. In hazarding conjectures of this description a wise reserve is therefore desirable; nor is it less difficult to arrive at probable suppositions as to the future retrogression of the immense cataract. In proportion as it moves further from the place where it actually escapes, the height of the precipice may increase or diminish in consequence of various modifying causes. However this may be, if in the course of years the falls of Niagara should reach Lake Erie, that lake would probably be dried up rapidly, for its greatest depth does not exceed the height of the falls. Its mean depth being about 120 feet, it may even be dried up some time before that event. The tourists

UPPER FALLS OF THE YELLOWSTONE.

and travellers of the next century will thus be deprived of one of the most beautiful spectacles which Nature can offer them amidst all the effects, so varied and changing, so picturesque and so grand, which she knows how to produce by means of the liquid element.

The Zambesi is also a striking example of vast excavations produced by the action of water. This great African river engulfs itself in a vast abyss, which it is incessantly deepening, and its fall produces torrents of froth and vapor which rise into the air and become well nigh lost amid the clouds. Picture to yourself a river much over a mile wide, which suddenly finds itself without a bed, and which falls into a deep and narrow ravine. The waters confined within this gulf boil up with so much energy that five vast whirlpools, called by the negroes who dwell upon its shores, "the smoke that thunders," rise up towards heaven in light and graceful columns which yield to the wind's breath; white at their base, dark at their summit, they resemble the smoke of a vast chimney. The immense fissure through which the Zambesi escapes, is a flaw in a long bank of basalt; this fissure is continued beyond the falls and forms a long zig-zag furrow in which the waters eddy and rebound with great force, part of its sides being carved and seamed by the ever-moving water, which wears and polishes them unceasingly.*

But it is especially near the falls of the Felou that

* Livingstone's Explorations in South Africa.

the most beautiful and sculpture-like effects of fresh water may be seen acting on a rocky substance. The Senegambian river flows between banks formed by natural embankments in stone. Its waters put in motion the pebbles of red quartz which they meet with in their course, and the rock, worn away as if by the action of the drill or the chisel, is cut into numerous holes. At the time of the year when the waters are low, we find at the bottom of these cavities or pot-holes, as we call them, piles of pebbles which reveal this mode of formation. In other places the rocks are carved into small fissures of every sort, and represent designs in intaglio, not less worthy our attention, "so much do they resemble miniature cathedrals, Prometheuses, Laocoöns, horses, men, strange and nameless animals, and antique sarcophagi, Gothic baths and human footprints. These marvels have exercised the imagination of the negroes and given rise to a host of legends."*

Switzerland and the Pyrenees both abound in similar marvels. Who has not heard of the beauties of the falls of the Rhine near Shaffhausen, and can there be anything more sublime than the ten or twelve torrents which throw themselves from the heights of the Circus of Gavarnie? Imagine a semicircular area enclosed by a wall over one thousand feet high, surmounted with snow; picture to yourself on the summit of this amphitheatre a series of battlements formed by the glaciers, which give birth to abounding torrents. The most considerable of the falls of

* Raffenel's Voyage in the Land of the Negroes.

FALLS OF THE ZAMBESE.

Gavarnie has an altitude of over 1,200 feet. "It falls gently as a descending cloud or as a muslin veil, which is being spread out—the air breaks its fall; the eye finds pleasure in following the graceful undulations of this beautiful aerial veil. It glides down the whole length of the rocks, and appears

Falls of the Rhine.

rather to float than to flow. The sun shines through its feathery waters with the softest and most agreeable lustre. It reaches the bottom in a form resembling a plume of light and softly waving feathers, and rises up again in a dense silvery dust; the cool and transparent vapors rise and fall gracefully around the wet stones, and their rebounding trail mounts lightly up along the precipice. The air is motionless, and no living creature exists in this solitude. Nothing is to be heard but the monotonous murmur of the cascades, which resembles the rustling of the leaves in a forest, agitated by the wind."*

Where great rivers are shallow, and pour their waters over low cliffs as over an irregular dam, the fall is called a cataract, such as the Nile forms in its upper part; while isolated cliffs, forcing the water back with great violence, and producing a rotary movement, cause whirlpools. Rapids, on the other hand, owe their origin generally to the sudden narrowing of the bed of a river, which is thus compelled to rush through the confined space with furious haste. The most remarkable are those of the Connecticut River, which, at one place, 400 feet wide, is all of a sudden forced through narrows leaving scarcely a space of fifteen feet; the waters are so forcibly compressed by the current from above, that lead and iron swim on them like cork, and even a crowbar cannot be forced down to any considerable depth.

---

* Taine, *Travels in the Pyrenees.*

CHAPTER II.

DELTAS.

"On the same principle by which waters are continually wasting away portions of our continents, they must be perpetually creating some portion of new land, proportionate in size to that which they carry away."—BEUDANT.

AFTER the melting of the snows, or after a violent storm, the water-courses become greatly increased in bulk; they overflow their banks, they spread out into the valleys and cover them with a large liquid sheet, which deposits a thick layer of mud. When the waters swell quietly in the bosom of lakes, they surrender likewise all these earthy substances which elsewhere are carried away by currents in their rapid course, forming thus deposits of a greater or less thickness. "When the rivers," says Cuvier, "have at length reached the sea, and when the rapidity which swept away the particles of clay has at length ceased, these particles are deposited on the sides of the river's mouth, forming thus gradually a soil which lengthens out the coast, and if the seaboard be of a form which allows the waves to cast upon it much mud, and in this way to contribute its share to such an extension, whole provinces and entire kingdoms are thus created, usually the most fertile, and whenever the government allows industry to develop itself untrammelled, the richest in the world."

The mud which the rivers set in motion is thus deposited in lakes and inland seas, and at the mouths of streams, which fall into the ocean, and gives birth to three distinct classes of deltas.

The alluvial soil which is formed at the mouth of the Rhone, towards the upper end of the lake of Geneva, affords a striking instance of the enormous size which superincumbent layers of mud may acquire in a short space of time. The village of Portus Valesiæ (Port Valais), which stood eight centuries ago on the very edge of the Swiss lake, is now actually separated from it by a tongue of land over 6,000 feet long. The sand and mud deposited by the waters have formed this vast territory, and we can even now see the liquid element daily as it gives birth to a great number of smaller deltas on the banks of the Lake of Geneva, perpetually invade the dominions of the blue and transparent waves.

Lake Superior, the largest lake in the world, which covers an area almost equal to that of France, sends forth from its bosom considerable quantities of earthy substances and of sediment which are regularly deposited in thick layers. Like the other Canadian lakes, Lake Superior presents upon its shores precious evidence of the work effected by its waters in times long gone by, and from these we learn that its waters attained formerly a very high level. At a long distance from its present shores we meet with parallel rows of pebbles and banks of shells, which form one above another superincumbent layers resembling the steps of an amphitheatre. These rows of pebbles washed up here by the waters, these collections of shells brought together by the motion of the waves, present a striking analogy with the banks which are now rising in like manner round a number of bays. They sometimes reach a considerable height, and some are found upon ground more than 45 feet higher than the present level.

The majority of rivers form at their mouths deltas larger or smaller, which infringe upon and modify the domain of the ocean by subjecting the outline of its shores to great and frequent changes. The account which Strabo gives us of the delta of the Rhone in the Mediterranean does not agree with its present configuration, a fact indicating the alterations which have, since the days of Augustus, modified the aspect of that country. The increase of this delta during the last ten centuries is however measurable, owing to the existence of certain structures which speak to us in clear language. Far distant from the present coast we can still see several rows of towers and nautical signal stations which were certainly erected on the coast itself. The peninsula of Mega, described by Pomponius Mela, is now inland, far away from the shores of the Mediterranean. The tower of Tignaux, erected on the coast in 1737, is now nearly 5,500 feet distant from the sea.

The Adriatic Sea presents a combination of all the circumstances which are most favorable to the formation of a delta. A bay which enters far up into the land, and a sea without either tide or currents, receiving the tribute of the Po, the Adige, and numerous other rivers, thus presents us in all its features, the spectacle of the work of forming a delta, as it is effected by the power of transportation possessed by fresh water courses. All the rivers which discharge their water into the Adriatic are incessantly making up mighty dams of mud and sand, torn from the lands through which they have passed. In this manner they form against the Adriatic a redoubtable alliance, a terrible coalition, in order to advance the line of coast. Adria, which in the time of Augustus was able to receive the Roman galleys in its port, is now an inland town, surrounded by fields situated at a distance of eight leagues from the coast. The town of Spina, which in the days of the Etruscans lay close upon the coast of the Adriatic, at the mouth of a large arm of the Po, is now four leagues inland, and Ravenna, in the Middle Ages a famous seaport, is now nearly five miles from the shore.

The Po, drifting down to its mouth enormous volumes of mud and fine sand, is constantly invading the sea, which, having no ebb and flow, is unable to offer any resistance to the intrusions of the stream. All those countries are incessantly exposed to extensive changes, such as for instance those produced by the river Isonzo, which has gradually abandoned its bed, driven from it by its own mud and alluvial deposit. It runs now above a league to the west of its former channel, and in the neigh-

FALLS OF FELOU.

borhood of Roncai an ancient Roman bridge has been found buried beneath fluvial mud.

The Nile, which, like the majority of great rivers, is subject, from the effects of the atmospheric variations, to periodical inundations and annual overflowings, spreads its waters in consequence of the gradual elevation of its bed over more and more extensive tracts, and the alluvium gains every year upon the sand of the desert. Antique temples and statues, which ten centuries ago overhung its waters, are now disappearing under a thick layer of mud. The priests of Egypt were therefore correct in terming their country "a gift from Heaven," since it owes its fecundity to the generous river which fertilizes its soil.

In consequence of the Nile depositing its sediments inland, it does not rapidly increase the great delta at its mouth; notwithstanding which some of the mouths of the Nile, mentioned by ancient geographers, are now completely closed, being stopped up by the mud. "The distance of the island of Pharos from Egyptus," says Homer, "is equal to that which a vessel can accomplish in a day with a favorable wind." At present a swimmer can, in a few strokes, reach this island, which has become united to the mainland by an artificial dam.

The "Sacred River" has thus raised its valley more than sixty feet, during the 160 centuries of its known history; for, by the aid of ancient historians, dating from the days of the Roman emperors, it can be easily ascertained how much has been gained since their time, and the same standard may be fairly applied to preceding ages. Occasionally, natural obstacles force the river to one side; in such cases it covers gradually the whole valley with mud and slime, raising it not unfrequently hundreds of feet, and changing its course. The Mississippi, it is well known, is continually "wandering" in this way, changing its bed more or less every season; the Gihon, which formerly fell into the Caspian Sea, now flows, pressed back by sand-banks, its own offspring, into Lake Aral; the Po and the Adige have raised their bed so that they are now higher than the adjoining plains, and in like manner, several canals in Holland are raised high above fields and meadows.

The greatest delta on earth is that of the Ganges, which measures over 200 miles in width and length. From the highest mountain range of our earth, water flows in a thousand tributaries toward the giant river, till, united with the Brahmapootra, it strikes the northern point of the Gulf of Bengal. The immense proportion of mud which it brings with it, often a hundredth part of its volume, is here deposited, arrested as it is by the inflowing tide of ocean, and forms a vast plain, known as the Sunderbund, consisting of swamp and morass, shallow lakes and immense jungle, the home of tigers, crocodiles and serpents.

When the rivers, instead of pouring their waters into inland seas, throw themselves into the ocean, they become subject to the influence of tides, and the deltas are in consequence less rapid in formation. The tidal currents maintain a fierce struggle with the river current, and often instead of the land making an inroad upon the sea, it is the salt water which penetrates far into the mouth of a fresh water river. The ocean thus intrudes into the continent and there forms a gulf, an estuary, in fact a *negative delta.*

But when the volume of the river is very considerable, when the velocity of its waters is enormous, the action of the tides may be neutralized, and the continental artery succeed in constructing its delta in spite of the wrath of the waves.

When the waters of rivers are low, the tide exercises its influence as far as the extremity of the delta, but when they are swollen by tropical rains, they rush forward with an impetuosity which is terrible, and they are capable of resisting the oscillations of the sea to repulse the mighty element and to surmounting every obstacle. The delta then increases in a short space of time, and rapidly advances against the empire of the waves. During the other seasons of the year the waves of the sea take a terrible revenge; the army of billows sweeps unhampered through the channels, drowning the alluvial plains, and the salt water makes reprisals at the expense of the fresh water.

CHAPTER III.

INUNDATIONS.

"It is an error to estimate the harmonies of nature by merely calculating what advantages may be drawn from them by man; for if nature be his auxiliary, she is at the same time his antagonist. He is constantly carrying on against her a war which admits of no truce, combating her with her own weapons, until the inevitable day in which he has to confess himself vanquished."—LAUGEL.

THE peaceful rivers of large plains occasionally have their times of wrath and passion. In times of peace, their wide, level bed affords them ample room; but when the windows of heaven, and the sluices of the earth are opened, these mighty arteries also swell, the rivers overflow their banks, and, like lakes, inundate boundless plains. Where rains occur periodically, inundations also accompany them regularly. The Orinoco rises from April to September, often nearly 100 feet, and then affords for months the magnificent spectacle of an inland sea, 100 miles wide, and more than 1,000 miles long, with countless whirlpools and waterfalls. Only in October it recedes, and resumes, in February, its former bed. The Ganges also rises in April, when the snows of the Himalaya swell its waters, and, uniting with the Brahmapootra, forms an immense lake, with here and there a town or a village rising like islands. .The inundations of the Nile are blessings, but the June-rise of our Mississippi turns but too often into a curse.

The Orinoco.

Not unfrequently sudden inundations become the causes of fearful disasters. Thus, in 1816, the White Mountains, in New Hampshire, were (after two years of drought) inundated by a deluge of rain.

The torrents thus formed, flowing rapidly along the sides of the mountains, rolled large stones down to the banks of the river Saco; their speed becoming accelerated from second to second, it was not long before they drew along with them earth and trees, which they had uprooted. One of these moving masses, measuring not less than 100 yards in extent, precipitated itself into the bed of the Saco, and produced a partial overflow, whilst other torrents also became visibly swollen under the influence of the rain. In a few hours several valleys were completely inundated, and from all parts, torrents came rushing down furiously, bringing with them uprooted trees and whole forests, torn from the ground, and falling like stalks of wheat beneath the scythe of the reaper. The rivers Saco and Ammonoosuck completely overflowed their banks, burst forth from their channels, and deluged the surrounding plains so completely, that in a short time many square miles of neighboring country presented a terrible scene of devastation.

In 1818 the valley of Bagnes was converted into an immense lake, owing to the stopping up of some outlets by avalanches. This lake was dammed up by glaciers and by embankments of snow, which melted in the spring, and the valley, full of water, became empty in less than half an hour. The waters formed across the open defiles a torrent of nearly 20,000 cubic feet in bulk, and, precipitating themselves with a speed of 30 feet to the second, they inundated, to a great distance off, the adjacent country, carrying with them houses, trees, rocks, and ploughed soil. The list of such disasters is, unhappily, but too long, and examples of the same description might be infinitely multiplied. In these catastrophes, water displays all the violence of its activity; sweeping away without pity the products of nature, together with the works of man, and revealing itself to us, to employ an expression of Pindar's, as "the strongest and most powerful of all the elements."

The Rhone, the Loire, and indeed most rivers are liable to frequent floods, with their well known melancholy consequences, and to prevent the return of such fatal occurrences has long been felt a necessity. But how can we meet so formidable an enemy? Ought we to erect perpendicular banks, or dig out vast basins? Ought we to construct veins? All these works may be attended with more or less happy results, but after all it is not so much the evil which we have to attack as the cause which we should study, so as to anticipate and prevent its working. The whole system of water-courses seems for some years past to have become extremely irregular; for while on one hand some rivers have become subject to sudden floods, and have overflowed their banks, burst all barriers, and deluged surrounding countries, others have become choked with sand, and abundant streams, and perennial springs have dried up. What has caused this disarrangement in the hydraulic system—this disorder in the arteries of whole continents? In order to answer these questions, we have only to walk through forests that are being cleared, and look at the trees on the mountain sides falling under the wood-cutter's axe, and there we see at work the fellow-laborers of the inundation. The effects of this system of clearage are nowhere more manifest than in America, where natural phenomena are, so to speak, amplified, and for that reason more easily explained.

In the year 1800, Humboldt sought, near the city of Nueva Valencia, for the lake of Valencia, of which he had found numerous descriptions in the works of old writers. But the lake of which so much had been said was now nothing more than a pool, and the islands on it were mere hillocks. The change was easily explained by the fact that during the intervening two centuries, numerous clearings had taken place in the neighborhood. Twenty-five years later M. Boussingault visited the same region, and the lake seemed to have regained its former size; for twenty-five years of neglected cultivation—the result of civil war—had enabled the neighboring forests to provide shade with their thick branches. In Ascension Island the same phenomenon has been observed. A mountain was cleared of its wood, and in consequence, an abundant spring in the vicinity dried up. Later, however, the spring re-appeared, with the trees, which had been permitted to grow again. In other regions, also, the cutting down of forests is followed by frequent inundations, while in still others, where the trees are preserved, the system of water-courses remains unchanged. On the road to Quito, for instance, is to be seen the Lake of San Pablo. From the period of the first invasion of Peru, the country has remained the same; the trees have been respected, and the lake has never varied. These facts prove that clearings favor the evaporation of the water, render the rain-falls irregular, and cause the drying up of lakes and of water-courses. When, on the contrary, a country is well planted in trees, the rain-water remains on the surface of the earth, each tree surrounding itself with earthy matter which has been carried along by the water, and which, in its turn, stops it and directs it into a series of little channels. If these trees are cut down, torrents will, during the heavy rains, sweep down the mountain slopes, and, not meeting with any obstacle, they will cause the rivers to overflow. But more important still is the influence of forests. Their leaves condense during the night the vapors of the atmosphere; they deprive the air of its moisture, and render the rains less violent; in a word, forests regulate the distribution of water, put obstacles in the way of the soil being washed away, and prevent, or at least retard, the rivers becoming obstructed by sand banks.

The importance of forests for an adequate supply of water cannot well be over-estimated. On bare ground, rain-water runs off quickly, and often in torrents, to the brooks and rivers, which suddenly rise and inundate the plain; while the sheltering shade of trees keeps it from immediate evaporation, and the rich wood-soil holds it in its moss and turf as in a sponge, and thus gives it time to sink slowly into the soil. Hence, well-wooded regions invariably abound in springs. But forests act indirectly toward the same end: on days when the atmosphere is damp and filled with vapors and mists, they condense the latter on their branches and leaves, so that tree and bush hang full of welcome drops, though no rain has fallen. The services which forests thus render were well known to the ancients; Seneca and Vitruvius both praise them for their usefulness to man. Hence, also, Æmilius Paulus, the Consul, insisted upon it that there must be springs near Mount Olympus, because it was so well wooded, and though no trace appeared at first, upon digging into the ground an abundance of water was procured.

Unfortunately, other nations have not been as wise as the Romans. In Spain, vast districts, once covered with golden harvests, year after year, are now utter deserts, all the woods having been cut down for miles around. Very different was the policy of the Turks. Near Constantinople rises a magnificent forest of oaks and beeches, which is held sacred, stringent laws prohibiting the cutting of a single tree. This forest feeds the springs which furnish the great city with its supply of water.

Our own people are but very slowly learning the lesson, and many a farmer in the West has painfully to plant young trees again on the very spot where his father's narrow-bladed Yankee axe cut down giants of hoary age. When every foot of arable land was covered with trees, and when behind every tree lurked an Indian, it was quite necessary, no doubt, to chop and shoot indiscriminately. But by cutting down trees thus upon every mountain-side, and in every ravine, we have inevitably entailed two great evils upon posterity—scarcity of fuel and scarcity of water. More especially is this the case where a railroad or smelting furnace has created a profitable market for fuel; in such regions the trees have gone, and with them the water, and the meadows and fields are dry and parched.

There is folly in this haste to be rich. A keen axe, in a stout woodman's hand, will destroy in an hour what it has taken a century to produce, and what a century cannot replace. A few cords of wood represent a snug sum, but what are the dollars in comparison to a perpetual fountain? A few acres added to a farm are dearly purchased by cursing the land for generations with drought and barrenness. It is gratifying to find that the good common sense of our people has led them, to some extent, to see the evil that is done, and to repair the injury. In Ohio, in one or two of the New England States, and especially in the young, vigorous States of the Northwest, large plantations are beginning to grow up, which, there is reason to hope, will soon add to our supply of wood, and prevent the distressing droughts of our summers.

The history of the Isthmus of Suez has taught us, recently, a striking lesson in this respect. A few years ago the whole region through which M. de Lesseps' famous canal now passes hundreds of richly laden vessels, was a sterile desert—the rainfalls amounting often to less than an inch during the year. There were no trees to be seen far or near. When the energetic Frenchman began his gigantic enterprise, he at once directed thousands of trees to be planted in proper localities; they grew up, thanks to careful irrigation, and now the astonished eye of the traveller beholds blooming prairies and stately forests, where once all was waste and wild desert. But a still greater change has come over the climate: rain falls now frequently and abundantly, the soil produces richly; and if that man is to be counted a benefactor who can make a blade of grass to grow where none could be raised before, true glory belongs to him who has thus created, as it were, a fertile land, capable of maintaining thousands of industrious and happy citizens.

CHAPTER IV.

CHEMICAL ACTION.—PETRIFYING SPRINGS—CAVERNS —STALACTITES.

"Certain waters have the power of petrifying and converting into marble the substances which they touch."—OVID.

THE effects produced by so-called petrifying springs have, at all times, attracted the attention of naturalists. "At Perperene," says Pliny, "there is a fountain which petrifies all the earth which it waters, which is also the case with some hot springs at Delium, in Eubœa, for at the spot where the water falls, stones are formed one above another. At Eurymenes, the garlands which are cast into certain fountains become petrified. At Colossa flows a river which turns the bricks that are thrown into it, likewise, into stone. In the Mines of Scyros all the trees washed by the waters there become petrified, with all their branches."

This idea of *changing a body into stone* by contact with certain waters, has been handed down from one age to another, and even in our own days numbers of persons imagine that the so-called petrifying springs transform organic substances into stone. This is, of course, a mistake.

The liquid, charged with carbonate of lime, deposits the salt, which it holds in solution, on the surface of organic bodies, animal or vegetable, and covers them with a solid layer, a coating of stone, a chalky varnish, which adapts itself to the external form of the object which it covers, but does not take the place of the material of which it consists. Thus, organic substances become clothed in a solid envelope, and may be preserved for a long period in an unchanged form.

In France, near Clermont (Puy de Dôme), at St. Alyre, at St. Nectaire, and in numerous other places, there exist springs and fountains which possess this incrusting property. Baskets of fruit, bird's nests, branches, and various other objects are placed in the water, and in a very short time become covered with a stony coating. The waters of Hieropolis, in Asia Minor, present one of the most beautiful phenomena to be met with anywhere in connection with incrustation; they run down the slope of a mountain and form there a series of beautiful cascades in stone. It is well known that waters in the great caves of our Union, like the Mammoth Cave of Kentucky and the smaller caves of Virginia, possess the same remarkable properties.

The water from the clouds, charged with the carbonic acid of the air, often has to pass through thick layers of calcareous soil, and dissolves large quantities of carbonate of lime by means of the acid which it holds in solution. By its weight it sinks into the ground, and should it meet in its progress caverns and chasms, it evaporates on coming into contact with the air, losing its carbonic acid, and the limestone which it held in solution produces fantastic ornaments, to which nature delights in lending a thousand fantastic forms.

Natural caverns are thus frequently adorned with stalactites, deposits conical in their form, resulting from the infiltration of mineral waters through their walls, and forming vertically from top to base, in a shape similar to those needles of ice which we see on the eaves of our houses in winter. The formation of stalactites remained long unexplained, it being supposed that stones sprouted and vegetated like plants, and for a time no one traced these marvellous vegetations to the agency of water. Stalactites are generally formed of carbonate of lime, but some are formed which consist of flint, or of malachite, etc.; as however in all cases their method of formation is the same, we will confine our description to the carbonate of lime. This substance is indissoluble in pure water, but dissolves in water charged with carbonic acid. Let us imagine that water of this nature filters into the earth and penetrates into the fissures of rocks, which form the walls of a grotto, or oozes through their porous texture; some drops will remain for a time suspended, and they will successively evaporate and leave the carbonate of lime which they held in solution. The first drop will leave an almost imperceptible deposit of an annular form, the second will add to this deposit, and so will the others, until the whole assumes the form of a quill of a feather, till the successive and continuous evaporation of other drops will at length stop up the orifice. The water now trickles along the sides of the quill, which increases externally, and as the deposits are more abundant towards the base than at the extremity, in consequence of the progressive impoverishment of the fluid, the stalactite will speedily present the appearance of a greatly elongated cone.

The water in escaping from the upper portion of the vault falls vertically upon the ground. Arrived there it evaporates entirely; the same takes place with regard to the other drops, which form underneath the stalactite a deposit of the same nature, called a *stalagmite.* The stalagmites rising from beneath can in time reach and meet the stalactites, which form downwards, and in this manner are formed the fantastic columns which decorate the interior of such grottoes, the apparent draperies and waving folds, the cascades suddenly petrified—in one word, all the vagaries which chance delights in moulding and fashioning after every imaginable pattern; producing almost always most singular effects by giving them a grotesque resemblance to real objects.

If the feeble stream of water does not drop from the ceiling, but flows slowly along the surface of the rock, enough lime is still left behind to mark its devious path and thus to form a network of delicate tracery, adorned here and there, where water abounded, with graceful fringes. At times, again, large, quantities of water come flowing down simultaneously, and, when these are very rich in carbonate of lime, form apparent cascades, curtains or masses of driven snow. In the course of time—and who can tell how many centuries must often have passed before whole vast caves are thus filled with wondrous works?—the roofs, the walls, and the floor are all ornamented in lavish profusion, and scenes of beauty created such as man's sublimest genius could never produce.

In France, especially in the Pyrenees and in the neighborhood of Besancon, there are several of these grottoes, in which the water is incessantly employed in the construction of fantastic ornaments. The grotto of Antiparos, in the Greek Archipelago, which has been visited and described by the celebrated naturalist Tournefort, is probably the most remarkable in the world. After that may be ranked "Han's Hole," in Belgium; the Grotto des Demoiselles, in the Hérault; those of Arcy in Savoy, of Kirkdale in England, and Baireuth in Bavaria, and those of our own country.

One of the finest, though by no means the largest of these fairy scenes, is the famous cave of Bellamar, near Matanzas, on the island of Cuba, probably unsurpassed in the world by the beauty and marvellous variety of its crystallizations. The happy manner in which stalactites and stalagmites here blend is one of the chief wonders of the place. Now they form, jointly, rich curtains of white, delicate lace, woven in patterns such as human ingenuity never devised, and again they hang like motionless cascades, suddenly arrested by the magician's wand.

One of the latter, the Diamond Cascade, is especially beautiful, resembling strikingly a casket of diamonds poured out profusely over a gentle slope, and resting there in a glittering shower forever suspended in the air.

The Grotto of Han is situated in the Province of Namur. A little river, the Lesse, penetrates into a rocky cavity at the foot of an eminence and disappears in the depths of a dark gulf with a deafening roar. It reappears again a mile off on the opposite side of the hill, and its waters, so agitated a while before, are now as calm and limpid as if they had issued from a fountain of crystal. What road can they have travelled in the bowels of the earth? No one can tell. If floating bodies are thrown into the Lesse on the side of the hill where it loses itself, they are never found on the other; and if the waters at their entrance are troubled and blackened by a tempest, they take an entire day for their transparency to be defiled at their exit.* Beneath the rock from which the Lesse issues to continue its course, reigns a fearful gloom. All is dark, and a deep gulf has to be penetrated ere we can explore the wonders of this curious cavern. The grotto of Han is composed of 22 different chambers and numerous narrow and very long passages. These cavities are no doubt the result, in the first instance, of earthquakes and

* This fact, which is common to some other rivers, such as the Rhone, etc., may be easily explained if we suppose the water to pass, during its subterranean journey, through a rock pierced with small holes, a natural filter which, whilst it gives passage to the liquid, retains the heavier substances.

the vibrations of the soil; they afterwards became polished, the interior being worn away by the constant action of subterranean waters, and gradually began to bristle with deposits of stalagmites.

PISOLITES—OOLITES.

The water which holds solid matter in solution, gives birth also to other concretions, termed by geologists "pisolites" or "oolites," according to the size and shape of their grains. These globular stones are formed under the influence of whirlpools which gush up in the basins in which incrusting waters

Pisolites and Oolites.

meet. These latter, by their motion, lift up and keep suspended in the liquid, particles of sand, which become centres of attraction. The dissolved calcareous matter deposits itself upon them and surrounds them with a film, which gradually increases and in time becomes a thick envelope. Meanwhile the grains, as they become heavier and heavier, sink to the bottom of the water and become welded together, agglutinate and produce granular masses. We can follow in our own day the formation of such stony masses in the calcareous waters of Vichy, of Carlsbad in Bohemia, of Tivoli near Rome, and others.

While pisolites, or pea-stones, never form any but very small concretions, oolites, on the contrary, although their grains are no larger than the roe of fish, have given birth to entire mountains. In this case, of course, other and powerful causes must have been brought to bear, but we can only form conjectures as to the nature of this singular formation, which doubtless originated in ancient geological epochs. This much alone is certain, that here also the action of water has been busily at work. Some geologists are of opinion that these concretions must have been produced in tranquil, and rather shallow waters, where they were at first deposited on the surface of the liquid, thanks to their extreme delicacy in the beginning. Other savants, however, imagine them to have drawn their origin from the bosom of the liquid itself, and consider the calcareous matter to have moulded itself round a number of small ovoid bodies similar to the eggs of fishes. Others, again, like Delafosse, have had recourse to mechanical action, and attribute the formation of these strange concretions to the action of the waves upon a consolidated calcareous sediment. Whichever of these theories be the true one, water is certainly the skillful artisan that has moulded these singular stones, and has agglutinated these myriads of small grains of which certain rocks are entirely formed; and if we do not know how the artist has accomplished the task, we should not the less admire the work.

Water charged with carbonic acid has also the power of dissolving limestone rocks, and thus frequently produces deep excavations. It has been suggested that the celebrated natural bridge of Ain-el-Liban is the result of such causes.

STANDING WATER.

After having seen water in motion, hard at work, let us take a glance at these vast marshes in which the liquid element is in stagnation, and where it spreads inert and lifeless over a uniform and level soil. Widely different is the work which it accomplishes, but not less important is the effect produced.

Organic substances, vegetable debris of all sorts, the remains of reeds and other marsh plants, are found collected in stagnant water, which disorganizes and decomposes them. Genuine fermentation is thus produced in these ponds and morasses where no current comes to renovate the waves reeking with the corpses of the vegetable world. Noxious miasmas, mephitic gases rise from these immense vats in which nature accumulates aquatic mosses of every sort, which in their turn perish and add their share to the general fermentation. The remains of trees and plants become partially carbonized and form at the bottom of these marshes enormous deposits, which dry up during the progress of ages, and are transformed into peat.

Such is a hasty sketch of the effects produced in the epidermis of the earth by the labor of water.

To recapitulate, the liquid element in its unwearying movement acts as a mechanical force in diluting the soil, which it moistens, in polishing stones, and in transporting mud, slime and clay; as a physical force, by dilating in congelation, and in thus giving an impulse to avalanches which cause rivers to overflow and to produce inundations; and finally as a chemical force in dissolving rocks and minerals. On the continents, as out at sea, the action of water is both destructive and reproductive. It carries away the earthy particles, but it desposits them again elsewhere. The mountains feed the delta. It dissolves limestone and floats it down to the sea, but it offers it to the polypi, which seize upon it and build with it in the midst of the ocean atols and immense banks of madrepore. Thus existing continents furnish the materials for future continents.

The sight of all these forces constantly at work before our eyes, is an evidence of the admirable mechanism which regulates the world. We see by what a sublime law of compensation nature keeps up the harmony of things, and how she succeeds in maintaining by counterpoise the equilibrium of the universal balance.

CHAPTER V.

YESTERDAY AND TO-MORROW.

"The world does not always present to us the same aspect; where we are to-day treading the soil of a continent, these a has flowed, and will one day flow again; the region where it flows now has once been and will again be a continent. Time modifies all things."—ARISTOTLE'S TREATISE ON METEORS.

"As I was one day passing through a very ancient and densely populated city, I asked one of the inhabitants if he could tell me when it was founded. 'It is,' replied the man, 'a great city, but to inform you how long it has existed would be absolutely impossible, and of that our ancestors were as ignorant as ourselves.' Five centuries later I revisited the same spot, and finding no vestige of a town, I inquired of a peasant, who was gathering herbs on its site, how long a time had passed since its destruction. 'By my faith,' he replied, 'you ask of me a strange question. This country has never been anything different to what it is now.' 'But was there not once a great city here?' I inquired. 'Never,' he replied, 'as far as we can judge by what we have ourselves seen, nor have our fathers ever told us anything to the contrary.'

Another five centuries passed, and again I revisited the spot—now the sea covered the site. Seeing some fishermen on the shore I asked them how long it had been since the sea had invaded this district. 'A man like yourself,' said they, 'ought to know better than to ask such a question. This place has always been what it is now.' Again, at the end of another five hundred years I returned once more. The sea was no longer there, and I was desirous of knowing how many years before it had retired. A man whom I accosted answered to my question as all the others had done, that is to say, he said that things had always been just as I now saw them. Once more, after a similar lapse of years, I returned for the last time, and found instead of a desert a flourishing city, richer, more populous and more magnificent than the first which I had seen. Being desirous of ascertaining how long it had existed, I questioned the inhabitants on the subject, and they replied: 'The origin of our city is lost in the night of ages; we do not know when it first arose, and on this subject our fathers knew no more than we do ourselves.'" *

Thus speaks Kidhz, an allegorical personage introduced in the writings of a very ancient Arab poet, Mohammed Kaswini, who flourished toward the end of the 13th century, and this graceful apologue

* The narrative which we have quoted is taken from a very valuable MS. in the possession of the Bibliothèque de Paris, translated by Messrs. Chézy and Sacy. It has been recommended to the attention of geologists by William E. Beaumont, in 1832, and Sir Charles Lyell reproduced it in his "Principles of Geology."

sets forth in a manner both elegant and original the reciprocal changes of position which the continents and oceans have experienced.

From remote antiquity philosophers have recognized that great changes must have taken place on the surface of the globe, and the ancient systems of Egypt and India have connected these changes with deluges, but at that time every belief was based upon superstition, and they imagined that the gods interfered directly in all great cataclysms. It is not long since these confused theories have assumed a more practical shape, and it is from the last century only that we can date the birth of geology. In studying the archives of the primeval world, in whatever part of the terrestrial globe they are found, we discover that a large portion of the present soil has been formed at the bottom of the ocean. The sea shells found in it attest that fact by irresistible evidence. It is well known that the ordinary stone of some localities is crusted all over with shells visible to the naked eye, and if we examine a piece of chalk with a magnifying glass we are amazed at the number of broken shells of every sort which we discern in it. The calcareous soils which extend over the surface of our continents are in fact aqueous deposits. The sea formerly flowed over them, and the deposits which it gradually formed, increasing with every age, produced at length layers of considerable thickness, consisting entirely of debris of animals, which lived in those remote epochs.

In digging into the soil of Paris successive layers are found, each of which speaks to us a different language, and the vestiges discovered there may be regarded as so many hieroglyphics graven by nature upon the superincumbent strata of the terrestrial epidermis. A careful examination of these layers has brought us to know the deposits which have gradually covered the primeval soil, and enabled us to fathom the mysteries which presided over their formation. It is thus that geology has been able to retrace the past, and to unveil the history of the formation of Paris soil. Excavations made into the Buttes of Montmartre have brought to light the following series of deposits: 1. A layer of marine animals, indicating that this was once the bed of an ocean. 2. A layer of soil which, containing remains of land animals, made it evident that the sea must have retreated from the place which it had previously occupied. 3. A second layer of shells and marine animals, showing that the waters had regained their former dominion, doubtless in consequenc of the subsidence of the soil. 4. A second layer of debris of creatures which live in the open air, and some of which are almost identical with existing species. 5. A layer testifying by new marine deposits, to a fresh invasion of the ocean. 6. The soil has once more been exposed to light, and debris of our own animals, and of the implements of human industry, indicate the commencement of the modern epoch. By examining in this manner all over the globe the vestiges of extinct worlds, by tracing in various countries layers of the same nature and date, geologists have been able to reconstruct the map of Europe as it was before the advent of mankind. The site now occupied by Paris was then buried beneath the waters, and the shape of the ancient continents bears no resemblance to those of any countries now existing.

It is probable that we shall one day succeed in solving the enigmas that conceal from us the mysteries of the past, while on the other hand the history of former revolutions on the face of the globe, and the study of the past, may, to a certain point, enable us to divine the future. Nevertheless we must acknowledge that a thousand causes as yet unsuspected may destroy the most beautiful hypothesis, and we must content ourselves with merely touching in passing on a question which gives such wide scope to the imagination. It is certain that all here below is doomed to incessant change. The face of the globe is for ever passing through a continual metamorphosis, and the oceans of our day will be the continents of the future. But changes even more extensive are probably in store for our planet. It is possible that the ice which lies piled up at the north pole may cause, according to the opinion of Agassiz, a sudden movement in the axis of the earth, and that by the changed position of its centre of gravity our globe may suffer a terrible shock which would cause the instantaneous death of every living being by causing the sea to overflow the land. Or it may be that the epidermis of the earth, (which is after all nothing more than a crust congealed by the action of cold,) will increase so much that on a certain day lowered temperature may convert all the water on our sphere into a vast mass of ice. Let it be added, however, that if these predictions can ever be realized, it will only be after the lapse of many ages, for geology teaches us the immensity of time just as astronomy teaches the immensity of space. Mankind will in the meantime have had time to disappear from the stage of the world, and perhaps give place to some other race of purer essence.

But, it will be said, without travelling so far from the present epoch, is it not possible to ascertain whether these deluges, which are not so far distant from us, can cccur in our own days? Can science reassure us on this subject? or must we live in a state of constant anxiety from dread of the possible encroachments of the sea, which might result from an earthquake? Before answering this question it is necessary to know whether the revolutions on the earth's surface have been sudden or gradual, and that is a grave question which has been the subject of eager discussion between most distinguished scientific men. It is probable that both hypotheses are true, since in our own days the shores of certain continents are rising gradually and progressively, and in the course of ages this insensible movement, continued without ceasing, may become the cause of radical changes. On the other hand, the rising of mountains, and earthquakes, must have before this wrought upon the face of the earth convulsions both sudden and terrible. When the chain of the Cordilleras first rose as an immense protuberance on the surface of the globe, the terrestrial epidermis must have been violently shaken, and the sea, thrown suddenly out of its bed, must have produced frightful inundations and terrible deluges.

Will these violent phenomena be reproduced? Probably not; for the crust of the earth, augmenting its bulk in proportion as the globe grows colder, in consequence of radiation, opposes an obstacle, ever stronger and stronger, to the subterranean fires. On the other hand, it is certain that our planet is destined to lose its oceans and its atmosphere, and to pass gradually into a condition similar to that of the moon, for the waters will become absorbed in proportion as new rocks are formed by the consolidation of the mass, which now is in a state of fusion. The solid surface of our planet is a porous mass, through which the water, insinuating itself by a thousand tiny openings, travels slowly, but surely, towards the centre of the earth, and disappears in proportion as the vast domain of fire diminishes. We have already seen that the rivers and lakes have diminished in volume since the geologic ages; it is very probable, from the calculations of scientific men, that the seas themselves will disappear whenever the solid pellicle of the earth has attained a thickness of about 93 miles. Then the dried-up earth will behold all life disappear from its surface; the atmosphere will no longer oppose any obstacle to the solar rays; icy nights will succeed burning days, but our planet will not the less continue its course around the sun, like a corpse taken in tow by another corpse, till, at a yet more remote time, the freezing chill will have reached the sun himself, and he also will be extinguished—cold and darkness reigning then in the midst of all this dead world. And what will become of all these ruins? Here, necessarily, Science must be silent. Whatever we can do, we always perceive in the future, as in the past, a mysterious horizon, which recedes further and further in proportion as as we advance, and which irresistibly attracts our gaze.

> "We may laugh, we may weep, we may boast of our power,
> But can ne'er make thee speak till thine own fateful hour,
> Or compel thee thine hands to unclasp;
> Oh! thou phantom so mute—our host and our guest—
> Thou masked spectre, that haunts us and leaves us no rest,
> Thou, To-morrow, we never can grasp."
>
> VICTOR HUGO.

IV.

THE PHYSICAL AND CHEMICAL PROPERTIES OF WATER.

"No desire is more natural than the thirst for knowledge. We use every method which can be employed in our endeavors to attain it. When reason fails us, we try experiment."—MONTAIGNE.

CHAPTER I.

WHAT IS WATER?—THE LABORATORY.

"We shall see that, for us, water is no longer an element."—LAVOISIER.

AFTER having examined the part that water plays in nature, and the mission which it fulfills on our globe, let us pursue our investigations more closely, and employ such apparatus as science brings to bear on the study of the substances which make up this wonderful element.

Let us enter the laboratory, that best theatre for the display of the facts which we are about to study. But before opening the door, I must warn you that you will not find there that fantastic apparatus which you are perhaps expecting to see, and with which the alchemists were in the habit of astonishing their visitors. The crocodile has long ceased to yawn from the ceiling, and the broken wind-bellows no longer blow up the glowing furnace with horrible sounds. The master has thrown aside his long gabardine, and is no longer half hid in a labyrinth of dusty tomes, which lay in disorderly piles within his sanctuary. Instead of hunting amid the inextricable medley of old books for the truth which is so rarely found there, his efforts are now directed to the study of nature itself, and to a search after facts by means of experiments; and in this way, climbing laboriously the steep path of methodical study, he at length reaches, by means of observation, truths which thus only can be discovered.

We shall find in our laboratory phials in readiness to receive fluids which are to be poured into them, glasses, receivers, and retorts, destined to be subjected to the action of fire. In a word, vessels of every sort will lend their aid to the necessities of our study. Gas stoves will be lighted by the touch of a match, furnishing us instantaneously with a high temperature without the aid of the traditional bellows. Machinery will give us, as we require them, either a powerful electric current, or an intense luminous spark. A pneumatic machine will produce a vacuum, if we need one, for our experiments. A chemical balance will assist us in our analysis; a barometer will indicate the atmospheric pressure, and a thermometer and other instruments will each in turn supply our wants.

Perhaps, my reader, you rather regret the old alchemist, with his strange apparatus and the dust which covered everything. If you have a taste for the picturesque, you doubtless deplore the absence of the crocodile stuffed with hay, and you regret seeing nowhere the serpent, preserved in spirits, the stuffed pelican or the skeleton, and a thousand spiders' webs—no local coloring in fact.

Our laboratory has laid aside all the charming mysteries which once surrounded these studies, but instead of speaking confusedly to your imagination, it will address your reason in clear language. Science will no longer appear to you half hidden under a thick veil, a perplexing mist; she has been stripped of the rags which only disfigured her fair proportions. This half light, this mysterious shadow, which hung over the sanctuary of the alchemist, was nothing less than superstition casting her mantle over everything; it was the false dominating over the true. These fantastic ornaments represented that element of the marvellous which always surrounds the first footsteps of science and retards its development. That old philosopher, who has for sixty years been trying to decipher the same musty work of Black Art: what is he but a representative of misdirected science? of man asking the truth of his fellow-man, who is as ignorant as he himself, instead of sitting down to learn it at the feet of nature, which conceals it indeed, but will assuredly reveal it to the patient seeker.

Our laboratory, clean, well lighted and orderly, is naught else but modern Science, simple, accurate, stripped of unintelligible jargon, of repulsive aspect, offering to all, the secrets she formerly kept for the initiated few. She is no longer in love with abstract terms, with mysterious and high sounding phrases, with formulas bristling with hard words; she has torn off all these trappings and addresses herself to all, and aims at being understood by all.

The days have gone by, when the question: What is water? could be answered by the simple words: It is an element! We have already seen how many generations of men were content with such a reply, and yet how utterly erroneous it really is; still, till down to the middle of the last century this view prevailed almost universally. The great philosopher, Thales, six hundred years before Christ, looked upon water as the only genuine element, from which all life upon earth was derived, and after Aristotle, some three hundred years later, confirmed this view, the doctrine was blindly adhered to for twenty centuries. Diodorus even believed that water could be condensed into an earthy matter, and considered crystals as such petrified water. Other naturalists looked upon quartz in the same light, and firmly believed the change possible. Even in 1750 alchemists were still eagerly at work to force water, by constantly grinding it in a mortar, to form a deposit of earthy matter! The great Newton and the acute Leibnitz shared this opinion, and the few who dared to doubt fared badly with learned men. It was finally due to the experiments made by Cavendish (1766), Volta (1777), and Lavoisier (1781) that the true nature of water was discovered.

What then is water? To learn this, let us begin by decomposing water—that is to say, by submitting it to analysis.

ANALYSIS AND SYNTHESIS.

Here is a glass vessel, and a voltaic battery; we will fill the former with water, slightly acidified with sulphuric acid. By the aid of a galvanic pile we pass through it an electric current, conducted by two platinum rods (or wires) which traverse the mastic bottom with which our apparatus is furnished. Thus the water is decomposed and the wires are immediately covered with little gaseous beads, to which the water has given birth. How can we collect and examine these gases? Nothing more simple. We place in the basin above the platinum wires two little test glasses which soon become filled with gas, and we observe that the volume of gas which escapes from the rod corresponding with the negative

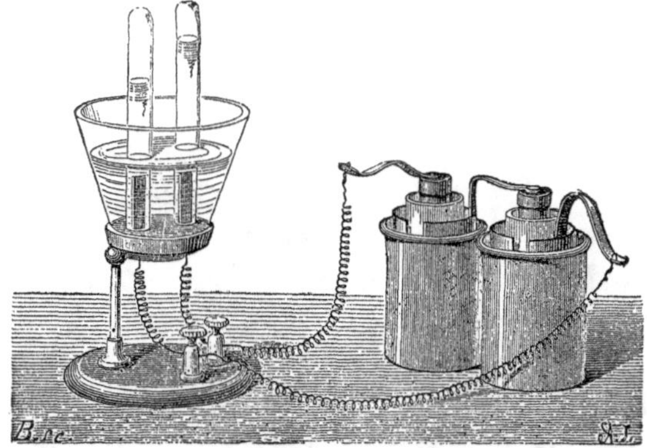

Decomposing Water by a Voltaic Battery.

pole of the pile is twice the amount of that of the other gas issuing from the positive pole. If we remove the first test glass from the voltaic battery and then apply a lighted match to its orifice, the gas it contains becomes immediately ignited, with a slight detonating sound.

If we plunge into the second test-glass a match, so nearly extinguished as to offer a simple incandescent point, it is immediately relighted and burns brightly. The gas it contains, though not itself inflammable, can yet produce combustion.

In this experiment we have decomposed water,—and have extracted from it two distinct gases, one of which burns with a dull flame, that is hydrogen—whilst the other, which does not take fire, but excites combustion, is called oxygen. Water can by various other means also be decomposed. If we pour into a flask with two tubular orifices, containing zinc, water mixed with sulphuric acid, the zinc,

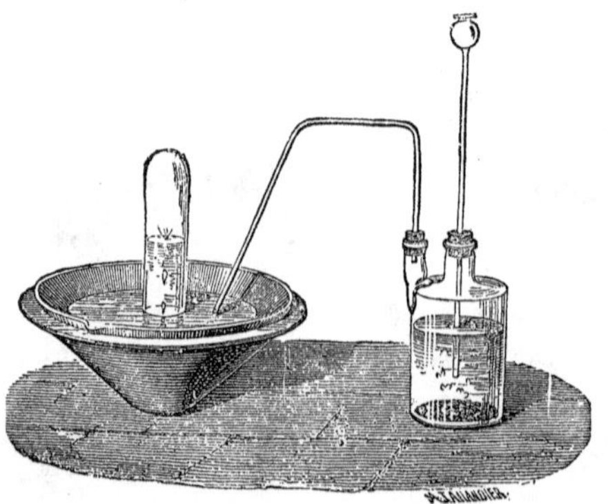

Decomposition of Water by Zinc and Sulphuric Acid.

under the influence of the acid, takes up one of its elements, oxygen, and the hydrogen thus set at liberty can be collected in the test-glass. The other constituent of water, oxygen, can be produced by heating in a retort chlorate of potash with binoxide of manganese. Oxygen is thus very easily obtained so as to enable us to study its properties. This gas, as we have seen, can maintain combustion; sulphur and phosphorus burn in it much more freely than in the air and if a piece of tinder fas-

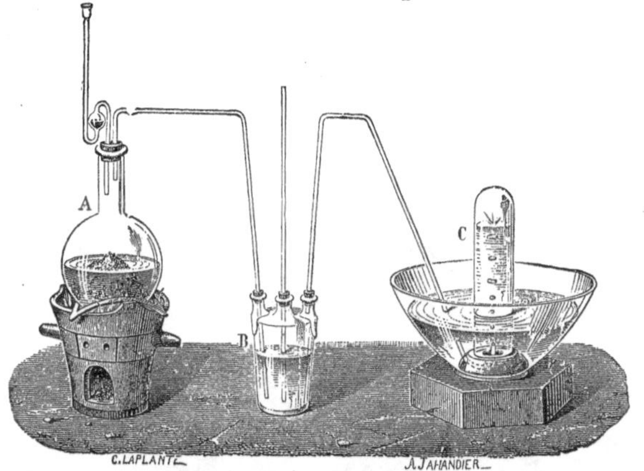

Preparation of Oxygen.

tened to a steel spring is set on fire, we see the

Combustion of Steel in Oxygen.

metal burning with great brilliancy, numerous bright sparks escaping from the incandescent steel. Other metals, such as iron, decompose water by their mere contact; but they have to be heated to a red

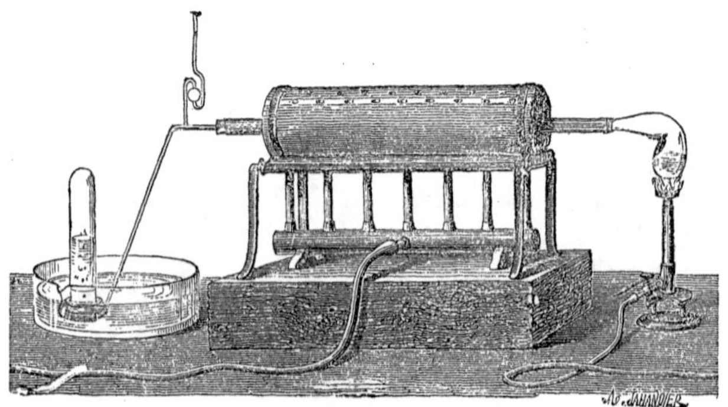

Decomposition of Water by Hot Iron.

heat. If we introduce steam into a tube filled with iron rods heated by gas-burners, the water becomes decomposed by contact with the incandescent metal, and the oxygen becomes solid in the form of oxide of iron. Meanwhile the hydrogen becomes eliminated, and passes through a tube into a test-glass placed in a basin filled with water. This process of decomposition may be thus represented:

Water { Hydrogen............Hydrogen.
Oxygen }
Iron.......... } Oxyde of iron.

Chlorine, a greenish yellow gas, also decomposes water by the aid of a high temperature, but it com-

DECOMPOSITION OF WATER BY CHLORINE.

bines with the hydrogen and sets the oxygen at liberty. The decomposition is effected in an earthenware tube, filled with pumice stone, made red-hot in a furnace. The chlorine is produced in a glass receiver of a spherical form containing peroxyde of manganese and chlorohydric acid; it passes through a glass retort containing water heated to boiling. Chlorine and steam pass through a column of pumice stone made red hot—the hydrogen of the water combines with the chlorine and gives as its result chlorohydric acid, which passes with the isolated oxygen to an earthen pan filled with water, into which a test-glass is plunged. The chlorohydric acid becomes dissolved in the water; the oxygen, which is scarcely solvable, fills the test-glass.

We have thus decomposed and analyzed water, which is not, as the ancients believed, a simple body, an element, but, on the contrary, consists of two distinct elements. Till now we have been content to destroy; we may be compared to children who break their toys to see what is inside, but can the fragments be reunited in our hands? Can we make artificial water out of oxygen and hydrogen? Nothing is simpler.

The illustration (see next page) shows us an apparatus by means of which this problem can be solved. A flask with two tubular orifices contains the combination which produces hydrogen; the gas is disengaged and passes into a test-glass, furnished with a foot, through pieces of chloride of lime—it eliminates itself at the extremity of a bent tube, where it is set on fire. A bell glass is then placed beneath the flame and soon becomes covered with a cloud of steam; a few drops next trickle down its sides and fall into a vessel beneath. This liquid is nothing less than water artificially produced. The hydrogen, as it burns in the air, unites with the atmospheric oxygen, and together they produce water.

We have thus made the *synthesis* of water.

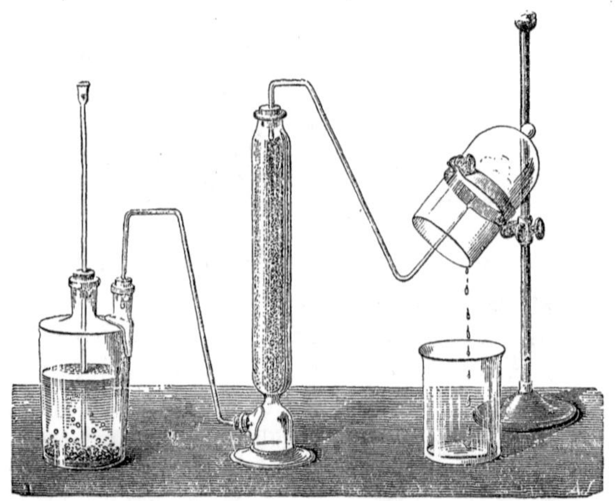

Formation of Water by burning hydrogen.

Can anything be simpler than these experiments, in which the nature of water shows itself with clearness and with certainty? And yet it has taken centuries to arrive at this point, and the doctrine of the four elements maintained itself age after age, till it was demolished as recently as the days of Lavoisier, less than a hundred years ago. The fact is, the method of arriving at truth by experiment has only very recently been taught mankind by those gifted pioneers of modern science, Bacon, Descartes, Galileo, Newton. More than three centuries have elapsed since the earliest of these mighty masters first threw open the gates, which were to make the highways of so extended a sphere of knowledge accessible to our race. Previously to that period human thought had been hemmed in between narrow barriers; men were accustomed to think only as earlier, and in their eyes infallible, guides had thought before them, and the most convincing experiments failed to carry conviction to the minds of the multitude. The opinion of Aristotle on the subject of the four elements was to the ancients as indisputable a truth as any axiom in mathematics, and no one dared even to discuss the conclusions at which the illustrious tutor of Alexander had arrived. The injurious effects of this blind adherence to his views necessarily impaired free thought and prevented all progress in science, which was forced to follow forever the beaten track first marked out for her by the Stagyrite. It is needless to dwell on the inconvenience of so circumscribed a method of studying nature. In her domains nothing is speculative, nothing is true but what can be demonstrated, and experiment must always come forward to confirm theory.

Chemistry, in thus dissecting substances aims at unveiling the constituent parts, at penetrating into these mysteries which matter, whether inert or organized, conceals from our view, and at ascertaining their true nature. She commences by destroying, but only in order to reconstruct—she separates the elements in order to combine them once more, and thus destroys in order to create anew.

Looking upon that infinity of living beings, of inert bodies, which cover the surface of the globe, of plants of every description, of animals of endless variety, of mineral substances of every kind, one might feel tempted to believe that an endless number of distinct elements composed this vast array of bodies and substances. But such is not the case. If we analyze all the substances in nature, if we pass through the crucible of science trees and animals, stones and rocks, water and air, we reach after all only a small number of elements, which united by twos, by threes, by fours, form the infinite variety of objects which constitute the magnificent spectacle called the Universe. The air we breathe is formed by the union of two gases, nitrogen and oxygen; water consists of one of the gases of air, united to another gas, hydrogen; vegetable and animal substances are again formed of hydrogen, oxygen and nitrogen, combined with a third substance, carbon. If we add to these elements sulphur, phosphorus, potassium, sodium, aluminum, calcium, silicum, iron, and a few others, we have the complete list of bodies which by their union form the whole series of beings, living or inanimate.

Wheat and hemlock, food and poison, consist of the same primal elements; animals and plants nearly all contain the same fundamental substances, and it may be said, speaking generally, that 64 bodies have given birth to the universe and all that is therein.

It is possible, if not probable, that what we call elements, are not primal elements of nature. The day may come, perchance, when science will subdivide our so called simple substances as we are now dividing water, which the ancients considered an element, into oxygen and hydrogen. The chemistry of the future will proclaim, perhaps, as an obvious truth, the unity of all matter, modifying and transforming itself incessantly under the unwearying play of physical forces. However that may be, with our present appliances, we have a vast field for our wonder and our curiosity in the constant metamorphoses of matter; and nature, to use the language of a profound philosopher, seems to us like a self-devouring monster; for in this unending bringing forth of new beings, matter is constantly modified, transformed, and metamorphosed, while ever revolving in a circle alike wondrous and sublime.

There is, however, nothing so very astonishing in the diversity of beings produced by a few elements. The disposal of the arrangement of the various atoms is the sole cause of this diversity. The diamond and the coal, the precious stones and worthless clays, Iceland spar and common building-stone, all have the same chemical composition and yet present as much diversity of appearance as exists between an animal and a plant.

Are not the twenty-six letters of our alphabet sufficient to produce an infinity of words, which paint every shade of human thought? The primitive elements are the letters in Nature's alphabet. Living beings and inert bodies may be considered as the words in that great book of Nature, which strikes our imagination and speaks to our reason by its sublime language and the grandeur of its style.

So is it with the eight notes of music, which by their combination produce every harmony that can charm the ear, and with the seven colors of the rainbow, which produce every tint in earth or sky.

THE COMPOSITION OF WATER.

We have found water to consist of oxygen and hydrogen, but in what proportion are these two

Mercurial Eudiometer.

gases united? That is the question on which we are now about to enter. We introduce into a eudiometer plunged into a mercury bath two volumes of oxygen, and two of hydrogen; by means of an electric machine we cause an electric spa k to pass into the mixture of the two gases; they unite and form water, which becomes condensed and causes in the apparatus a vacuum immediately filled by the mercury. After the experiment there remains in the eudiometer one volume of oxygen, and hence we conclude that two volumes of hydrogen have combined with one of oxygen in order to form water. This result may be verified by a celebrated experiment, due to Mr. Dumas, by means of an apparatus represented on this page, and the principle of which we shall content ourselves with describing. A current of pure hydrogen passes over an ascertained weight of oxide of copper held in a special glass receiver,

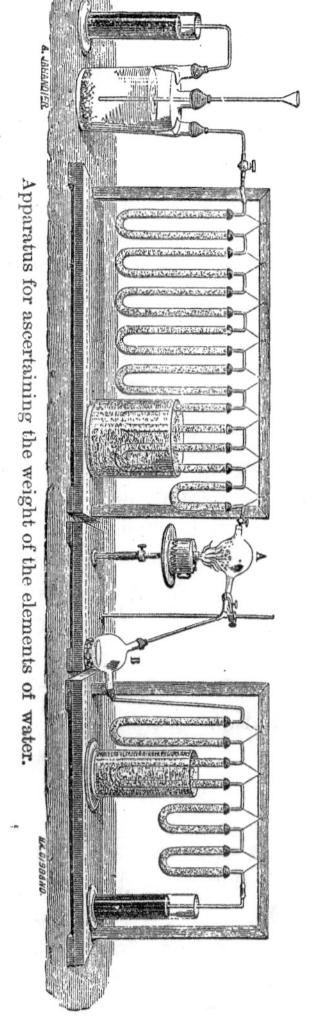

Apparatus for ascertaining the weight of the elements of water.

A. The oxide of copper becomes reduced—that is to say, its oxygen unites with hydrogen to form water, which water is condensed in the glass receiver B. In weighing the reduced copper after the experiment, we obtain the weight of the oxygen combined with an equally well known weight of water, that is to say, we have by ascertaining the difference, the weight of hydrogen contained in the water. These investigations have proved that nine parts of water consist of eight parts of oxygen and one of hydrogen.

The composition of water may thus be described in a couple of lines, but what a long array of centuries, what an army of pioneers passed away, before these simple facts became known to mankind! Cavendish, Lemery, Lavoisier, Volta, Humboldt, Gay Lussac, Dumas, each were the intellectual laborers, whose persevering and incessant toil was needed to reveal to us the nature of water. What labor, what disappointments, what doubts, but also what joy and what triumph! What ineffable happiness a single conquest in the material world brings! What a glorious victory is that achieved by the patient seeker, who, after innumerable days of hard work, and nights of watchfulness, succeeds at length in lifting the veil which conceals a new truth!

Two gases, oxygen and hydrogen, are they really all that is needed to produce water? Water, when *chemically pure*, certainly contains nothing else; but *pure* water does not exist in nature. The water of springs and rivers dissolves salts and, little by little, melts away the rocks which it meets in its course—it dissolves the gases of the air, oxygen, nitrogen and carbonic acid—it contains common salt, sulphate of lime, and calcareous matter—in one word, it contains all that is soluble upon earth.

CHAPTER II.

THE INFLUENCE OF HEAT—EBULLITION.

HEAT acts upon the majority of bodies, and usually changes their form, that is to say, it melts solids and causes liquids to evaporate. Water comes before us under three aspects, solid, liquid and gas; heat melts ice and causes it to pass into the form of water, and again it volatilizes water and causes it to pass into the form of steam.

In order that we may better understand the action and effect of heat, we warm some water in a glass vessel, and then plunge into it a thermometer to indicate its temperature. The thermometer rises gradually until the water reaches the boiling point. It is then at 212°, but from that moment ceases to rise. Yet the fire furnishes still the same amount of heat. What becomes of this heat? It is concealed, absorbed by the liquid. Heat is a force which displaces the molecules of water, causes them to pass into the gaseous state, and while engaged in this task it is insensible to the thermometer. As long as water is thus volatilized it does not become warmer.

We see thus that water expands under the influence of heat so enormously as to assume the shape of air, and yet it is in this almost invisible form that it exercises its power with greatest violence and pitiless passion—tearing open the surface of our earth, causing huge craters to sink in or new mountains to rise from the bosom of the sea, shaking whole kingdoms by terrible earthquakes, and destroying in a few hours the lives of many thousands. If such are the fearful effects of a sudden conversion of water into vapor, the gradual transition produces not less striking effects. To it we owe the protecting canopy of clouds that shelters us from the destroying heat of the sun, to it, thunder storms and hail storms, indeed the almost endless series of continual changes in the world around us, which add to its beauty and please the eye, while they give food to the mind, and cause us to admire the great Maker of all, who directs these agencies and makes them subservient to His will.

Water does not boil at the ordinary temperature when it is in contact with the air, because this air weighs heavily on all objects on the surface of the earth; it weighs heavily also upon the water, and to some extent compresses the molecules of this liquid, so as to prevent their separating and passing from the fluid into the gaseous state.

Let us take a spherical glass receiver full of water; let us form a vacuum with the aid of an India rubber tube, fastened to our pneumatic machine. The water boils up at once and is changed into steam, simply because the air has been driven out and no longer opposes any obstacle to this transformation.

When the barometer marks 29½ inches of pressure, water boils at a uniform temperature, and it is the same with all liquids. The boiling point of

Ebullition of Water in a Vacuum.

water under a pressure of 29½ inches, has served, as is well known, as a term of comparison; it is the hundredth degree of the centigrade thermometer. If the pressure on the contrary is not uniform but varying, if it is increased or diminished, the boiling point rises or falls in the same proportion. When the pressure increases water boils only at a temperature above 212° F.

There is a well known apparatus, which was invented by Denis Papin. It is a close copper vessel half filled with water and then heated. The steam which is produced, finding no issue, compresses the water and prevents its boiling at 212° F; it is thus possible to keep water still liquid at a temperature of from 392° to 572° F.

If two pounds of mercury, at 212°, be mixed with two of water, at 32°, the mixture will be found to have a temperature of 37°; the degree of heat which maintained the mercury at a temperature of 212°, heats the water only up to 37°; this liquid has therefore "a great capacity for retaining heat."

This explains why islands and countries surrounded with water have a temperate climate, and enjoy a nearly uniform temperature; in summer the water of the sea lays up the heat of the sun—absorbs a large amount of it—and thus softens the rigor of the winter; this is why the Gulf Stream—a long distance away from its hot birthplace—is still warm when it reaches the polar ice.

When steam cools off, when it loses the heat that has volatilized it, it returns to the liquid state. We boil some water in a retort, furnished with a long glass neck, and a receiver. The steam set free, cools off in the receiver, and condenses into the liquid state; but in taking the form of gas it gives off all the substances which it held in solution, and returns thus to a state of purity. Hence it is that the vapors which escape from the sea form pure water in the clouds.

The operation we have just described is *distillation*,

and chemists frequently employ a distilling apparatus when they wish to obtain pure water. The process of distillation was well known to the ancients, particularly to Aristotle, who says, "Sea-water is rendered wholesome for drink by boiling, and all

Distilling Apparatus.

liquids, after having been transformed into steam, can return to the liquid state."* But the accomplished tutor of Alexander stopped at this statement, and did not think of inventing a distilling apparatus. Three centuries later, Pliny described a process by which resin might be distilled. He heated this substance in a pot with an orifice, over which was a covering of wool. The vapor became condensed in the porous stopper, and after the experiment, no-

* See Aristotle, on Meteorology.

thing was needed but to squeeze the wool, which was found saturated with oil.

Now, when we wish to obtain distilled water in large quantities, the following apparatus is employed. A copper cauldron contains the liquid which is to be distilled; it is capped by a glass head, a movable part of the machine, which forms a kind of retort. The neck is connected with a bent tube, called a serpentine, which passes through a vessel of cold water, or cooler, intended to condense the vapor, into which cold water is introduced at the lower part, whilst the hot water escapes through the upper part, and may be made use of to feed the cauldron.

The first portions of the condensed vapor are of no use; they contain the gases held in solution by the water; those that are collected afterwards are pure. This apparatus proves that steam, while condensing, throws off heat. This explains how it is that a cloud, when condensing to form rain, produces heat, and it may with truth be said that it transports the solar rays of the tropics to cold countries.

CHAPTER III.

INFLUENCE OF COLD.—AN EXCEPTION TO THE LAWS OF NATURE.

"We here detect nature in the act of making a halt in her accustomed march, and of reversing her ordinary habits."—TYNDALL.

WHEN a body is heated, whether it be solid, liquid, or gaseous, its volume increases—it expands; whereas, when it is cooled off, its bulk diminishes—it contracts.

Let us chill, at the same time, three spherical glass receivers, A, B, C; the first of which contains mercury, the second, water, and the third, alcohol; let us plunge them all in the same vessel, which we have filled with water, and into which we will throw pieces of ice. Let us begin by noting the temperature by means of a thermometer, starting at 59°; the three liquids will become cold, their level will perceptibly sink lower and lower, and the phenomenon will continue, in all alike, till the thermometer has reached 39°; but at this temperature of 39° water ceases to act like the two other liquids; for, while they continue to contract, water, on the contrary, expands, and its level continues to rise in the tube.

At a temperature of 39°, therefore, water ceases to contract; at 39° it has reached its minimum bulk, or, in other words, its *maximum density;* its molecules have drawn closer to each other, and it has become heavier. Below 39° it expands more and more, till at last it congeals and solidifies. As soon as it becomes ice its expansion is sudden and considerable. This fact at first seems a singular anomaly, which does not at once strike us as remarkably interesting; but we shall see, presently, that this property is of an exceptional importance in the economy of nature.

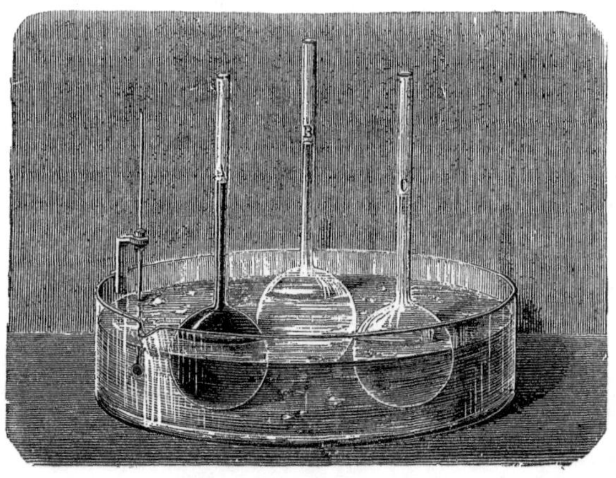

Maximum Density of Water.

Let us, for instance, examine what occurs in a lake, exposed to the cold of winter. The surface of the water cools and contracts down to 39°. At that point it becomes heaviest, and sinks from the excess of its weight, and is replaced by lower and less heavy layers. These new liquid strata, coming in contact with the icy atmosphere, speedily attain, also, a temperature of 39° ; they fall in their turn, and so, in succession, until the moment when the entire lake has reached the same temperature of 39°.

The upper strata continue subject to the influence of cold; but below 39° they increase in volume, become lighter and lighter, and remain on the surface of the lake. At 32° they become congealed and the ice floats upon a mass of water of a temperature of 39°, which is sufficiently high for the living creatures which it contains, to prolong their existence. Were it otherwise, if water like all other bodies diminished its bulk down to 32°, the ice, becoming heavier, would sink to the bottom and there form a solid mass perpetually increasing in thickness through all the winter months. At length a moment would come when all the great reservoirs of water in nature would be frozen, and the consequence of this entire solidification would be the instant death of every living creature which finds here the conditions of its existence. Rivers and water-courses would present to us, during severe winters, the appearance of enormous veins, hard frozen, and causing by their complete solidification the most deplorable disasters. To avoid this, when the peril is most imminent, nature obliges the water to expand under the influence of cold; hence the ice soon floats upon the rivers, covering them with a protecting mantle which shelters the living creatures and screens them beneath its kindly folds.

The expansion of water by freezing produces an irresistible force, capable of breaking the most solid substances, and hence we derive our popular expression, "It freezes hard enough to split stones." We take a tube of welded iron or a common gun barrel, fill it with water and stop it up hermetically by means of a firmly fixed screw. If it is then placed in a freezing mixture of pounded ice and common kitchen salt, the water in it will soon sink to a temperature of 39°, when contraction ceases. It goes down to 37°, 35°, 34° and 32°, and meanwhile its bulk increases. It passes slowly from the liquid to the solid state. In order to effect this molecular change, it requires more space than its narrow prison affords, and the iron tube refuses to yield. But we find that it cannot be held by the iron walls which seek to confine it. It reaches a temperature of 32° and congelation is inevitable. The water bursts its iron walls; the liquid atoms have acquired irresistible strength, and nothing can any longer withstand its molecular force. The tube flies into pieces under the play of the tiny icy crystals. If we increase the resistance, if we imprison the water in a cast iron cannon, in a mortar, a shell, the effects will be exactly the same. The resistant force of the metal will be utterly impotent in this struggle against atomic force, which has been estimated to reach a pressure of not less than 1,000 atmospheres.

This explains how it is that during winter our metal pipes are burst by the frost. The ice breaks the pipes, and when the thaw comes on, the water trickles through cracks opened by the tiny ice crystals. This is also what makes flowers and vegetables unable to resist the action of frost. The sap which circulates through stems and branches speedily solidifies. It increases in bulk and soon breaks its frail covering, dealing at the same time a death blow to the plant to which hitherto it has given life.

CHAPTER IV.

ICE—THE ARCHITECTURE OF ATOMS.

"This block of ice does not appear at first sight to be more interesting than a block of glass, but to the enlightened mind of the philosopher, ice is to glass what an oratorio of Handel's is to the cries of the market and the street. Ice is as music, glass as the mere noise ; ice is order, glass confusion. In the formation of ice, molecular forces have learned the art of weaving a regular embroidery."—TYNDALL.

THERE are coarse yet showy works of art, which at the first glance attract our admiration, but do not bear close inspection. Others again, like the carvings of a Cellini, have to be examined closely to be enjoyed. In examining the details of such a work, we find that the smallest portions of it have been wrought by a master's hand, and that the least prominent parts, even, have received most careful attention ; we discover everywhere traces of a conscientious artist in love with his work. But the hand of Nature is far more skillful yet, and delights in elaborating the most insignificant details of her work with matchless art. Our eye is unable to follow her into these minute details, and some of her loveliest masterpieces can only be seen with the help of a microscope. But even the microscope only reveals to us the outward form. The secret of her handiwork is as yet unfathomed. Science has not yet taught us how it is that the mutual friction of gaseous vapor-bubbles produces electric sparks; nor can it tell us why the same tiny bubbles, suddenly cooling off, assume the form of a snowflake or change into ice. The beautiful snowflake, as it falls silently from the darkling sky, is a mystery still, and the countless particles of ice, which sparkle in the cold winter air, betray the working of powers which have not yet been revealed to our knowledge. Nothing is more insignificant than the diminutive dust of such icicles, nothing more terrible to life; for, by means of their marvellous smallness, they penetrate into the interior of houses, pierce through the thickest fur clothing, enter the very pores of the skin, and make their way even to the lungs of man, causing fatal diseases, so that the dwellers in Arctic regions never go out during violent winds.

If, on the contrary, these icicles fall in less frigid zones, several unite and form the well known stars of startling beauty; if the air be damp, they collect in a large flake or the poor little star dissolves in a drop of rain, so that frequently it rains in the valleys while snow is falling on the mountains.

This snow, as we have already stated, is not a confused aggregate of solid particles, but is formed of a number of aqueous atoms symmetrically grouped and possessing an infinite variety of forms. If it is examined with a magnifying glass, a flake of snow will present the appearance of a regular geometrical pattern symmetrically arranged around a centre. One will perhaps resemble a flower with six petals, another a hexagonal star cut with the most exquisite delicacy; still another flake will present itself to eye under the appearance of a graceful arabesque, and there are snow stars of every variety of shape.

Nevertheless they are all constructed on the same model, fashioned after the same type. From the

Snow Crystals.

central cone radiate six needles, at angles of 60°. From these needles start out others of smaller size, which again send forth, to the right and the left, branches a thousand times slenderer, but still faithfully tracing their angle of 60°.

All these snow flowers affect the most marvellous forms, and present the most varied aspects; one might mistake them for the ever shifting images of the kaleidoscope. They are cut out of the most delicate material, embroidered on the daintiest muslin. The atoms become soldered together; they are attracted mutually to one another, and thus they unite to form rosettes, branches, stems, stalks, corollas and geometrical flowers.

This is what may be seen in snowflakes; but your observation must be very rapid, for this divine structure, these invisible monuments of which every block is an atom, have but a short duration. A single gleam of sunshine is sufficient to destroy all this harmony, and the mere heat of your body may melt the fragile flake. Instantly the atoms separate and the stars disappear; a drop of water takes the place of the fairy spectacle.

Ice, like snow, possesses a structure of admirable regularity. It consists of geometrical crystals, which can be shown by the aid of heat.

Let us pass a ray of electric light through a piece of ice. Its luminous intensity is not changed after traversing the transparent block, but its calorific intensity is noticeably diminished, as we can easily ascertain by the aid of a thermometer. A certain amount of heat has remained in the ice and will there act the part of a skillful anatomist, dissecting in a marvellous manner the block of solidified water.

If a lens be placed before the block of ice, in the centre of the ray of light, so as to project the image of the ice on a screen, we shall see here also stars with six rays, and flowers with six petals. The luminous ray acts as the messenger who informs us of the work of dissection which has been wrought by heat in the block of ice. The heat melts the water which has become solidified on its way—it destroys the structure of ice; it carries away, one by one, the blocks which formed so admirable a structure; and it separates the molecules which the atomic forces had heaped one upon another.

As in almost all the manifestations of Nature, Beauty and Power go hand in hand, solid water also presents us both features in striking contrast. Few things on earth are more truly beautiful than a fresh-fallen snow-flake—few are more terrible than a few of these flakes frozen together in a ball. In this shape we call them hail, and find them endowed with a surprising power of destruction.

ICE AND GLACIERS.

These small crystals of ice form, in time, these fields of ice surrounding the poles. They cover the Alps with a stainless garment, and become metamorphosed into water when the rays of the sun strike the white and shining surface, in spring. But this melting of the snow is always incomplete. Beyond a certain limit, which is called the "snow-line," begins the kingdom of everlasting ice. Below that line the prevailing heat causes the snow formed by the cold of winter, to melt completely. But if above this boundary line every winter were to bring a new accumulation of snow, the mountains would, in the course of ages, be charged with an enormous weight. If the layer of snow merely increased at the rate of three feet a year, the deposit, which would have gradually been formed during the course of eighteen centuries, would amount to nearly 5,000 feet; and if, instead of limiting ourselves to historic ages, we went back to geological periods, we should have to assign to the covering of snow resting on the shoulders of mountains, a height absolutely prodigious. But no accumulation of this kind can ever take place; and it is out of question that the sun should continually place on the summits of the mountains the water which he is forever taking from the ocean.

But by what mechanism are the summits of mountains freed from the excess of snow which crushes them beneath its weight? Immense masses of snow and formidable glaciers are constantly detached, and form avalanches which are precipitated into the valleys, where they return to the liquid state; but this rude and accidental motion is not the only one with which glaciers are endowed. They descend the mountain slopes slowly and progressively; whilst their upper part is situated in the domain of ice, above "the snow-line," their feet touch the warmer regions, where their snow is constantly melted by the action of heat.

We know how easy it is to agglomerate snow by pressing the flakes together in the hand, and how, by a powerful pressure, they can be made perfectly hard. A snow-ball is merely ice in process of formation. Ice itself is capable of yielding to pressure, and if, consequently, a thick coating of snow is spread over a layer of ice, the latter, bearing the weight of snow, will be pressed down and packed;

and if it lies on a slope it will not long resist the force which propels it, but will begin gradually to descend.

This movement is always taking place on the slopes of mountains which are covered with snow; the glacier gradually slips down the side of the declivity on which it came into existence, and thus reaches warmer regions, where it is soon changed into water. Between the snow and the glacier is to be found what is technically termed the *névé*—this is ice in process of formation, agglomerated snow, solid and opaque, such as is to be met with in all high mountains.

Glaciers are endowed with a singular property, which has often been noticed by tourists: that of fitting themselves into the grooves in which they move, and penetrating into the irregularities of the soil. They exactly reproduce the form of the ground on which they are placed, as if they consisted of a viscous mass of molasses or soft wax, which, without being absolutely liquid, is soft, and takes the exact shape of the solid layer of earth or of rock on which it rests. The glacier becomes flattened, spreads out or contracts, stretches as if made of India rubber; its centre always advancing with more rapidity than its melting sides. Attempts have been made to explain this curious fact by attributing a property called "viscosity," to ice; but this so-called explanation cannot be admitted without actual proof; and even if we were perfectly sure of the fact that solidified water yields to traction, spreading in the same manner as honey or tar, we would be none the less compelled to seek elsewhere for the cause of this faculty of extension possessed by ice, since a name is not a theory.

If you take two pieces of ice, and hold them for a few moments touching each other, their surfaces will soon unite, and the result will be a single block of ice, perfectly homogeneous. This experiment alone can furnish us with an explanation of what takes place in nature; but we will approach this important subject step by step, and first inquire why these two separate fragments became united.

In the same manner as steam always escapes from a free liquid surface, and as the molecules of the surface become changed into gas sooner than those of the interior of the liquid mass, so, also, the external particles of a piece of ice change into water, and melt before those of the centre. Two pieces of ice, at 32°, begin to enter into fusion on the surface; if we hold two of their faces together, we thus place these two surfaces in the centre of a new block, which we have formed; the fusion of these two surfaces can no longer go on, because they touch one another they congeal and become glued to each other.

We owe this curious experiment to Faraday—it is known under the name of "regelation;" we owe the explanation to Tyndall, who has verified the fact by other interesting experiments. "During a hot day in summer," says the English philosopher, "I went into a shop in the Strand, in the window of which some pieces of ice were exposed for sale, in a basin. With the permission of the owner of the shop I took them into my hand, and, taking up the topmost piece, I used it to draw all the rest out of the dish. Though the thermometer at that moment was at 86°, the pieces of ice had become welded at their points of junction."

The regelation of ice is effected even in hot water; two distinct fragments, held to each other in a liquid as hot as the hand can bear, will, in a few seconds, freeze and unite in spite of the heat. It is by virtue of this regelation that ice acts in a manner similar to a viscid body; it breaks as easily as a piece of glass, but the broken pieces become welded one to another, and can contract and expand under the law of gravity, or under the weight of snow which they support.

A bar of ice, compressed successively in a series of moulds, each more bent than the last, can be transformed into a circular ring. The bar breaks in the mould, but has scarcely broken before it freezes again, and forms a single mass, homogeneous and unchanged. It is the same principle which presides over the formation of snowballs, squeezed between the hands. If we forcibly compress a large snowball in a mould we can obtain a cup of ice, perfectly transparent, and resulting from regelation. If a spherical mould be filled with snow and then compressed by a hydraulic press, we obtain a ball of ice, solid and transparent,—a snowball somewhat different from those that schoolboys are in the habit of making.

Mountaineers, though uninitiated into the theories of physical science, frequently avail themselves of this property of regelation, possessed by solidified water, in order to cross deep crevasses, by means of snow-bridges. By walking cautiously on a bridge, formed of agglomerated snow-flakes, they force them to harden, and the compressed snow assumes, under the influence of regelation, a hardness and rigidity which renders it capable of supporting a heavy weight. Some of the guides, in Switzerland, are in the habit of crossing, fearlessly, in this manner, on snow bridges, very deep gulfs; and if ever you see them making these dangerous-looking transits, instead of trembling with apprehension of what their fate may prove, make yourself perfectly easy about them, think of the regelation of ice, and follow their example by trying the experiment yourself.

You understand by this time, dear reader, how a glacier makes its way through the defiles of the Alps, insinuates itself into the inequalities of the soil, penetrates into narrow gorges, bends and winds backwards and forwards over the shoulders of mountains, takes the impress of the furrows which it meets with, adapts itself to the movement into which all these objects urge it, and even sinks into the crevices of rocks, without necessarily possessing that property of *viscosity*, for which M. Jorbes and Bishop Rendu have given credit.

The ice, in its course, wears away and polishes the surfaces over which it glides, for its lower part is filled with pebbles, which act the part of the hard fragments adhering to sand-paper. The ground becomes lightly fissured by these small stones, which progress slowly with the glacier.

When the glacier has ceased to exist—when it is converted into water, by the action of solar heat—it leaves on the place of its existence incontestable traces of its former presence, and its native soil is covered with the marks which it has traced.

In all mountain chains, in every country, we see in a number of different places, deep flutings furrowing the soil, and smoothly rounded off surfaces, which tell the eye of the observer, in clear language, that a glacier must have formerly existed in the place where he is now standing. The valley of the Grimsel, in the Bernese Oberland, presents an aspect highly characteristic of the passage of glaciers; the rocks are rounded off and polished, and everywhere traces are found of the furrows formed by the pebbles which adhere to the ice. The same characteristics are to be found in the valley of the Rhone; on the slopes of the Jura; everything in these regions proclaims the existence of former glaciers—formidable and powerful—veritable giants, when compared with our modern glaciers.

North America and certain parts of Asia were once upon a time covered with ice, and the cedars of Lebanon now flourish over the morains of prehistoric times.

The whole of our continent, between Newfoundland and the Upper Mississippi, is thickly strewn with innumerable blocks torn from regions near the pole and transported southward, not only on the plains, but often raised to an altitude of 500 feet. All these erratic boulders, as they are commonly called, lie on the southeast side of the mountains from which they come; some, torn from Canada, have been carried as far as Ohio; others, from Labrador, have been cast on the southern coast of the Gulf of St. Lawrence; and red sandstone, plucked from Prince Edward's Island, now lies in Nova Scotia. New England can show blocks of huge size lying four hundred feet higher than the rocks from which they come. In Europe enormous masses, detached from the mountains of Sweden and Finland, are dispersed in prodigious numbers over Germany, Poland and Russia. Nor is this all. Immense tracts of transported materials, consisting of sand, gravel, clay, mud, and all sorts of sweepings of the face of the earth, and incrusted with erratic boulders, cover vast regions to a depth which attains as much as three hundred feet, forming sometimes grand horizontal plains, sometimes tiers of hills, stretching along from north to south. Mysterious marks, stripes, furrows and flutings, often two feet deep, have been scooped out by an irresistible chisel in the granite flanks of mountains, that have been ground down, smoothed and polished, by the agency of an anonymous workman.

All these erratic blocks, vast deposits and inexplicable marks, are, according to Agassiz's theory, the result of the action of grand polar glaciers.

The ice of glaciers, snow and the *névé*, are not the only forms of solidified water which nature presents to our view. Glaciers frequently contain cavities full of water, on the surface of which layers of ice form themselves of quite a different character to the glacier-ice; this water-ice is more compact than the latter, and does not contain any of the capillary tubes which give to ice the beautiful blue tint so much admired by tourists.

At the bottom of rapid rivers, such as the Rhine, are sometimes found collected together fragments of a kind of spongy solidified ice, known to the dwellers on the banks of these rivers as "*bottom-ice.*"

The ice which is formed on ponds and rivers is naturally that variety which has been most carefully studied. We have shown that this ice has a crystalline structure—a fact which can be easily ascertained by examining the motley designs which are to be seen on our window panes during severe frost.*

Ice has, finally, often been met with in real crystals, formed by hexagonal or triangular prisms. Dr. Clarke took from under the bridge at Cambridge several large rhomboidic crystals of ice. These cases, however, are exceptional, ice seldom presenting a more crystalline structure than glass.

---

* Mr. Haas has discovered a process by which the frost designs may be retained upon a window. He exposes to the cold a horizontal glass plate covered with a thin sheet of water, holding enamel powder in suspension. The hoar frost, keeping the powder of enamel imprisoned, forms and traces out numerous ramified arabesques. When the water is evaporated by carrying the glass plate to the stove, beautiful aborescent designs of enamel remain, and the crystallizations formed by the hoar frost are fixed forever by the enamel melted in the stove heat.

CHAPTER V.

THE PART WHICH WATER PLAYS IN CHEMISTRY.

"Water is the principle of all things,—plants and animals are only water condensed, and it is into water that they are resolved after death."—THALES.

1. DISSOLUTION.—This phenomenon, common and well-known as it is, is nevertheless of great interest.

We throw a handful of saltpetre (nitrate of potash) into a vessel filled with water; this salt dissolves like sugar. We then throw into the vessel a second handful of the same salt, then a third, then a fourth, and they will all melt and disappear, little by little, like the preceding. But at last a moment is sure to arrive, when the liquid will refuse to dissolve the fresh salt which will be thrown into it, and leave it unchanged and solid, at the bottom of the vessel.

The water is now said to be saturated. If we heat this water, the salt, which is in excess, and lying on the bottom, dissolves under the influence of heat; and when the liquid is in a boiling condition we can cause it to absorb a much larger quantity of the salt than it did at a lower temperature.

Water, when hot, usually possesses a greater solvent power than when it is cold; notwithstanding which, certain products—such as common kitchen salt—dissolve as well in cold as in boiling water. If we allow a basinful of water, which had been saturated when warm, to cool off and to rest a few hours, it will relinquish the excess of salt, and deposit it in the shape of geometrical crystals of various sizes. Carbonate of soda, sulphate of copper, and alum, crystallize with great facility in water, and carpet the bottom of the vessel in which they are placed with needles and prisms of the most remarkable appearance. Water does not dissolve all

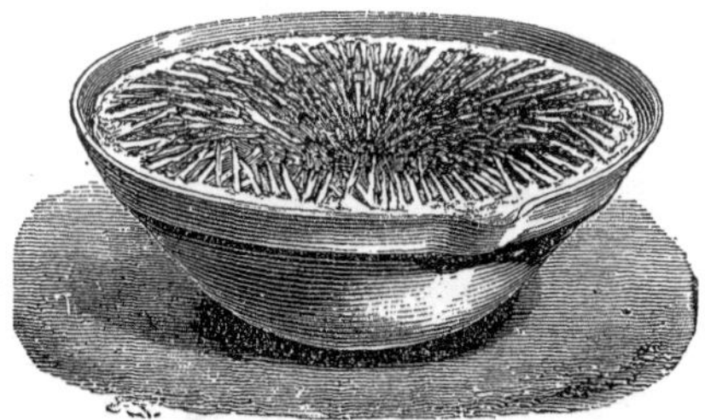

Crystals of Saltpetre.

salts in like proportion; a pint will take up more than two pounds of sulphate of soda, but cannot dissolve more than two grains of sulphate of lime. Water charged with carbonic acid acts upon a great number of stones; it dissolves with ease, as we have seen, carbonate of lime, (chalk, and common building-stone,) and can even decompose granite rocks; and the carbonic acid, which it holds in solution, is thus found fixed in the solid state.

Dissolution is frequently accompanied by a chemical phenomenon,—a more or less considerable escape of heat,—and it is thus that water, which has no effect on some substances, such as gold, silver, quartz, carbon, sulphur, etc., is decomposed by potassium and sodium; it is thus that it unites with lime and anhydro-sulphuric acid, and that, in the act of uniting with lime, it raises the temperature more or less, while giving birth to a new composition—a true chemical combination.

Action of Water on Lime.

Nor is the solvent power of water less wonderful when applied to other substances. Few of us, surely, imagine that the glass which contains the water we drink is soluble by the latter; and yet it is well known that the stained-glass windows of Westminster Abbey have all been honey-combed, and in many places nearly eaten through by the rain! The great chemist, Lavoisier, moreover, found that the glass retorts, which he used in distilling water from its constituent gases, lost much of their weight, while that of water was correspondingly increased by an impregnation of the elementary flint and alkali of the glass. Nor is granite itself exempt from the mastery of this marvellous solvent. An object dipped in the silicious waters thrown up by the hot springs of Iceland, from the depth of the Plutonic strata, becomes coated with a flinty deposit identical with the silicate of glass.

In like manner, water is capable of absorbing astonishing quantities of various gases; of ammonia, the gas exhaled by spirits of hartshorn, not less than seventy-six times its own measure. To this absorbent power of water is owing the frequent contamination of London water by the coal-gas, which, leaking from the gas-pipes into the soil, is drawn into the water-pipes, sometimes to such an extent as actually to ignite at the hydrants! In other cases, water has absorbed large quantities of the foul gases exhaled by sinks and cesspools, and led to fearful diseases and grievous loss of life among those who drank it, unconscious of its contamination.

2. The Color and Transparency of Water.—Who would believe that colorless water could tinge, or render transparent, the salts which crystallize in its bosom? Nothing, however, is truer, as very simple experiments prove.

We take some crystals of sulphate of copper, which present an admirable shade of dark blue;

their brightness and their transparency are remarkable, and they reflect the light which falls upon their regular faces. If we confine them in a stove, heated to a temperature of 248°—a degree at which water evaporates and abandons the sulphate of copper—we shall find that, at the end of a few hours, the salt will be thoroughly dry; but the crystals also are destroyed, the structure broken up owing to the departure of the water; color and transpa-

Oven for drying Salts.

rency alike have fled with the liquid element. These crystals, blue and regular when they contained water, are, now that they have become dry, changed into a white, opaque powder.

We next take transparent crystals of carbonate of soda. If we dry them they will, in like manner, assume the appearance of a white and shapeless dust, as soon as they lose their water.

The water thus imprisoned in the mass of various crystallized bodies is not mixed; it is combined—united—according to positive laws, with the molecules of salt, which it colors and renders transparent; for instance: seven molecules of water unite with one molecule of sulphate of copper to form the beautiful blue crystals, which make so striking an ornament in some chemists' shops.

A large number of stones also contain this *water of crystallization*, which gives them their beautiful transparency. The translucent gypsum, which is so frequently met with in the quarries near Paris, is a hydrated sulphate of lime, having a singular crystalline form, and presenting the appearance of the head of a lance. This gypsum, when calcined, gives out the water which it contains, and changes into a white dust—called plaster of paris. Azurite (or lazulite), one of the most beautiful stones of which the mineral world boasts, and which has a regular crystalline form, of beautiful dark blue color, contains, also, waters of crystallization, and is destroyed as soon as it is dried, losing, as it does, the tint of azure, which gives it its name.

3. Plants and Animals.—Much more important is the chemical part played by water in the animal and vegetable kingdoms. We all know that the liquid element nourishes plants, and we shall now find that it almost entirely constitutes the trees of our forests, the fruit and seeds of those trees, and the bodies of every living thing. The philosopher Thales, the celebrated head of the Ionian school,

said, two thousand years ago: "Water is the principle of everything; plants and animals are merely condensed water, and it is into water that they will be resolved after death." This statement is not so exaggerated as might appear at first sight.

If we heat in a stove a handful of green herbs which have been carefully weighed, and after the water has had time to evaporate, cast our eyes upon the remains of the dried plants, we shall find that these herbs, so recently green and brilliant, fresh and living, are now dead and calcined. Their weight is diminished by four fifths; and in depriving their substance of the water it contained, we have taken out of them all that contributed to their life; we have destroyed the sap, the coloring matter, in fact, the whole organism.

All animals, including man, consist in like manner almost entirely of the elements of water. A few globules are all that is needed to change water into blood, and a few mineral and organic substances transform water into sap or into milk. Natural milk contains 85 per cent. of water, and the blood of animals 97 per cent.!

If a beefsteak be strongly pressed between two sheets of blotting-paper, it will yield nearly four fifths of its own weight of water, while the experiments of Berzelius and Dalton prove that of the human frame, including the bones, one fourth is solid matter, the rest being water. "If a man, therefore," says the Swedish savant, "whose weight is 140 pounds, were squeezed flat under a hydraulic press, 105 pounds of water would be expressed and only thirty-five pounds of dry residue, composed chiefly of carbon and nitrogen, would remain. The living organism is thus to be regarded as a solid mass dissolved in water." And Dalton found by experiments made on his own person, that five sixths of the food taken day by day to repair the human fabric is also water; of potatoes, again, no less than seventy-five per cent. is water, and of turnips, at least ninety.

If, as some say, iron is the bone of the earth, then water is the blood—the ceaseless ebb and flow, the endless evaporation and return, corresponding to the throb and pulse of the human heart and its life blood. The very air, even when crisp and dry, has one fifth per cent. of moisture in it, and without water the whole earth, Himalayas and Andes included, would be but a handful of dust, a gigantic heap of dry powder, on which not even the most rudimentary lichen would exist. The ancients built altars to Diana and worshipped the mother Moon. For Diana and the Moon emblemized the water principle, without which Nature would have no plastic force, and the fair earth no form, no life, no loveliness.

Without water not only the oceans would dry up, but the rivers, streams and brooks which course through all the lands, would present the appearance of dried-up furrows; the little brooks would cease to purl and murmur. Trees, plants, vegetables of every kind would be utterly destroyed; losing the water which they contain, they would lose both their sap and their life—the noblest trees of our forest would be transformed into a confused heap of shapeless dust.

Even the majority of stones would change their appearance—transparent gypsum would become white powder, blue carbonate of copper and the green stalactites of malachite would be changed into colorless ashes; building-stone, slate, the strata of coal, all would wear an appearance totally different from that which they now present.

The air, deprived of vapor and of the clouds which float in it, would no longer present the magnificent spectacles which result from the play of light; the sun would no longer, as he sets, tinge the massive banks of clouds with crimson and gold; the entire surface of the globe would present a terrible picture of desolation, and with the disappearance of water all organic life would perish.

V.

THE USES OF WATER.

"There are few substances of which so many uses have been made as water."—THENARD.

"The uses of water are innumerable, and they increase in number in proportion as the human intellect develops itself, and discovers new services which this agent can render."—JEAN REYNARD.

CHAPTER I.

WATER AND AGRICULTURE.

"To ameliorate the water-system of the world in such a manner as to cause it to subserve public utility to the highest degree possible, to extend the numerous agricultural expedients for turning running water to account, is to open up sources of prosperity so numerous and so great, that the science of the engineer could not be directed towards an object more entirely in conformity with the general interest."—NADAULT DE BUFFON.

"The liquid element is to the dry a constant remedy, protecting it against aridity."—MICHELET.

WHEN the summer sun has for a long time been burning the parched earth with its pitiless beams, when the sky has refused to bestow the blessings of rain upon the earth, trees, flowers, and all vegetation appear to mourn and languish; the leaves wilt, the branches droop, the meadows lose their brilliant verdure, and grain stalks bend under the weight of their ears, while at the same time all noxious plants increase with startling rapidity in the fields which they invade. If the sky becomes dark, if thick clouds begin to burst, pouring upon the parched ground a profusion of rain, then vegetation rapidly revives and drinks in joyously the precious blessing. Everything seems as though newly awakening to life. But the sky does not always grant so freely its treasures, and the husbandman cannot always afford to wait till the clouds bring him that water which is the very life of his fields; he must learn how to prepare for the inclemency of the season, and to provide against drought. Has not Virgil already said: "Next to the gods there is nothing so all-powerful as agriculture?"

Plants, like animals, are born, grow, reproduce themselves and die; like animals they breathe; like animals they requre food. Their leaves are their organs of breathing; they absorb the carbonic acid of the air, and under the influence of the solar rays, they exhale oxygen and assimilate the carbon which they require for their development. Their roots are the organs of nutrition; they search in the soil for such elements as are necessary to feed the plant, and it is water which brings these to them in a state of solution. The food of plants consists of hydrogen, obtained through the decomposition of water; nitrogen proceeding from the ammonia contained in every kind of water, even in rain-water and certain mineral substances, such as soda, potash, lime, silica, magnesia, etc. It is hence not every kind of water that can fertilize the soil and aid vegetation; there are some even which being injurious to the development of plants render the earth barren. The stagnant waters of marshes and peat bogs put an end to organic life; for being charged with astringent matter they wither the foliage and paralyze vegetation. Water which has been flowing through a very shady country, or even under large trees, is cold, and retards rather than advances the growth of plants; it carries into the fields the seeds of weeds and noxious herbs, which soon spring up and thrive to the great detriment of the cultivated plants. If water should have imbibed any of the acid which is to be found in soils formed by the debris of organic matter, it may be highly deleterious.

Water from badly aerated springs also, like that which is formed from the melting of snow-water, is injurious both to plants and animals, and can be used for irrigation only after it has been exposed to the air for a considerable time. Plaster is beneficial to a larger number of plants, and water charged with plaster, is therefore good for watering. Not so that which holds any calcareous matter in solution. According to Sinclair, water impregnated with iron has the same effect upon plants as upon animals, and serves to imbue grass and herbs with tonic qualities. Water which contains an appreciable quantity of sulphate of iron is injurious, and carbonate of iron is still more so; it covers the tissues of plants with a crust, closes their pores, obstructs their cells, and gradually kills them. Brackish water and even sea water produce good results if applied cautiously and in due proportion to the dryness of the climate. Every one knows what beneficial effects salt meadows have upon cattle, and the improvement they cause in the quality of the meat. River water and that of well aerated springs are alike beneficial and enrich the soil. From these the husbandman draws his wealth:

> "When 'neath the burning sun the scorched herbs die,
> I see swift rushing down a soft descent

> A limpid brook, which on a rocky bed
> Falls, foams, and flowing with a gentle murmur
> To each parched mead, brings back the vanished green."
>
> VIRGIL.

It is curious that the importance of water in connection with agriculture has been nowhere more fully appreciated than by the French, and is nowhere more grievously neglected than in our own country. The unfortunate French, the race of contrasts by eminence, combining rare talents with sad defects and fatal passions, have studied the subject of irrigation thoroughly, and possess the best code of laws controlling the use of water known to our day. The famous works by which the muddy, fertilizing water of the river Durance, near Marseilles, is distributed by a vast net of canals over an enormous district, dates back to the twelfth century. At that time their neighbors, the Moors in Spain, taught them the great art of irrigation ; their works being of such surpassing merit, that quite recently Prussian engineers were sent to Southern Spain, there to study the scanty ruins which still speak eloquently of the marvellous skill of the Arabs. Even now large portions of the kingdom are cultivated by the aid of constructions belonging to those days. The traveller who reaches Granada and visits the Alhambra, hears of an evening, as the sun sinks in a flood of gold beneath the horizon, a large bell striking three, four, five times, and then deep silence falls upon the city. After some minutes a few more strokes, but in a different rhythm. That is the Bell of the Moorish Kings, which now, after so many centuries, tells the peasant far out on the vast Vega, that he can open the sluices of his canal, and then bids him close them again. Every five minutes the signal is repeated, from sunset till sunrise; its solemn sounds are heard far away in the hot summer night, and all over the plain it sets the blessed waters running and purling merrily, bringing new life to the thirsting fields.

Nor is Italy behindhand in this branch of art, for here above all, hydraulics have been proved to be an art like all others, since some of the greatest painters, a Leonardo da Vinci and a Guido Romano, a Raphael even, and a Bramante, have lent their genius to the construction of great works of irrigation. Northern Italy, especially, is covered with a multitude of canals, watering a plain of two million acres, the grandest of which bears the name of her illustrious statesman, Cavour, and has cost more than fourteen million dollars!

It is certainly not peculiarly creditable to our nation, that the advantages of irrigation are as yet so imperfectly appreciated in this country, although the natural fertility of the soil and the facility of obtaining virgin land for cultivation explain this neglect in part. The Mormons seem to have been "wise in their generation" in this respect. It is one of the beauties of their great city that the clear, fresh water is running through all the streets, and from the main channels conducted into every garden and field—the supply being strictly regulated by law and carefully watched over by "water-masters."

IRRIGATION AND DRAINAGE.

Have you never found pleasure, dear reader, in cultivating a plant in a flower-pot, on your window-sill? Did you lavish your care on the little shrub while anxiously watching its progress? You noticed the birth of the first little bud, you saw it change into a beautiful flower with fresh and vivid colors, and again and again you admired its graceful petals at the moment when they opened under the caresses of the sun. What made that plant thus grow beneath your eyes? *You* ought to know better than any one, for you it was who every morning supplied the food it needed in the form of water. In the evening the leaves and flowers, exhausted by the heat of the day, had lost their smiling beauty and seemed to droop; but a little water speedily revived them.

Did you never remark that the earthen pot which contained your plant, was pierced at the bottom with a small hole? Did you not observe that the saucer, which held the flower-pot, often filled with water while you were watering your plant? The water which had been poured into the pot had passed through the small supply of earth in which the roots were spread out; it had been thus filtered, and the surplus of liquid which was not absorbed by the roots, settled in the saucer by means of the hole at the bottom. Without this outlet the water would have remained in the midst of the roots, which would have quickly rotted, thus causing the death of your plant. Well, your agriculture prospered because it was in conformity with the rules of irrigation and drainage; and the husbandman should arrange the fields he cultivates on the same principle as the flower-pot. It is by an artificial watering, by irrigation, that he must improve his soil, but the water has to be distributed with prudence, or else the remedy may prove a poison; it can kill as well as cure. After having watered the soil, after the ground has absorbed the water which has been so abundantly poured upon it, it becomes necessary to relieve it of the excess of liquid. Irrigation must be succeeded by drainage.

Irrigation is useful to all soils, but especially to sandy soils, and if the water used for the purpose contain some earthy elements, it not only enriches the land by the manure it brings, but it also lessens its too porous character by means of the sediment which it deposits. It is very important to understand thoroughly what amount of water is requisite for the purpose of irrigation; the volume of water supplied, the rapidity of its flow, the absorbent capacity of the soil, and the climate of the locality, all should be the subject of the farmer's most attentive study. In warmer climates the amount of water usually employed is equal to the extent of land which is to be irrigated, but the quantity differs naturally very much in various parts of the world. Northern France, for instance, requires nine to ten times as much water for the acre as southern France, while on the other hand the quality, that is, the fertilizing power of some rivers differs so much from others, that frequently one kind of water is worth ten times as much as another.

The water being conveyed to the head of a piece of land, the question next arises, "How it is to be used so as to spread uniformly over the whole surface, and thus to benefit all the plants?" We shall not attempt to describe the various methods of irrigation that have been tried, but shall content ourselves with briefly pointing out those that have been found most successful. The figure below represents irrigation by infiltration; the water arrives by a feeding-trench A, and is distributed into other

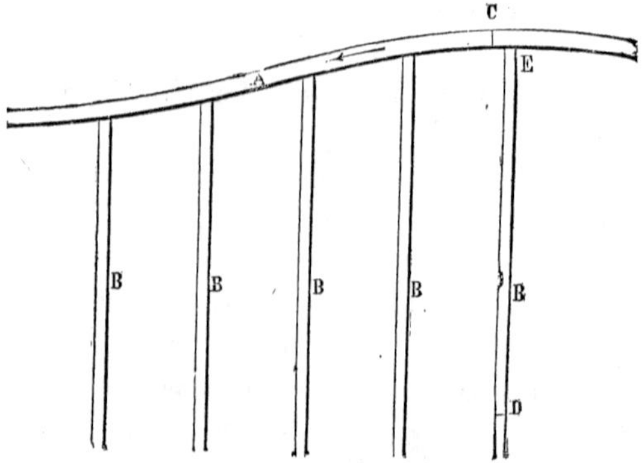

Irrigation by Infiltration.

secondary trenches B B; the latter are simply deep open furrows between those formed by the ploughshare or the drill for cultivation. Water is successively let into all the secondary trenches; for instance, a beginning is made in the trench which meets at E the principal feeding-trench; the latter is closed at C, and the water soaks into the soil as far as D. Frequently a field that is to be watered is entirely submerged, and this mode of irrigation is called submersion, immersion or irrigation by shelving beds. It not unfrequently happens that the water occupies a lower level than the field which is to be irrigated, and then it becomes necessary to raise it by means of machines such as pumps and hydraulic rams.

The most famous of all systems of irrigation is, of course, the watering of Egypt by the Nile, which overflows the whole vast plain on both sides of its banks, and leaves behind a thin layer of incredibly rich deposit. Embankments cross the country in all directions; villages and towns are built on natural or artificial eminences, and while the land is under water, all intercourse is carried on by boat and ferry. Thus, Egypt is perpetually changing; to-day a lake, to-morrow a blooming garden; now a land of morasses, teeming with malaria, and now a parched desert. As its very life depends upon this system of irrigation, and the needful supply of water, the inundation has been celebrated from time immemorial, by solemn ceremonies and national rejoicings. As soon as the river begins to rise, public criers proclaim the joyful fact, passing through every district and town, calling out: God has been merciful to the fields! Day of joyful news! At the same time they recite animated dialogues with the accompanying boys, changing their tenor daily with every inch that the Nile has risen, and receive in return a small fee from the grateful peasants. When the river has at last risen 20 to 21 feet, the time has come for piercing the great dam, at Cairo, and once more the criers are seen waving flags and reciting sacred songs of praise.

After a night, spent by the majority of natives in anxious watchings and superstitious worship, the Government orders, on the appointed day, the great canal to be opened. The embankment is massive below, but dwindles to a width of nine feet at the top, which, though 22 feet above low-water mark, is not quite 20 feet above the canal, the banks of which are higher than the embankment. On these banks of the canal lie the ruins of a stone house, from which the chief officers of the government used to witness the great ceremony. Nowadays a tent is erected here for the officials, whose presence is required; and all around, numerous other tents are opened for curious spectators, who are all well provided with vast quantities of rockets, Bengal lights, and other fireworks, by means of which the night is turned into day. Venders of coffee and sweetmeats abound, and the whole scene is striking and eminently picturesque.

In the afternoon, already, numbers of boats crowd around the place where the embankment is to be pierced; all are adorned with countless flags and bright bunting; but above all shines a larger vessel literally covered with flags and lanterns, which carries several small guns, and has a silk tent on deck for the ladies. All night through songs and laughter, music and solemn anthems, fill the air, while on shore an immense multitude is moving restlessly to and fro, in anxious expectation of the coming ceremony. In the meantime, laborers have been at work making a breach in the massive rampart, so that, an hour before sunset, only a few inches of soil restrain the waters of the Nile. Now the high officials come down from their tent to the embankment, sign a document stating the precise height of the water,—which has to be sent to Constantinople,—throw a few purses, filled with gold pieces, among the workmen, and, as soon as they have disappeared, a government boat is driven hard against the embankment, and glides down with the overflowing river, followed by all the gaily-decked vessels. Thundering guns, shouting crowds, and bursting rockets are mingled in one great explosion. Thus, an event which everywhere else would be a source of terror and infinite suffering, becomes in Egypt a blessing and a cause for universal rejoicing.

A system of drainage serves to carry off the superabundant moisture, which might otherwise injure the development of plants. Trenches or drains are dug, and cylindrical tubes are laid on the bottom.

The earth which has been excavated is thrown back into the drain, and no trace remains on the surface ; but the superabundant water trickles through the soil, sinks to the bottom of the drain, and enters the pipes by way of their joints. These pipes, laid slanting, carry the water outside of the field, where they are emptied. Occasionally gutter drains are employed, (see Fig. 2,) in which a stone channel is substituted for the earthen or glass pipes, and cobble drains, as seen in Fig. 3. As the drain is always

Fig. 1.—Tubular Drain.

under ground, and it is still necessary to know how it works, openings are left at the places where the

Fig. 2.—Gutter Drain. Fig. 3.—Cobble Drain.

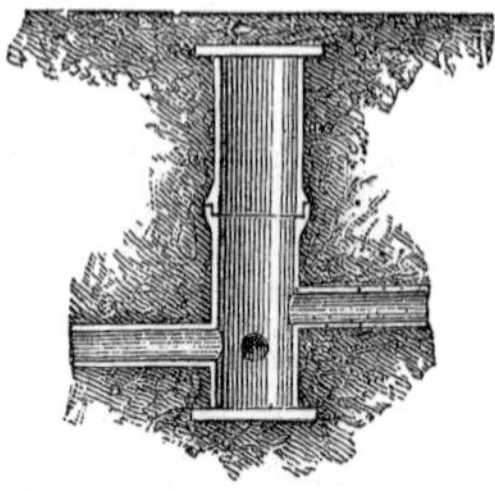

Fig. 4.—Drain Well.

pipes enter the main trench, (see Fig. 4). A few spadefuls of soil are removed, which cover the opening, and it is easily ascertained whether the water runs off, by the noise which it makes as it falls from the smaller into the larger pipe.

"COLMATAGE," OR THE DRAINING OF MARSHES.

We have seen how, every year, the Nile overflows its banks, and, spreading its waters over the adjoining fields, deposits on them a precious mud, which, by its fertilizing properties, constitutes the wealth of the immense valley. Nature does in Egypt herself what man performs in other countries by a process which is termed "*colmatage*." The object of this operation is to cover a certain portion of land with muddy water, so as to render it fit for cultivation. The waters are allowed to stand upon it for some time, and a sediment is deposited; the pure water, relieved of its earthy particles, is then let off, and replaced by new sheets of thick, muddy water, and this process is continued until the soil has been sufficiently raised. This process is thus the means of creating, at little expense, a new and fertile soil: it is thus, for instance, that the valley of the Isère, in France, has been rendered so productive. All who dwell upon the banks of great rivers can, in this manner, derive wealth and prosperity from the water-courses at their feet. Agriculture has still to discover the means of utilizing the beds of marshes and stagnant pools, where the water covers the land with a miry and unwholesome liquid. These noxious pools must be drained, and then the place where now useless reeds and marsh-plants, poisonous and noxious herbs, grow in hideous luxuriance, will be filled with the golden stalks of wheat; the ripening fields will sway to and fro under the soft breath of the breeze, and their ever-changing surface, agitated by the air, will resemble the undulations of the ocean.

CHAPTER II.

SALT WATERS.—SEA SALT.

"Nothing in nature is worthless; and there is no substance which man cannot turn to account."—JEAN REYNAUD.

AMONG the most important industrial products, a prominent place must be given to sea salt, or chloride of sodium. It is water which furnishes us with abundance of that valuable substance, which, under the name of kitchen salt, appears at all our meals and is daily employed in domestic economy, to season our food and preserve our meat. A large quantity is annually used in agriculture, also; and the industrial arts employ a considerable amount in producing sulphate of soda, chlorohydric acid, and several chlorids of great importance in connection with chemistry.

Chloride of sodium is procured from three different sources; from *beds of rock salt*, from *salt springs*, and from *sea water*. In the first case, when rock salt is pure, pits and subterranean galleries are excavated, and miners set to work to bring to light this valuable commodity. But when the salt is not of such quality as would repay this method of working the mine, a simpler and cheaper way is chosen. Instead of sending miners into the bowels of the earth, fresh water is made to do the work of man. In the neighborhood of Salzburg, in Suabia, and in a number of other localities, they merely sink narrow shafts going down into the salt beds, where they end in empty spaces, compartments termed dissolving rooms. Into these chambers water is poured, which dissolves the rock-salt and becomes thoroughly saturated with it; it is then pumped up to the surface, and made to evaporate under the action of heat. Thus, at a small expense, crystals of salt are obtained, which has been brought up from the earth's bowels by the agency of water.

Salt springs result from the infiltration of water, which in its travels through the bowels of the earth has encountered beds of rock-salt. These waters are rarely saturated with salt; generally they contain not more than three to four per cent., and as in this case the volume of water to be evaporated would require too large an expenditure of caloric, the saline solution is previously subjected to a process of concentration, by exposure to the air in an apparatus known under the name of *Graduation Buildings*.

These structures consist of walls formed of bundles of brushwood within wooden frames and surmounted by a small wooden channel, which runs the whole length of the building. The upper trough throws the salt water, brought up by the pumps, sometimes to the right and sometimes to the left, and this water, after passing through the mass of brushwood falls drop by drop through its whole thickness.

Constantly in contact with currents of air, it is subjected during its whole passage to considerable evaporation, and reaches the lower basin in a highly concentrated state. If the operation be repeated many times, and if the walls be situated so as directly to face the wind, the evaporation takes place very rapidly. In the salt works of Sooden, near Allendorf, in Hesse, a water which contains only four per cent. of salt before percolating for the first time through the graduating building, contains twenty-two per cent. after having been filtered half a dozen times. This mode of extracting salt is in frequent use in many countries, and may be seen, in vast proportions, in the interior of the State of New York. Here lofty walls are erected which attain at times a length of over fifteen hundred feet, by nearly forty feet in height and twelve in width. The salt water may be seen trickling slowly through the piled faggots, then gradually concentrating till it becomes sufficiently saturated to be subjected to evaporation by fire. When the water is at length found to contain from fourteen to twenty-two per cent. of salt it is exposed to the action of the heat, which causes first a deposit of all the impurities it contained, and then of pure chloride of sodium.

The richest and most abundant source of salt is, however, the ocean.

In every pint of sea-water there is more than half an ounce of solid ingredient, which would be left as a dry, crystalline powder on the liquid being evaporated by heat. If all the water of the Atlantic were steamed away, there would remain enough salt deposited from it to cover an extent of seven millions of square miles, one entire mile deep. This substance consists mainly of common salt, compounds of lime and magnesia in a soluble form, and compounds of potash and soda. A little of iron and still less silver make up the whole. The question naturally arises: Where has the ocean procured this large quantity of solid substance, these dense compounds? No one knows how far away it may have commenced its terrestrial career as salt brine, but it is easily seen that its liquid floods never could have been pure water. Rivers themselves, we have seen, are not pure; they are fed by rains, and these rains wash down with them, as they course through the river-channels, everything which they can dissolve during their progress. All these dissolved matters are carried with these streams into the ocean. Fresh water evaporates from the ocean continually to form the clouds and to supply the fountains of the rain. These vapors, however, cannot carry up with them a single particle of saline or earthy material. As the rivers, therefore, bring down to the sea, day by day, fresh stores of dissolved saline solids, and as none of these stores can be dissipated under evaporation, it follows that from this agency alone the sea must at length become salt.

In almost all Southern regions, in Europe as well as on our own seacoast, sea-water is evaporated in vast natural reservoirs, called salt-marshes, by the action of heat, which the sun lavishly supplies. Upon the shores of the Mediterranean and on the seacoast salt water is made to flow into vast basins where it evaporates rapidly, and when the liquid has attained from twenty to twenty-four degrees by the famous salt-meter of Beaumé, it is made to flow into other basins, where it leaves its sea-salt.

These works are of the greatest importance, for the sea-water does not merely contain chloride of sodium, but holds in solution many other salts from which industry may materially profit.

The following table will show the ingredients of two quarts of sea-water:

		OCEAN.	MEDITERRANEAN.
		gr.	gr.
Chloride	of sodium	25.10	27.22
	of potassium	0.50	0.70
	of magnesium	3.50	6.14
Sulphate	of magnesia	5.78	7.02
	of lime	0.15	0.15
Carbonate	of magnesia	0.18	0.19
	of lime	0.02	0.01
	of potash	0.23	0.21
Iodides, Bromides and organic matters.		?	?
Pure Water		964.54	958.36
Total		1000.00	1000.00

Certain lakes contain a much larger proportion of sea salt.

The two most remarkable lakes on earth—not only on account of their biblical importance, but simply in their physical aspect—are the lakes of Tiberias and the Dead Sea, connected with each other by the river Jordan. The level of the former, surrounded by the most picturesque heights on earth, is 308 feet lower than the Mediterranean, and the Dead Sea, with its bitter saline water, lies as it were in a huge pit between rugged rocks, salt cliffs, and desolate barren slopes, at a depth of 1,231 feet below the level of the sea. Instinctive dread seizes the traveller as he enters this low, doomed region, where no life stirs, and not a sound is heard, and he feels that he stands on a scene where nameless crimes were punished by a fearful judgment.

Salt lakes of like character seem to be a characteristic feature of Asia: the lakes Urmia and Wan in the Taurus are both so saturated with salt that no fish and no mollusks can live in their waters, and the only large lake of which Persia can boast, called Urumiah, though receiving seventeen rivers, is for the same reason lifeless, while for miles around the whole country is covered with a snowy white efflorescence. Russia derives nearly its whole supply of salt—over 100,000 tons annually—from a single source, Lake Elton, which, although only 130 square miles in area, is so full of salt that its surface is perpetually covered with a thick layer, shining brightly in the sunlight, and thus procuring for it the local name of the Gold Lake.

The waters of the Great Salt Lake of Utah, which is some forty miles in length, and has a bottom of fine white sand, and a margin of encrusted salt, will float the most unskillful of swimmers. They support no living thing, and the banks are barren of vegetation and as desolate as those of the Dead Sea.

The waters of salt marshes, after having abandoned the chloride of sodium which they held in solution, contain, beside sulphuric acid in the form of sulphates, soda, potash, and magnesia, commodities which cannot be obtained in some countries, and have to be imported from abroad at a high price. Hence, great efforts are made, for instance, in France, to obtain these valuable ingredients from the sea directly, and immense amounts of capital and skill are applied to these new branches of industry. Sulphate of soda is employed in the manufacture both of soda and of glass; it is one of the most important chemical products, and the discovery of a method by which it can be extracted from the ocean most therefore be considered as one of the most satisfactory results of science of our age. In order to isolate this salt, the temperature of the salt marsh waters has to be lowered to zero, a process which formerly entailed considerable expense, but which is now effected at a much cheaper rate by an ingenious contrivance for producing artificial cold, which we will describe in the following chapter.

CHAPTER III.

ICE AND ITS ARTIFICIAL MANUFACTURE.

"Some physicians consider ice, which is one of the most refreshing and useful tonics in hot countries, as being also a powerful sedative."

EVERYBODY is familiar with the varied uses of ice, and knows, also, that it preserves organic bodies from putrefaction. The decomposition of organic substances requiring a certain degree of heat and fermentation, becomes impossible below a certain degree of temperature. If, therefore, ice is placed in small quantities round fresh meat, fish, etc., these perishable articles of food may be kept for several days, and when the temperature is below that of melting ice, the length of time during which they can be preserved is still more considerable. In Russia and Siberia animals intended for consumption are slaughterd at the beginning of winter; they are frozen, and the cold preserves them a long time; in this way people save the food which the cattle would otherwise have required during the winter. In the far north, in Greenland, and Davis's Straits, those English sailors who are engaged in the seal fisheries, expose beef to the icy air, and are in this way able to have fresh meat during the whole of their long voyage. In Siberia fossil elephants and mammoths have been found, admirably preserved in ice; the flesh of these antediluvian animals, kept during many thousands of years in its thick wrapping of ice, was as fresh as that of animals killed at the moment.

In domestic economy ice is daily used for the pre-

Cream Freezer.

paration of cooling drinks and for the manufacture of sherbet, of which such quantities are consumed during the summer months. The juice of fruits and the cream, which are to be used, are put in a freezer and frozen by plunging into a refrigerating mixture of broken ice and salt. Medicine also finds in ice a valuable specific against certain maladies, a tonic and a preventive against hemorrhage of the lungs, nausea, etc. The enormous quantity of ice taken

South every year at great expense, in ships from all the northern countries, shows the great importance which machines for the artificial production of ice have recently acquired.

Drinks cooled by ice are, however, by no means a fashion of yesterday; for the ancients enjoyed anything cool in summer as much as we do now. The Romans had learned how to preserve snow and ice in caves which answered the same purpose as our ice-houses, and snow-water was a favorite beverage. At night, carts covered with straw, brought the snow of the Apennines to the ancient capital of the world, and galleys came to Italy laden with snow from Sicily, which was considered superior to any other by the gourmets of that day, because it was found in the vicinity of burning craters, filled with boiling lava. A temple had been erected specially to keep snow during the summer, and the priests of Vulcan derived from its sale an enormous income. Christian priests afterwards kept up this good custom, and the Bishop of Catanea, as late as the latter part of the last century, obtained 20,000 francs a year from the sale of a snow-bank which he owned on Mount Etna. At the present day, as in classic times, the Ural and Mount Caucasus provide for the East. Ice packed in felt cloths and covered with straw, is transported on horseback. In Europe the consumption of ice has not as yet become general; but in our own country it has attained enormous proportions. Collected during winter in the lakes of Canada and the Northern States, it is cut into blocks by means of saws, and transported to Boston, whence ships convey to the Antilles, the Cape, the East and West Indies, and even to Australia. The city of Boston alone consumes annually several hundred thousand tons of ice, and nearly 10,000 workmen were employed last year in this single branch of commerce. In New York city, in 1870, the consumption of ice amounted to thousands of tons, a large amount of which was exported. Norway is the ice-house of Europe, and furnishes the South with that refreshing commodity, supplying even more northern countries, and often Paris itself with ice, when the Seine and the lakes of the Bois de Boulogne have been scarcely congealed in consequence of too mild a winter.

Goubaud's Apparatus.—Family Refrigerators.—In order to convert a certain volume of water into ice it is necessary to freeze this water, or in other words, to subtract its heat. Cold is not, as was long imagined, a special physical agent, with properties exactly opposed to those of heat; on the contrary, it is a purely relative quality, and we only say that a body is cold when we compare it with a warm body. How is the water which we wish to freeze, to be cooled artificially? How is it to be deprived of its heat? Nothing is simpler, if we only know how to apply certain physical laws. It is well known that whenever a substance changes its physical condition, when it passes from a solid into a liquid, or from a liquid into a gaseous state, it draws heat from that body with which it is in contact, and consequently cools it in proportion. If you let a drop of ether fall on your hand, the liquid will disappear from your sight; it will become volatilized, and pass almost instantaneously from the liquid to the gaseous state; but in the very act of volatilizing it will deprive your hand of its heat, and thus give you the impression of a sudden chill. If you throw a handful of nitrate of ammonia into

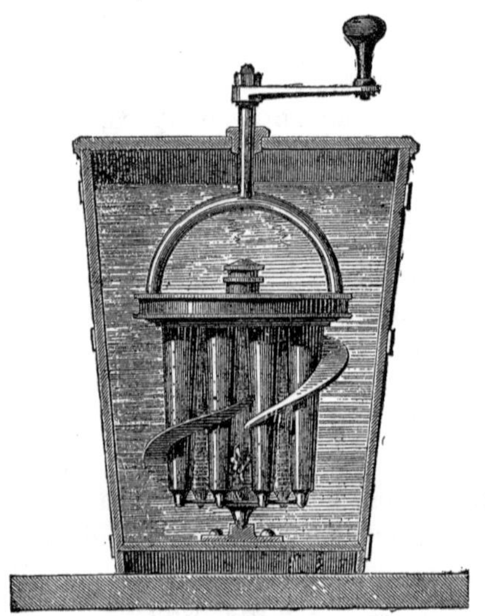

Goubaud's Apparatus.

a glass of water, the salt will dissolve by the mere action; from a solid, it will pass into a liquid state, and a considerable lowering of the temperature will accompany this change. These simple experiments form the basis of all freezing machines. The above illustration shows a number of tin cylinders, so arranged, in a wooden tub, as to revolve round an axle turned by a handle. Into these cylinders the water is poured which is to be congealed. The external tub is full of water, into which a small quantity of nitrate of ammonia is thrown. The salt melts and absorbs the heat from the cylinders, with which it is in contact, and from the water which they contain; and if we turn the handle in such a way as to make the salt melt more rapidly, by the agitation produced by means of spiral metal-screws, it will not be long ere we see blocks of ice formed in the cylinders, originally filled with water.

On this same principle househould freezers are made. Several concentric spaces are alternately filled with water, and with a refrigerating mixture.*

* There are various compositions which may be made use of in preparing a refrigerating mixture.

MATERIALS USED.		LOWERING OF TEMPERATURE.
Sea salt, ...	— parts.	From 50° to 10°
Powdered ice, ...	— "	
Water, ...	10 parts.	From 50° to 3°
Nitrate of ammonia, ..	5 "	
Saltpetre, ...	7 "	
Water, ...	1 part.	From 50° to 14°
Nitrate of ammonia, ..	1 "	
Sulphate of soda, ...	8 parts.	From 50° to 2°
Chlorohydric acid, ...	5 "	

The employment of acids is always disagreeable or dangerous, and should, if possible, be avoided. Nitrate of ammonia is preferable. When the solution is no longer cold, it is advisable to evaporate it, and thus to produce salt which will be good for any other purpose afterwards.

The water in A and in B is surrounded by the freezing mixture, C, O, and is speedily transformed into ice; in the lower part of the apparatus a valve, opened by means of a small lever, permits the

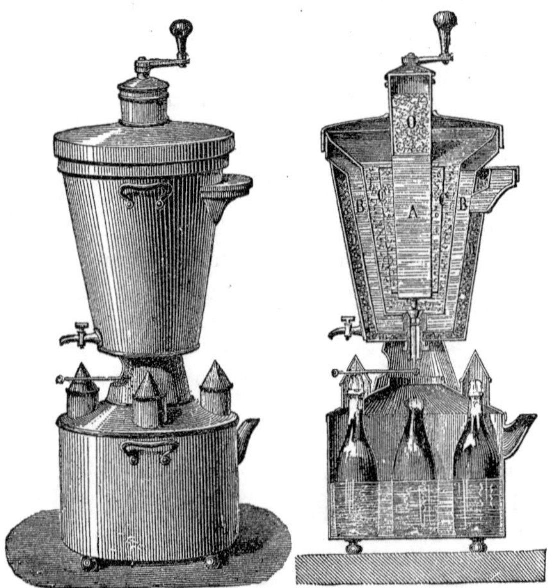

Household Freezer.

melted ice-water to flow out, and it falls into a basin in which are placed the bottles of wine, which are speedily iced by the action of the cold.

Carré's Apparatus.—Neither of the apparatus which we have just been describing, is by any means perfect, and their practical use does not correspond to their theoretical value. The one we are about to describe is very different. It consists of a cylinder, in communication, by means of tubes, with a vessel in the shape of a truncated cone, having a cavity in the centre. This apparatus, every part of which is kept close, is furnished with a thermometer which, without communicating with the interior of the cylinder, indicates its temperature. We first

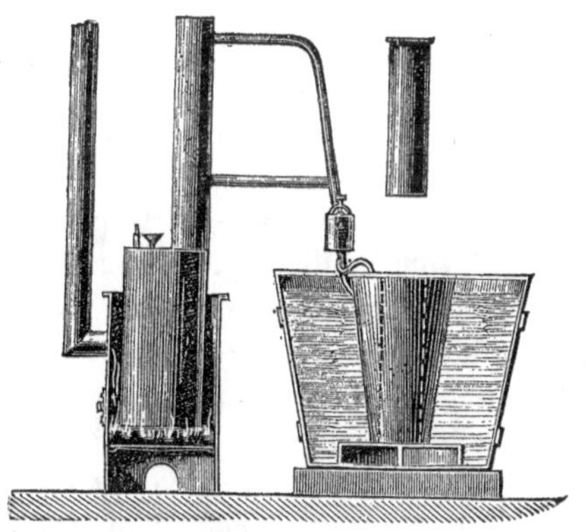

Carré's Apparatus.

heat the cylinder, whilst the truncated vessel in the centre sinks into the cold water of a large tub; in its central cavity is placed a metallic cylinder, filled with water. When the thermometer reaches 266° the furnace (a stove or pipe) is replaced by a tub of water; the vessel cools off perceptibly, and soon we are able to take from the cavity a block of ice. Ice can thus be produced by means of a few pieces of coal, and the apparatus, after having once worked properly, is ready to begin again without the necessity of changing anything. All that is needed is to heat once more the large cylinder. But how does this apparatus work? Let us explain. Its mechanism is extremely simple. The cylinder contains ammoniac gas, dissolved in water. When it is heated, the gas escapes from the liquid and passes into the receiver, after having passed through all the connecting tubes. But on arriving there it finds no outlet; nevertheless, the heat continually disengages from the water fresh quantities of ammoniac gas, which thus accumulates, and, being subjected to considerable pressure, becomes liquefied. This is the moment when the generating cylinder is plunged into a cold tub; and, thus chilled, the water is capable of dissolving once more the ammoniac gas.

The gas which is liquefied in the receiver, returns to a gaseous state, and a corresponding absorption of heat accompanies this change, at the expense of the water contained in the central cavity; this cooled-off water now changes into ice. This shows how extremely simple this apparatus is, and how ingenious its mechanism, which leaves all previous inventions far behind. It is still, however, capable of improvement, as its inventor, Mr. Carré, has himself proved. Its small dimensions prevent its furnishing large quantities of ice at once; it cannot be made to work continuously, and could never be of much industrial value. Another apparatus, however, has been invented, constructed on a much larger scale, and has successfully solved the important

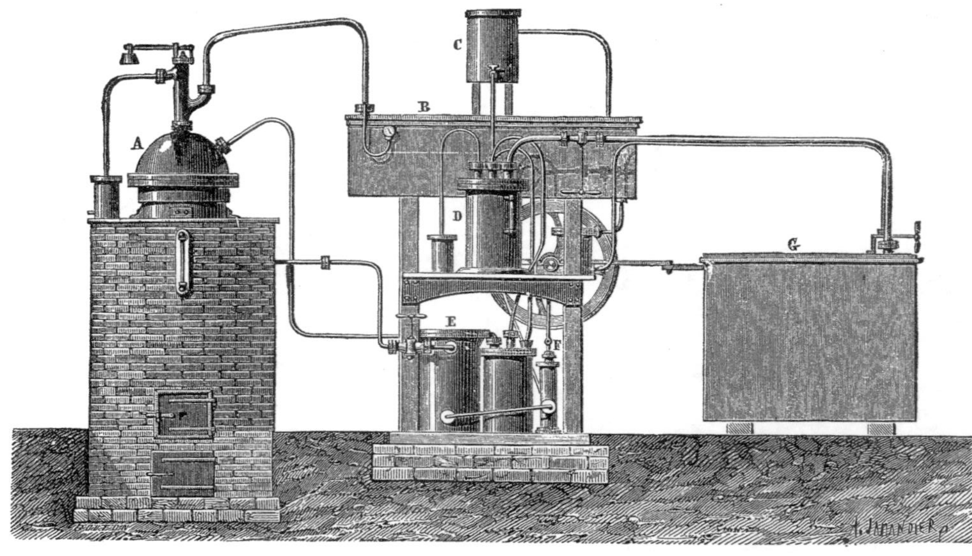

CARRE'S LARGE APPARATUS FOR THE MANUFACTURE OF ICE.

problem of the artificial manufacture of ice, or, what amounts to the same thing—the production of cold. A large boiler, A, contains the solution of ammonia. The gas escapes, and becomes liquefied, in a reservoir, B, cooled off as it is by the water, which falls from a reservoir, C. The liquid ammonia penetrates into the hollow sides of the refrigerator, G, which contains cylinders filled with the water that is to be frozen. During this time an especial arrangement permits this exhaust water (or waste water) of the boilers to penetrate, after having cooled off, into a vessel, E, connected with the cylinder, D, in which the ammonia is distilled, that has been volatilized in the refrigerator. The original liquid, thus regenerated, is conveyed into the boiler by means of a pump, F.* This apparatus acts with great regularity, and it is astonishing to see large blocks of ice issuing from this refrigerator, which are formed as if by magic, without any visible agent to show the secret of their formation.

* A detailed description of the numerous parts of this apparatus requires too voluminous an explanation for our space. But further details may be found in the Report of M. Pouillet, in the Publications of the Society of Encouragement, for 1863. Paris, 1863.

CHAPTER IV.

MINERAL WATERS—POPULAR ERRORS.

"There are to be found in certain localities waters either warm or cold, which, by their properties, show that they are beneficial in cases of sickness, and which appear to issue from the earth for the sole benefit of mankind."

PLINY.

NOTHING has more exercised the talents of inventors of incredible stories than the origin of springs and mineral waters. The proof of this is found in the many miraculous stories and strange statements which have been borrowed from ancient authors, who are the best interpreters of popular credulity.

According to Theophrastus, the Crathis, a river in Magna Græcia, turned the animals white who drank of its waters. According to Ovid, Vibius Sequester, and Antigonus, the waters of the Sybaris dyed the hair a golden-yellow:

"Electro similes faciunt auroque capillos."

OVID.

Shepherds who wished to have white sheep led them to drink from the river Aliacmon, while those who desired them black or brown watered them in the river Axius. The waters of the Alcos caused hair to grow on the body. In

Bœotia, near the temple of Trophonius, opposite the river Orchomenos there were two springs, one of which had the power of quickening the memory, while the other destroyed it. One was called Mnemosene the other Lethe.

Varro states that near Cessus there flowed a brook called Nous, the Greek word for Mind, the waters of which made people bright, while on the other hand there was, in the Island of Ceos, a spring which rendered him who drank of it stupid. There was still another at Zama, which endowed the human voice with an admirable strength and tone.*

The waters of the Lyncestes, in Thrace, produced a slight intoxication, while on the contrary, according to Eudoxius, the waters of the Clitorius made wine distasteful.

Theopompus, the celebrated author of the "Wonders of Nature," quotes, besides, a great number of examples of intoxicating waters. Mucian goes still further; he seriously affirms that in the Isle of Andros a fountain consecrated to Bacchus furnished real wine at certain seasons of the year. At Cyzicus Cupid's fountain cured love. Cresias states, and Antigonus of Carystus confirms the fact, that there existed in India a pool called *Side*, on the surface of which nothing—not even a dead leaf—could float. Perjured persons could not endure the waters of the river Olachas, in Bithynia; they were burnt therein as in boiling oil. In Thrace certain waters brought instantaneous death to those who drank of them.

* Vitruvius, Book VI., ch. 14. Agricola explains this property by supposing that it was due to the sandaricum contained in the waters.

If we believe Vibius Sequester, persons who bathed repeatedly in Lake Triton, in Thrace, were changed into birds. The inhabitants of Lycia, according to Pliny, consulted the Fountain of Limyra on the subject of future events, by throwing food to the fish which dwelt there. If the response was favorable the fish eagerly seized their prey; but if otherwise, they pushed the offering aside with their tails. At Colophon, there was a fountain which endowed with divining faculties all who drank of it, but shortened at the same time the thread of their life. This fountain was situated in a cavern consecrated to the Carian Apollo, and Tacitus tells us that it was there Germanicus received the prophetic intimation of his premature death.

The springs of Hippocrene and Castalia inspired poets. The Fountain of Diodona revealed the future by the soft murmurs of its waters, and an aged priestess constantly seated on its banks interpreted the mysterious language which she alone understood. The Fountain of Patras foretold the fate of sick people. A mirror was placed on the surface of the water, and after an invocation to the Deities, the image of the sick person appeared and was beheld dead or alive, according to the turn which his malady was to take. The Fountain of Apone, near Padua, had a great renown among the ancients, who consulted it frequently. Playing-dice were thrown into it, and the number thus obtained furnished the answers.

Nor is it only from the records of ancient Greece and Italy that we derive accounts of such superstitious legends. Mediæval tradition and the folk-lore of every time and country abound in similar belief concerning the healing efficacy of certain waters. A great number continue still in force in certain parts of Europe, and the ignorant peasantry of many a country believe in curious tales on the subject, which they relate with a sense of awe, and never doubt for a moment. The pure waters of our springs and mirror-like lakes, however, conceal no longer such mysteries. The sources whence the ancients drew are dried up for us, or rather, their waters no longer give forth the same murmur. Farewell then, lovely Naiads, timid nymphs, who used to hide among the reeds, farewell! Farewell, graceful Undines, charming divinities of the waves! We shall never behold you more. Touching poetry of fables, ingenious dreams of our fancy, your reign has passed away forever!

THE UNCERTAINTIES OF SCIENCE.

Extremes meet. To exaggerated credulity succeeds an equally exaggerated skepticism. After having too easily admitted the most marvellous stories, a thorough change came about and the health-bringing action of mineral springs was completely denied. Nowadays, however, we have returned to more reasonable views; and no one at present doubts the efficacy of mineral springs in a great number of maladies. It is, however, a very generally prevailing opinion—and not without good reason—that this efficacy of the waters is due in a great measure to the beneficial influence of a pleasant journey and to the salubrity of the country, in which health may be as contagious as sickness is elsewhere. For naturally seasons of repose and a change of scene with a busy man living in society and agitated by a host of artificial or natural passions, heal or at least sear over the wounds of the soul and react upon the body. But after making every allowance for such causes, independent of the healthful action of the waters, it must be admitted that certain waters have genuine medicinal virtues—virtues attested even by animals, on whom imagination cannot very well be supposed to react.

How do mineral waters act? Doubtless through the salts which they contain, but on this delicate subject there prevails still much uncertainty. The analysis of mineral waters is for the chemist a difficult problem to solve; he may find in the water carbonic, sulphuric or silicious acid, etc., chlorine, iodine, potash, soda or magnesia, but how are these elements combined? It is this which cannot certainly be known. We have, indeed, in our hands the disjointed materials of the building; but how are these materials combined and connected with each other? If we knew this, we might hope to find that there existed between the water and its constituent elements a relation, which might permit us to divine its medicinal properties beforehand. But this is by no means the case; and observation usually contradicts the deductions of theory. There scarcely ever exists any continuous connection between the chemical analysis of a spring and its effects upon health. Mineral waters act by feeble doses; they are homœopathic remedies, and their action escapes the investigation of science. Their composition is, moreover, not yet perfectly well understood, as they generally contain certain indefinable organic substances, which chemistry has not yet analyzed. Many a mineral spring contains only a minute proportion of iron, and yet acts with more efficacy than all medicinal remedies. Frequently, when physicians find all specifics fail, they see unexpected effects produced by springs, and yet the invalid has probably taken only a few glasses of water each day; perhaps he has not taken more than the hundredth part of a grain of iron.

There is, therefore, in chalybeate and similar springs, something more than the mineral held in solution. They contain, besides, organic matter, and often in large proportions; this fact has been usually ignored, but we believe erroneously, since it is possible in these elements that the therapeutic efficacy rests, which is sought for in vain everywhere else. "A mineral water," as Dr. Constantin James has well observed,* "is not an ordinary saline solution; it is, on the contrary, a special beverage, which has its own elements and its special flavor, which Nature has mixed by a kind of occult chemistry, and of which she has till now preserved the secret among her treasures. Even if it were known, the difficulty of making up the prescription would still remain. For a long period, we fear, Chaptal's saying, so true

* See "A Practical Guide to Mineral Waters," by Dr. C. James, 1 vol. (Victor Masson, Publisher. We have made many extracts from that excellent work.)

and so frequently quoted, will still hold good: 'When we analyze mineral waters we dissect a corpse.' "

CLASSIFICATION.

It is well known that the temperature of our globe rises one degree with every one hundred feet below the surface. Now, although most springs begin their life on mountain slopes and in valleys, many also sink deep into the bowels of the earth, where they are heated by the central heat of our globe; when they come up to the surface they are hence often so hot that they require many hours before they can be used for the purpose of bathing. Hot springs come, consequently, from the greatest depths when their temperature is highest—unless, as is sometimes the case, they are heated by volcanic causes. All water we have seen is a solvent, but hot water possesses the greatest power of solution; hence hot springs are most apt to hold mineral substances which they have dissolved on the way, and now bring up with them for the good of man. The more ramified the system of these springs, and the richer the soil in mineral elements, the more powerful will be the spring in its effects upon health. Nor must it be overlooked that these mineral substances may, on the way, enter into chemical combinations with each other, and thus produce entirely new properties in the health-giving waters.

Some of these hot springs rise, strangely enough, under the ocean, others on the top of the Alps; on the Himalaya Mountains several gush forth from under perpetual snow, at a height of 12,000 feet. Generally they break forth from wild, deep glens, between gigantic, barren masses of rock, or they come flowing out from narrow passes inaccessible to man. Frequently these hot springs owe their origin to volcanoes in the neighborhood; for it has been observed that in such localities hot vapors arise from every cleft and crevice. Tuscany abounds in pools containing a dark, miry water, known as *Lagoni*. At short intervals hot vapors arise from the centre, accompanied by low thunder, and the water is thrown up in a conical shape. If there is no water in the pools, mud and even small stones are thus tossed up, or new openings are made in all directions, giving a hideous appearance to the country, and destroying by their sulphurous exhalations all vegetation within reach. The soil is burning hot and sounds hollow under foot. But even here man has known how to make nature subservient to his purposes: the water of these pools contains a large proportion of borax, which is carefully gathered and becomes a source of prosperity for a whole neighborhood.

Many mineral springs, wines from the cellarage of mother earth,

"Springing through the veins of the mountains,"

come up tolerably well iced; others froth over at various degrees of heat, from gentle warmth up to the temperature of boiling water. Some springs are bright and sparkling; others, like fruity port, are deeply tinged with alkaline and other earthy matter. But the greatest marvel is that each spring should absorb its definite proportion of solid and gaseous contents unchangingly through all time, so as to present always, like the ocean and the atmosphere, that identical character which constitutes its settled value: a prescription carefully and unfailingly prepared.

We give briefly the most familiar varieties of mineral waters, classified not upon direct scientific analysis, but according to their popular designation.

1st. Gaseous waters, generally cold, contain carbonic acid in solution; and as chemically pure water is unfit for use, these, on the contrary, are eminently refreshing, and when coming in contact with the air, set free a large portion of the dissolved gas, which rises in pearly beads similar to those on artificial seltzer water.

The water of the Bourboule, on the right side of the river Dordogne, gushes from the centre of an ancient Roman bath. It contains a large proportion of free carbonic acid. Seltz, Ems and Wiesbaden, in Germany, are also well known examples of natural gaseous waters. Ems is one of the most popular watering places on the banks of the Rhine; its numerous springs are gaseous and alkaline, containing carbonic acid, and besides a little iron, and some salts on a basis of lime and magnesia. These waters are almost always taken internally, though they are also sometimes applied externally, and have a reputation for removing sterility. Gerning informs us that Agrippina often frequented the baths of Ems, and that they perhaps had the melancholy honor of having led to the birth of Caligula.

2nd. Salt-springs may be gaseous or thermal. The waters of Plombières, belonging to this class, are thermal, and contain only a small quantity of saline matter, consisting of alkaline bicarbonates, of bi-carbonate of iron, and of sulphate of soda, etc. Plombières is situated in a very low valley crossed in its whole length by a torrent called "L'Eau Groune." The water of its spring is generally hidden from view and sheltered by a vaulted building. The Roman Baths, situated in the centre of the town, on the site of a Roman piscina, and the Napoleon Bath, one of the principal edifices of the town, are famed far and wide, and are constantly visited by numbers of patients, afflicted with diseases of the bowels, nervous affections, sciatic neuralgia, and with rheumatism or gout, who come here in hope of finding relief.

Bagnères-de-Bigorre, Bourbonne-les-Bains, Nères and Vichy, are likewise thermal saline springs. The celebrated waters of Vichy are the most popular not only in France, but in the whole world. Nor is this merely the result of fashion; for never was reputation based on stronger claims. They unite rare and valuable qualities, mainly ascribed to the bi-carbonate of soda which is found in all eight springs. What multitudes of sufferers have drank with success of the spring of the *Grande Grille*.

Madame de Sévigné wrote of Vichy, to her daughter: "The scenery alone would cure me," admiring so warmly what is in truth a very ordinary landscape. All the springs of Vichy are alkaline; they are gaseous, thermal and contain a large proportion of mineral matter, consisting of bicarbonate of soda, sulphate of soda, chloride of sodium, carbonate of lime, magnesia, silica, and peroxide of iron. The waters of Vichy have performed perfectly marvellous cures in cases of diseases of the digestive organs, gravel, gout, diabetes and various cutaneous diseases.

Grande Grille.

3dly. Chalybeate springs have a styptic flavor strongly resembling ink when exposed to contact with the air; they leave a flaky deposit of hydrated peroxide of iron. Almost all contain small quantities of arsenic, copper, lead, tin, antimony, all in themselves deadly poisons, though when taken in small quantities, they seem to be beneficial in their effects. When

PLOMBIERES.

it was first discovered that there was arsenic in the water of many of the natural springs, the patients became a little uneasy, but their fears are groundless, for the quantity of arsenic is extremely small and its combination with iron or lime sensibly diminishes its dangerous properties. What settles, finally, beyond a doubt, the harmlessness of this poison in such minute doses, is the continued and beneficial use of waters like those of Dussang and Vichy, which contain arsenic. It is very remarkable, moreover, that precisely those springs which have been famous for many centuries are those which contain arsenic. Nature, by her admirable process of metamorphosis, is thus able to transform poisons into remedies, a curse into a blessing.

The waters of Porla in Sweden, of Spa in Belgium, of Crausac and Foyes in France, contain a considerable proportion of oxide of iron, combined with acids, crenic, carbonic and sulphuric. All chalybeate waters possess much the same virtues. Their action is essentially strengthening; they assist digestion, purify the blood, and produce a real and beneficial change in the system.

4th. Sulphur waters contain soluble sulphurets, and principally sulphates of soda, as Glauber's salts, (Bagnères-de-Luchon Barèges), sometimes sulphates of magnesia, as Epsom salts, and others sulphates of iron. They are always warm and easily lose their peculiar properties in contact with the air.

Near the Salt Lake, in Utah, there exists a remarkable sulphur spring, so warm that it is always boiling, and throws into the air clouds of smoke.

The most remarkable of so-called sulphur-springs was no doubt discovered by A. von Humboldt, when he ascended, for the first time, the Purace, a volcano near Poxagen, in South America. He found there, on a table-land, 8,000 feet above the level of the sea, a considerable stream, forming three cascades, the water of which was strongly impregnated with sulphuric acid. The natives called it, hence, the Vinegar River; and the great explorer found that even at a distance of 20 miles, after mingling its waters with those of the Rio Cauca, it is still fatal to life, and drives every fish from that river.

The renown of Bagnères is not of recent date, for it has been a favorite summer retreat from the age of the Cæsars of old to the brief hour of the Cæsars of to-day; and there are still to be seen native tablets of the Roman era, dedicated to the nymphs presiding over streams, and manifesting gratitude for health restored. The famous springs of Barèges rise in the Pyrenees, at a height of 4,000 feet above the sea; and winter avalanches not unfrequently fall upon the site of the wooden barracks that are erected, every summer, down the one long street that forms the village. Its modern fame dates from the visit of Madame de Maintenon, with the young prince of Maine, who was club-footed, and sought health here in 1675. The waters are a sovereign remedy against old wounds, and would have been called, in the days of Rabelais, the "true Arquebusade Water."

Among the most renowned salt-springs of France is that of Bourbon l'Archambault, to which Madame de Montespan retreated, to end her life in repentance and devotion. Here it was that, on the night of her death, a cavalier dismounted at her door, and, hastily entering her chamber, withdrew the clothes which covered her bosom, and tore away a key that was suspended at her neck. Then, taking a casket from a drawer, without having uttered a word, he remounted his horse and returned to Paris. This was her son, the duke of Antin; but what mystery the casket concealed has never been revealed.

AMERICAN MINERAL SPRINGS.

The same beneficent Providence which has endowed our country with every gift that nature bestows upon man, has made ample provision, also, of health-giving waters. There is no lack of springs of every kind, and what makes the gifts more precious still, is the happy manner in which these healing waters are scattered broadcast over the great Union. From the northernmost regions of Canada to the shores of the Mexican Gulf, and from the eastern slope of the Appalachian range to the mountains that face the Pacific, everywhere, springs and groups, and clusters of springs abound in marvellous munificence, so that the United States can boast of at least one hundred and thirty springs and groups of springs within its vast boundary lines. Carbonated and chalybeate, saline—or alum, as they are called in the South—and sulphureted, all are as amply and as efficiently represented here as in

Europe; and to these must be added a perfect wreath of thermal springs, from the moderate sulphur springs, in Florida, with a temperature of 70°, to the marvellous hot springs in Pyramid Lake, Utah, at 206°. Even the rarest combinations are not wanting; even the familiar Saratoga Springs, for instance, presenting the remarkable feature of carbonic acid abounding in saline waters.

Here, as in Europe, the majority of mineral springs owe their first renown to accident; now the beasts of the forest were seen to make beaten tracks from all directions towards certain salt-licks, as they were called, and soon waters were discovered, impregnated with a variety of salts; and now, Indian experience, first sneered at by early settlers, would in the end be found valuable, and marvellous virtues were ascribed to the springs they had long frequented. In still other cases, the early settlers themselves had their attention early drawn to peculiar properties in neighboring springs, and from the country-people the reputation of the latter passed to sufferers abroad, after careful and scientific investigation.

Among the more renowned mineral springs of the Union, those of Saratoga are, beyond comparison, the most famous. The springs of New York lie on or near a junction of limestone, with a talcy slate, close to faults in the strata, wherever the rocks are much deranged in position; they are arranged in an irregular line, from Vermont to Rockland County, and a number of intermediate springs connect them, on the same great axis of disturbance, with the popular springs of Virginia, often called the Saratoga of the South. In the immediate neighborhood of Saratoga, however, a long range of springs, in the shape of a crescent, extends from Ballston Lake to the Quaker Springs, at Stillwater, in a southeasterly direction. All these springs, varying only in the proportions of substances they hold in solution, possess the same properties, and are evidently prepared in one and the same great laboratory. They are eminently gaseous at the same time, and present some curious features connected with this peculiarity; thus the Park Spring, at Ballston, sends up minute bubbles, without intermission, but at an interval of about a minute the whole is agitated by the evolution of a large bulk of gas at once. At greater intervals, of many years, powerful, almost volcanic, discharges of this nearly pure carbonic acid take place, producing sudden and violent convulsions. The Saratoga springs rise mostly from a low, marshy valley, and come directly from a bed of blue, marly clay, that underlies the valley and the sand plains of the vicinity; the Ballston springs, on the contrary, rise from a bed of quicksand, underneath a layer of clay, filled with pebbles, boulders and gravel, and hence the sand which they carry up continually obstructs the tubes. The springs are then lost, or springs of fresh water break into the wells and dilute the mineral qualities of the water.

Saratoga contains not less than ten principal springs, besides a number of smaller ones; of the former, *Congress* Spring has for some time had the preference with visitors, although it may be added that fashion directs not only the mode of living at this extravagantly fashionable place, but even the choice of the waters. The *Pavilion,* the *Union* and the *Iodine* springs have each had their brief reign of popularity; the *High Rock* Spring was the first discovered, the Indians directing the attention of the colonists to its remarkable virtues in curing rheumatism. Here also game frequenting the spot as a salt-lick, had first of all attracted the Indians to the place, who then, using the water, discovered its healing powers. The first white visitor was the famous Sir William Johnson, who came here in 1767 to be cured of gout, and never afterwards ceased to praise the blessed waters. The popular interest in this spring was much heightened by its singular appearance: it is surrounded by a conical rock of calcareous tufa, formed by deposits from the water itself; the diameter being at the base eight or nine feet, and at the summit five or six. It must not be forgotten, finally, that besides the admirable qualities of Saratoga water in which an extensive trade is carried on throughout the Union—the dry and bracing character of the air, and the balsamic, or rather turpentine qualities with which it is impregnated by the extensive pine forests around the beautiful village, contribute much to the astonishing cures, reported as proofs of its efficacy in countless diseases.

Sulphurous springs are even more numerous in the State of New York, the official geological survey proving that there is scarcely a single county in which springs of this class, impregnated with sulphureted hydrogen, are not found. Their water is generally dark, though limpid ; in the strata of the Niagara group it looks almost black, while in those of the higher strata it leaves in addition a black and red deposit and a whitish stain upon the bottom. Among them the springs of Sharon and Avon take the precedence. The former rise near a little village called Leesville, in the township of Sharon, exactly at the junction of the water-lime and Onondaga salt groups, from a heap of .pyritous slate. The *White Sulphur* is so richly impregnated that it leaves a deposit of sulphur on all substances over which it flows, even when mixed with common water, and for a distance of a quarter of a mile ! Then it falls perpendicularly over a ledge of rocks sixty feet high, and is already large enough to turn a grist mill. Sulphate of lime, in small but perfect crystals, is found near the spring in great abundance. A magnesia spring is not far from the sulphur spring.

The Avon Springs rise in one of the most beautiful parts of the justly famous valley of the Genesee River ; they lie between the village of Avon, which is handsomely built upon a high table-land with a magnificent view over broad, rich lands, and the river in the valley below. They were well known to the Indians, who had from time immemorial resorted to them for the cure of diseases of the skin, and even in our day a few sad survivors of that ill-fated race may occasionally be seen at their old haunts. As early as 1792 white settlers came there to seek a cure for similar affections and of rheumatism, and soon the renown of the three springs spread far and near. The *Third* Spring, originally a large pool of fifty feet diameter, was first used for bathing, and has always been more popular than the *Upper* and the *Lower*, as the others are called. Iodine springs abound in the immediate neighborhood, with a strong salt taste, owing to the large amount of chloride of sodium they hold in solution. The water of both the Sharon and Avon springs have remarkable stimulating powers; when they do not immediately act as purgatives, they quicken the pulse, cause a sense of internal heat, and produce sleeplessness and a state of excitement similar to that which follows the use of strong coffee, and may be increased to the extent of causing slight intoxication. The popularity of these springs, used for bathing as well as for drinking, is growing with every year, and ranks them at least as high as the far-famed sulphur springs of the Pyrenees.

Besides these principal springs the State of New York boasts of other sulphur springs at Clifton, which are so strongly impregnated that their odor is perceptible at the distance of a quarter of a mile; at Chittenango, where the water fresh from the spring has an opaline or milky appearance; and at Manlius in the shape of a sulphur pool, known as Lake Sodom. The lake is about a mile and a half in length and half a mile wide, with a depth varying from 25 to 165 feet; water drawn from this depth is found to be highly charged with sulphureted hydrogen and of deep green color, probably due to partial decomposition of the hydrogen.

Nor is New York wanting in springs which hold an excess of sulphuric acid, perceptible to the taste as well as to reagents, and often called *alum* springs, on account of the sulphates of alumina and iron which they contain, while the latter ingredient would entitle them to a place among the chalybeate springs. The most acid of these springs is probably one of a group rising in the town of Byron, Genesee County, which has an intensely sour taste, contains nearly pure though dilute sulphuric acid, and issues from the ground sufficiently strong to turn a mill near the fountain-head. Another such acid spring of some renown, is at Clifton Springs, twelve miles from Geneva. Lebanon Spring, with its temperature at 73°, and its slight saline impregnation, makes a delightful bath and breaks forth in such abundance that there is not only enough for all the visitors, but also for two or three mills, which are kept running even in midwinter. The water is, however, quite as serviceable when taken as a drink, and has effected remarkable cures in dyspepsia and gout. Among the curiosities of mineral springs in the State of New York, we must not forget the numerous and valuable wells which give out carbonated hydrogen gas, which in many places, *e. g.*, in the town of Fredonia, is turned to good account, and lights up the streets and houses.

No other state is so rich in mineral springs as Virginia, which, before the discoveries made in California and New Mexico, could justly boast of the greatest variety and largest number of thermal springs. Dr. W. B. Rogers, long the State geologist of the Old Dominion, enumerated not less than fifty-six such springs, copious and constant, all of which are truly, though slightly, thermal, and owe their remarkable uniformity of temperature to what he called "a deeply subterranean source."

Among all Virginia springs, the so-called White Sulphur are the most renowned, assembling every year large numbers of visitors from all parts of the country, though the majority are naturally from Southern States, and presenting southern society in its gayest and most attractive aspect. The water is the strongest, most active, and most stimulating of a whole group of similar sulphur springs, known as the Red, the Yellow, and the White Sulphur. The main spring rises at an elevation of 2,000 feet above the sea, bursting with unusual boldness from rock-lined apertures, and yielding, independent of dry or wet weather, an average of eighteen gallons a minute. The water is perfectly clear and transparent, depositing copiously a white, and sometimes a red and black precipitate, composed in part of saline ingredients. It does not, like other waters, lose its transparency by parting with its gas, nor does it deposit its salt when quiescent, and still the gas is speedily fatal to animals when immersed for a short time even; small fish survive but a few moments, larger ones die after a few minutes. Its virtues in all chronic affections of the organic system cannot be over-rated; at the same time it must not be forgotten that these very virtues and its great strength make it, when misapplied, the most mischievous of similar waters, and its use requires, therefore, the greatest caution.

This delightful place, with its cool, bracing air, its magnificent scenery and matchless variety of field and forest, forms the centre of numerous groups of other springs, stretching along a line parallel with the range of the Appalachian Mountains. Nearly every variety of mineral springs known to medical men may be found here, within a comparatively small compass, and everywhere the beauty of scenery, the salubrity of the air, and the abundance of homely but wholesome fare, aids the benevolent purposes of Nature, in providing a remedy for almost every ill that human flesh is heir to. Among these, the Red Sulphur, long the favorite resort of South Carolinians, is much renowned for its power to cure pulmonary consumption. Instances are recorded of its effects on the action of the heart, reducing the beats from 100 and even 120 and 130 to 70 and 65 a minute, while drinking it allays thirst and causes sleep. Men of science attribute much of the good effects of the water to an organic matter, called by Dr. Hayes a "sulphur compound."

The warm springs, on the other hand, afford probably the most delightful natural warm bath to be found in any part of the world. The large basin, thirty feet in diameter and five deep, fed by a source which gives out a thousand gallons a minute, furnishes the most luxurious enjoyment that can be imagined. The water largely evolves nitrogen, and carbonic acid in smaller quantities; its full value is hardly yet appreciated, for competent judges inform us that its medicinal virtues are in no way inferior to those of the far famed Wildbad in Germany. The same may be applied to the hot springs, which have a temperature rising to 106° and have effected cures of the most violent chronic rheumatism and kindred diseases, unequalled by the efficacy of any other waters of the kind in Europe. Their wonderful restorative powers are far superior to those of the springs at Bath, in England. A few miles distant are the Healing Springs, discovered only within the last few years, but already well known by the apparent wonders they have performed in cases of rheumatism and cutaneous diseases.

Besides the springs which we have mentioned, almost every part of the State of Virginia has some springs endowed with medicinal virtues. In Berkley County, the Bath spring resembles that which in England, by a strange blunder, is called the Bristol Hot Well, and produces striking cures in cases of aggravated chronic rheumatism; its visitors are mainly from Baltimore and Pennsylvania. For dyspepsia and kindred diseases patients resort in large numbers to the Capon Springs. The Bath Alum Springs, again, containing in a gallon not less than 55 grains of saline substances and of carbonic and sulphuric acids, are very active as a strong tonic and astringent, and have of late become very popular. The water of the Rockbridge Alum Springs is stronger in free sulphuric acid, but contains less iron than the Bath; nevertheless it has its fair share of patronage. Among the chalybeate springs of Virginia, Rawley's Springs hold the precedence; the water is a strong, simple chalybeate of great power in cases where its medicinal properties are in requisition. Nor is the eastern part of Virginia without its fair share of mineral waters, and what the sweet springs of the valley are to the west, the Huguenot and similar springs are to the eastern portion—the former, a sulphur spring, resembling the White Sulphur.

Among the saline springs of the West those at Harrodsburgh, in Kentucky, are probably the most generally known. Unlike most of the mineral springs of that State, which are found in deep valleys, they burst out near the summit level of the country, at an altitude of near a thousand feet above the Gulf of Mexico. There is no trace of malaria, therefore, in the neighborhood, and as the whole country around has been settled ever since 1774, none of the causes that commonly cause autumnal fevers, can be presumed to be active any longer. The water is so strongly impregnated that every tumbler of it contains nearly 16 grains of saline matter, over half of which consists of magnesian salts, and the patient who drinks four tumblers of what is called the Saloon Spring, takes hence nearly a drachm of sulphate of magnesia and a grain of bicarbonate of iron. The Harrodsburg waters are extensively exported, and may be found everywhere in the Southwest, having made their way even into many garrisons of U. S. troops. Other epsom springs abound in Kentucky, among which the Rochester and the Olympian Springs, the latter also known by their less poetical name of Mud Lick, are most famous. These are at one of the oldest and most noted of the watering-places of the West, and derive their classic name from a detached conical summit in the neighborhood, which has received the pretentious name of Olympus. Like the famous Cluster Springs of Virginia, which, within a few feet distance from each other, represent nearly all the leading varieties of mineral springs, this locality also has salt and sulphur, a white sulphur and a chalybeate spring in almost immediate juxtaposition. A feebler vein, near the principal well, is called the Vitriol Spring, and contains muriates and carbonates in small quantities. The Blue Lick and Lower Blue Licks lie in that central fertile region, called the Great Blue Limestone formation, rich in the fossilized remains of inhabitants of the deep primeval ocean under which they were evidently deposited. The water of these springs, on standing exposed to the air, becomes of a yellowish green color, which deepens on boiling it, and has given it the name of Blue Licks; this color is the result of a remarkable chemical change which takes place in the water upon exposure.

In Ohio, we learn from Dr. Drake, one of the first settlers in Cincinnati, and the author of a well-known valuable work on the Mississippi Valley, mineral springs are numerous, but neither greatly diversified in their properties, nor copious in the supplies they afford. The most common are chalybeate, and among them the Yellow Springs furnish a very pleasant tonic, while the Westport Springs contain sulphate of magnesia.

Pennsylvania, on the other hand, can boast of her Bedford Springs, the waters of which have acquired deserved celebrity in indigestion and similar affections, while gout and rheumatism of certain kinds also yield to their efficacy. Their discovery was due to an accident; a mechanic of Bedford, in 1804, happening to be attracted by the beauty and singularity of the waters flowing from the bank of the streams in which he was fishing. He had suffered many years from rheumatism and formidable ulcers, but after a few weeks' use of the waters, both internally and as a bath, he was entirely cured. The report of his recovery soon spread, and from that time an incessant stream of visitors has annually visited the beautiful valley in which the spring is situated. The waters, drank with proper precaution, and accompanied by a judicious use of the baths, have been found salutary in a wide range of chronic diseases, and their curative powers cannot very well be overestimated. Here, also, sulphur, sweet, and chalybeate springs are found in the immediate neighborhood, in the latter of which, singularly enough, part of a skeleton of a mammoth was found, when cleaning it out. The accommodations for visitors are excellent, and the beauties of the surrounding landscape have been skillfully brought out by large plantations and judicious improvements. The York Springs, formerly much visited, from Baltimore especially, are strongly chalybeate, while Carlisle Springs have a mild sulphurous water. Besides these, nearly a score of mineral springs attract every summer large numbers of visitors, and enjoy great local reputation; those at Gettysburg have come quite recently into renown, but, though useful for many purposes, owe their prestige mainly to the historical associations connected with the town from which they derive their name.

The chief watering-place of the neighboring State of New Jersey, is Schooley's Mountain Spring, a rill issuing from a perpendicular rock, forty or fifty feet above the bed of a brook which flows down into the channel beneath. It gives thirty gallons an hour, and does not vary with season or weather. The water is a pure carbonated chalybeate, depositing oxide of iron on troughs, baths and even drinking vessels. Here, also, the medicinal properties of the spring are aided and enhanced by the pure air of the mountain, which is over 1,000 feet above the sea, and the inducement to take much active exercise held out by the beauty of the surrounding landscape.

It would exceed the limits of our purpose to mention here all the more important mineral springs of the Union. It must suffice to say that Maine and Vermont have their saline and chalybeate springs, while North Carolina boasts mainly of her warm and hot springs, in Buncombe County, which has given its name to a favorite style of political oratory. The Indian and Meriwether warm springs of South Carolina are said to surpass, in medicinal virtue, the most famous chalybeate springs of the North, while the hot springs of Ouachita, in Arkansas, are unsurpassed in the world. The water, as it runs out from the foot of the Hot Mountain in copious streams, all along the slope, is hot enough to scald the hand, and to boil an egg hard in less than ten minutes. A dense fog continually hangs over these springs, and the side of the hill looks, at a distance, like a number of furnaces in blast. The mode of using the waters is by taking a steam bath, which, after a few minutes, produces a profuse perspiration; the effect is said to be at least equal, if not superior, to that produced by the waters of Baden-Baden, Wiesbaden, and Carlsbad, in Germany. The water is so strongly impregnated with lime and magnesia, that leaves, sticks, and similar articles exposed to its action, are quickly petrified, that is, covered with a thick layer of these minerals.

Among the two thousand mineral and thermal springs which the patriotic enthusiasm of a Southern writer claims for the State of Florida, the sulphur spring near Tampa is perhaps the only one the medicinal virtues of which have been fully authenticated. It is a white sulphur, bubbling up from the crevices of limestone, and forming a basin of eighteen feet, filled with beautiful, limpid water.

The whole Southwest is remarkable, among other natural peculiarities, for the number of mineral springs it contains; but their inaccessibility has so far prevented them from claiming the rank that is due them among the famous places of the world,—a difficulty which will soon be at least partially removed by the great Southern Pacific Railway. Perhaps the most remarkable among them are the

Beer Springs, so called by early voyageurs, which rise in the bed of Bear River, and owe their curious name to their active effervescence and acidulous taste. They were discovered by General Fremont, in his famous expedition across the Rocky Mountains.

The richest portion of our Great West, in point of springs, of every kind, is the region inhabited by the Mormons. It is well known that the great Salt Lake City itself, lying on the banks of the river Jordan, which connects the Salt Lake with the Utah Lake, is provided with an unfailing supply of fresh, pure water. By an ingenious mode of irrigation, mentioned elsewhere, this water is made to traverse each side of every street, whence it is led into every garden-spot, spreading life and verdure, health and beauty, over what was heretofore a barren waste. Numerous warm and hot springs, some sulphurous, and others chalybeate, issue in all directions from the mountain slope, which rises on one side of the ill-fated city; while salt springs and salt pools abound in every direction. The water of the great Salt Lake itself has proved, upon scientific investigation, to be one of the purest and most concentrated brines of the world, thus adding one more wonder to the many which nature seems to have delighted in crowding together in those regions.

At the Eastern base of the Sierra Nevada, between Mud and Pyramid Lakes, rise the most remarkable hot springs which we possess on this continent,—the so-called Hot Springs of Pyramid Lake. The basin of the largest has a circumference of several hundred feet, and at one extremity, in a circular spot, of about fifteen feet in diameter, the boiling water bubbles up at irregular intervals and with amazing noise. The temperature is 206°, but when the water is stirred with a pole it rises to 208°. There are but few hot springs on the earth's surface with a temperature as elevated as these boiling springs. The hottest in Europe, according to Arago, unconnected with recent volcanic action, are those of Chaudes Aigues, in France, in which the thermometer rises to 176°, and the hottest produced by modern volcanic action, according to Forbes, the Baths of Nero, at Baiae, in the Bay of Naples, which rise to the same temperature. The Geysers, of Iceland, a hot spring in the island of Amsterdam, in the Indian Ocean, and the sulphurous hot springs of Ussina, in Niphon, a part of Japan, are the only springs which rise to 212°, and thus surpass our own. It is however asserted upon good authority, that the Boiling Springs of Pyramid Lake also really boil up, in the centre, rising to a temperature of 212°, and are thus equal, in this respect, to the hottest springs known in the world. Countless hot springs abound all along the base of the Rocky Mountains, and recent explorations in the basin of the Yellowstone River have brought to light new wonders in the way of spouting hot sulphur springs, in vast numbers.

Thus it will be seen that this continent, favored beyond any part of the world in richness of soil, abundance of precious metals, and exhaustless stores of coal and valuable minerals, is by no means deficient in ample means to restore health and return of strength to the feeble and the infirm. This is especially apparent when we bear in mind that only a very small portion of these health-giving waters is as yet known to the world; countless mineral springs have never yet been analyzed; others are, as yet, more or less inaccessible in remote mountain fastnesses, and new discoveries bring, every year, new treasures to light.*

TREATMENT.

"When you arrive at the waters," says Alibert, "act as you would do if you were entering the temple of Esculapius, and leave behind you at the door all the passions, which have been tormenting your mind and agitating your soul. Once there, abstain from imprudence, and do not exceed the prescribed doses as so many invalids have done at all times, for Pliny already complained of the evil. 'Many sick people,' he says, 'take a pride in having remained for hours together in very hot baths, or in drinking unmeasured quantities of mineral waters, which are both equally dangerous.' Lead a quiet, calm, tranquil life, bathe and drink with moderation, and the water will gradually exercise its beneficial influence upon you. Your sufferings will insensibly pass away in the precious liquid, and your forces will become invigorated."

Formerly, invalids sent by their medical advisers to the waters, were made to undergo a severe pre-

* Full analyses of American mineral waters will be found in the Appendix.

liminary treatment. The illustrious Boileau gives us a proof in a letter written to Racine on the 21st of July, 1687. "I have been purged and bled," writes the author of L'Art Poétique, "and nothing more remains for me to undergo of all the formalities considered necessary before taking the waters. The medicines which I have taken to-day, have, as they tell me, done me all the good in the world; for they have caused me to fall down four or five times from weakness, and have thrown me into a state in which I can hardly stand upright. To-morrow I am to begin the great work; I mean to say that to-morrow I am to begin taking the waters." Poor Boileau! We can understand when we read further how well he foresaw what that great work would be! In other letters, he informs us that he takes, every morning, a dozen glasses of water, which have caused him, so to speak, to lose every part of his body, save the malady for which he took them."

Happily our physicians no longer resemble the contemporaries of Boileau, or those which Molière so humorously describes. The cures due to mineral waters are nowadays more frequent and complete. Let us, therefore, be grateful to Nature for her admirable medicaments which are able to procure us that greatest of all blessings—health. "A most precious possession," says Montaigne, "and the only one which deserves that we should lavish upon it, not only our time, wealth and labor, but also life itself; since without it, life is sure to be painful and distressing; pleasure and wisdom, science and virtue, all, without it, languish and at length perish."

CHAPTER V.

BATHS.

"In all times and among all nations, baths have been considered as an efficacious branch of hygiene."—DR. CONSTANTIN JAMES.

THE celebrated Medea, who in the time of the Argonauts astonished all Greece by the miracles which the art of magic enabled her to accomplish, owed a part of her success to the power she possessed of rejuvenating the old and infirm. Pilephates and other ancient authors state that she obtained this marvellous result by the use of baths of mineral waters with which she was familiar.

From the days of Homer, who represented his heroes as bathing in vast piscines, to those of the contemporaries of the fall of the Roman Empire, when all the appliances of unbridled luxury were found in the public baths, the use of baths has always played an important part among the customs of antiquity. The reader will doubtless remember the pools of the Spartans and the baths of Athens, of which Lucian has given us so complete a description. Much also has been written concerning the baths and *thermæ* of the Romans to which Latin writers continually allude, which are familiar to us by well preserved remains of many buildings still existing in Pompeii. Seneca and Lucian still awaken our astonishment by their descriptions of the refinements of luxury, which characterized these public establishments. None of the entrances were direct, the baths being thus screened from contact with the

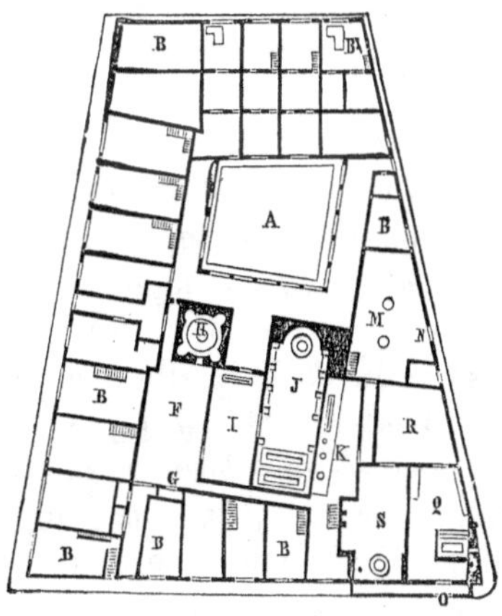

Plan of the Baths at Pompeii.

A, Atrium.
B B, Shops.
F, Spoliatorium.
G, Unctuarium.
H, Frigidarium.
I, Tepidarium.
J, Caldarium.
K, Hypocaustum.
M, Court.
O, Door of entrance to the women's bath.
Q, Spoliatorium and Frigidarium.
R, Tepidarium.
S, Caldarium,

air and observation from without. Two doors conducted you to the *atrium*, surrounded with long porticoes of graceful columns, under which the numerous bathers could comfortably wait their turn for entering the bath.* From the *atrium* you went into a hall called the *spoliatorium* or *apodyterium*, where slaves (*casparii*) disrobed the bathers, and kept watch over their clothes and valuables. An adjoining closet, the *unctuarium*, was devoted to perfuming the bather's body by means of oils and aromatic essences.

We should never finish our description if we were to enumerate all the arrangements which an immoderate love of luxury and comfort had suggested; if we were to mention every detail of the *frigidarium*, or hall of cold baths—the *baptisterium*, a pool of white marble surrounded with steps, on which the bathers sat—the *tepidarium*, a kind of vapor bath, kept at a gentle temperature—the *alipili*, who extracted all the superfluous hair—the *tractatores*, or shampooers, the heat-conducting pipes arranged beneath the pavements—the *labrum*, a kind of marble fountain, with its bronze jets, from which water flowed to wash the hands and face of the bather, who had been perspiring in the vapor-bath.

"A complete bath," says Galien, "is composed of four parts, each different in its effect. When you enter the thermæ, you are subjected to the influence of hot air; you are then wetted with warm water; after that you plunge into cold water, and last of all you are dried and rubbed." The order which

* Vitruvius. According to this author porticoes constituted an essential part of all baths.

Galien indicates was, however, constantly changed in consequent of the caprices of fashion and the fancies of the passing hour, and it is impossible at present to describe accurately the various processes of rubbing, shampooing and anointing, multiplied at pleasure by the effeminate descendants of the Romans of the republic. Publius Victor, in the fourth century, counted in Rome no less than nine hundred thermæ establishments, and the number of baths was still on the increase, when the advancing progress of Christianity came to stop a practice which had passed from the domain of hygiene to that of vuluptuous self-indulgence. In spite, however, of the opinion of Agathinius, the pupil of Athenæus, who saw in the use of warm-baths a thousand fatal dangers, the use of baths had followed the development of Roman society and could only perish with it. Doomed for a time to complete and general disrepute, the bath resumed its popularity once more under Charlemagne. Popular tradition shows us the Great Emperor of the West battling with his whole court in the baths of Aix-la-Chapelle. If we are to believe the legend, it is to a hunting-dog that we owe the use of mineral waters in modern times. The intelligent animal having escaped from the royal pack of hounds to bathe in a distant spring, and returning all dripping with a liquid smelling strongly of sulphur, suggested the idea of turning to account the hitherto unknown spring. But the use of baths is not limited to ancient or modern Europe. The oriental nations, Indians, and nearly all the savages of the earth, make frequent use of baths and ablutions. During the sanguinary wars which they maintained against the Christians, the ancient Moors were accustomed to plunge into every spring they met with in their way, and are said to derive signal benefits from the practice.*

Averrhoës recommends vapor-baths, and expresses his opinion strongly on the subject of their medical use. Alibert gives us a translation of a passage taken from the "Medical Observations" of the ancient Emperor Kang-Hi, which leads to the supposition that the qualities of mineral water must have been long understood in China. "Nothing is truer," says the royal author, "than that thermal waters are efficacious in the treatment of various diseases." In 1691, this Emperor undertook a long journey for the purpose of visiting and spending several months in a district situated to the north of Pekin, and celebrated for its efficient mineral baths.

In our own day nearly every nation has its own way of taking a bath. In the East the public baths are the places where the old and young assemble day after day to chat, to consult and to discuss public matters. Built of stone, they have marble floors, heated from below, and pipes passing through the walls to diffuse heat in all directions. The bather, undressed and wrapped in woolen blankets, is shown into the bath-room proper, where the perspiration soon breaks out from all pores; he is repeatedly washed with cold water while thus per-

* See Universal Dictionary of Mineral Waters by Durand, Tardel and Le Bret.

spiring, and then rubbed down dry, and anointed with aromatic oil. After this he lies down on a table, and is thoroughly kneaded in all his limbs by the attendants, who continue to pour the warm water over him and try the elasticity of his muscles and sinews to the utmost. This apparently merciless treatment produces a sense of voluptuous delight, during which the bather is carefully dried, the hard skin being removed with brimstone, once more anointed with oil and ointments, and at last led to a luxurious couch, where he rests and reposes himself with his pipe and cooling sherbet.

The Russian prefers steam, and loves his bath so dearly that no village in the whole empire is so poor but it has its own establishment. The unpretending building consists generally of a large room furnished with broad benches placed against the walls, on which the peasant lies down undressed. Hot water is then poured continually upon red hot stones, till the room is filled with dense, white vapors, and the pleasure-seeker breaks out in violent perspiration. During this time ice-cold water is repeatedly thrown over him, he is bathed in soap and beaten with softened birch-twigs till he has enough, and crowns his enjoyment by suddenly jumping into a bank of snow or a river.

The Esquimaux, the Finns, the Greenlanders, the Norwegians, the Samoyeds, all make use of vapor-baths, constructed, it is true, upon a most simple and primitive plan. A hole dug in the earth and a few stones made red-hot at a fire, constitute the bath and the stove ; the bather creeps into this orifice, and the steam, caused by the moisture of the soil when warmed by the hot stones, suffices to provoke an abundant perspiration. The Missionary Loskiel describes similar practices as prevailing among the North American Indians; a custom which is still in force with the majority of our Western tribes.

The ordinary bath is the most useful form in which mineral waters are taken. Non-escaping cold chalybeate waters and a few bicarbonates are used in preference as a beverage. Warm waters, slightly mineral, are employed almost exclusively as baths, (Néris, Bains, Chaudesaigues, etc.,) and it is the same with highly mineralized non-gaseous waters, such as Kreusnach and Salins.

Besides the topical action of baths, and the absorption of considerable portions of the water by the human body, mineral baths act medicinally also by the actual effect of the substances which they contain. All the waters which hold in solution a perceptible quantity of organic matter, produce upon the skin a soft and unctuous sensation which refreshes and renders it supple. Waters which are both sodic and sulphuric act as stimulants and produce irritation and eruptions upon the surface of the skin. The characteristic of thermal baths is their imparting to the bather a feeling of strength, and at the same time of comfort, while fresh water, and still more sea water baths can only be used by constitutions capable of resisting their depressing influence. But is there not much in the ordinary use of baths with which fault may justly be found? If the Romans abused the bath, may it not be said of us moderns, that we do not make sufficient use of it? Where are the magnificent public baths and pools full of bathers every hour of the day? They have been replaced by a narrow cell, a miserable bathing tub; bran has been substituted for perfumes and aromatic oils, and our baths have neither couch to rest on, nor appliances for friction or for shampooing. Where are those halls, so spacious, so well warmed and ventilated, where the bather could dry himself gradually before encountering the external air? All the baths of our day expose us to a sudden and dangerous transition from the heat of the water to the cold air without.

It would be a grave mistake, finally, to suppose that the internal or external use is the only advantage man derives from these mineral springs. If the latter are of endless variety, bringing life or death, heat or cold, fire or mire from the unknown depths of the earth, man, on the other hand, forces them to serve him in a thousand ways. Here he evaporates saline waters to obtain salt, there to win alum, glauber salts, iodine or borax; in some places, as in the Hartz Mountains and the Apennines, he gathers the limestone deposited by the water, and uses it under the name of travertine, to build his houses and churches; at other places, as in the Auvergne, he forces a river to build itself the bridge by which it is to be crossed. The "Sprudel," at Karlsbad in Bohemia, furnishes a variegated stone resembling costly marble, and a similar spring in Peru is made to run through moulds which it fills with its delicate deposits, and when the form is broken, a beautiful statue is the result!

FRESH AND SEA WATER BATHS.

All medical authorities are agreed in recommending the use of cold baths, and the inhabitants of large cities, situated on great rivers, have always been accustomed to bathe in the cool water during the heat of summer. In the country when the sun is darting his burning rays upon the earth, the bather finds a salutary repose in the waters of the river; he can there allow himself to be rocked by the waves, or, following the current as it glides down, shaded by thick willows, he swims along the health-giving river, his pores eagerly absorbing the refreshing liquid. In towns, bathing is a diversion at once less healthy and less agreeable, and the numerous bathing establishments which block up great rivers, afford by no means the same benefit or enjoyment. Still, Paris, for instance, may boast of having had cold river baths long before other towns, for it is not a thing of to-day, for the Parisians to make use of cold baths; they had them already in 1760, and before that time they took their pleasure in the open river. Bassompierre relates that in 1608, the heat was such that during a whole month more than five thousand human heads a day were counted on the Seine between Charenton and the Isle of St. Louis. In ordinary summers the bathers went into the water above the bridge of Tournelle, and La Bruyère reproaches the great ladies of his day with the pleasure they found in walking or driving in that direc-

SEA-BATHS — BIARRITZ.

tion precisely as similar sarcasms have been aimed at the fair visitors of the beach at Newport in our day. "Far otherwise," says Michelet, "is the breath of the sea; of itself it purifies. A seaside life is a struggle, but a vivifying struggle to all who can bear it."

The first immersion in the sea is almost invariably unpleasant, but the comfort one soon experiences causes the disagreeable sensation to be quickly forgotten. Swimming is so easy and the expenditure of muscular force so inappreciable, that the bather is tempted to abandon himself for a long time to the charms of such pleasant exercise. Its duration, however, has to be carefully regulated; the body, suddenly plunged into the cold, is apt to take a chill, and the circulation, slackened or even partially suspended, does not recover its equilibrium, if the bath lasts too long. Upon leaving the water, reaction takes place, the skin resumes its former color, the blood rushes back to the surface, and the beating of the heart becomes freer. For the rest, to use the words of Galien, uttered more than a thousand years ago: "Experience itself can be our only guide as to how long it is advisable to remain in the water. If when we come out of our bath the skin soon returns to its former good color after being rubbed hard, we may feel safe in remaining long in the water; but if it takes a long time for our skin to become warm again, and to lose its pallor, we see a sure indication that our bath has been too long. Its duration must henceforward be shorter."

Sea water is a true mineral water, marvellously

rich in saline principles; it is a vital source from whence the feeble may draw strength, and sufferers of every kind may derive health. It holds in its bosom nearly all remedies,—nearly all medicaments which are most valuable. "We ought," says Russel, "both to drink sea water and to bathe in it. We ought to saturate ourselves with it, in order to repair the injuries done to our bodies. The sea holds the carbonate of lime, which can give strength to our weak and nerveless bones; it holds the iodine which purifies our blood, the heat which our frame so much needs, and, above all, that mysterious something which penetrates so wonderfully, that gelatine, that mucous, which envelops vegetables and marine animals, and lavishes upon them strength and life."

"Whatever principle," says Michelet, "exists in you, that grand, intangible personality, the sea, possesses, in minute subdivision. She has in her your bones, your blood, your fibre, your vital warmth,—every element in your constitution, which has its representative in one or other of your children, exists also in the ocean. But she possesses what you have not,—an excess, the overplus of force. Her breath imparts a mysterious something,—active, energetic, creative,—which might be called *physical heroism*. With all her violence, the great mother is none the less prodigal, with her fierce joy, her lively and quickening alacrity, her wild and burning love, that beats in her own mighty heart."

THE WATER CURE.

There exists in Germany a celebrated school of medicine, which affects to cure all diseases by the mere use of water. Cold water for the healing of wounds; thermal and mineral waters, ice and snow, variously applied,—these, we are told, are the only weapons which physicians should make use of in curing the ills to which flesh is heir. Water is thus made a veritable panacea. It is, however, only the extreme Dr. Sangrados of this school, who have ascribed a German origin to the water-cure; for this important branch of the healing art has, in reality, nothing new about it but the name.

Naaman was told by the prophet to wash in the waters of Jordan; and Seneca has told us, in so many words, that cold water restores the patient suffering from syncope. Does not Homer show us Patroclus washing the wound of Euripylus, received at the siege of Troy, with cold water? Have we forgotten Hecuba's cries for water to wash the wounds of Polyxene? Do not these facts prove that the ancients employed water with excellent judgment? Douche-baths were fully known to them, and it was at Rome, in the reign of Augustus, that the hydropathic system was originated, under the happy inspiration of a freedman—Antonius Musa. This physician prescribed water as a drink, in baths and in shower baths, and he found in this simple remedy the secret of a new system of therapeutics. Augustus had but just been chosen Consul for the eleventh time, when he fell ill with a dangerous sickness. Seeing his end approaching, he assembled the magistrates, the senators, and the principal knights, and then, having conferred with them on the affairs of the Republic, he placed the seal of government in the hands of Agrippa. It was at this moment that Antonius Musa undertook to cure him by his new method, and the Consul was cured by means of cold water, applied both externally and internally. Augustus, full of gratitude, bestowed on Musa a large sum of money, the gold ring of a knight, and ordered his statue to be placed beside that of Esculapius; at the same time he conferred upon him, and all who then exercised, and hereafter should exercise the same profession, nobility, and an exemption from taxation. (See Dio Cassius, quoted in Dr. C. James' Guide to Mineral Waters.) Musa was not slow in acquiring an immense reputation. "Oh, Musa!" exclaimed Virgil, "No one may flatter himself that he will ever surpass thee in science." And thus hydropathy replaced, for a time, all other systems of therapeutics. Horace himself soon after resorted to this famous physician, and the graceful poet, after having sung the praises of the Falernian wine, thought of nothing else than to look for the best cold water; he set out for Velium, where Musa prescribed for him a hydropathic treatment, and after that he took the sulphur baths of Baiæ.

But fortune was not always prodigal of her favors to the celebrated Musa. Being called in to attend the young Marcellus, whose life was in danger, he felt bound to apply his favorite system—he recommended cold water and Marcellus expired. This was a terrible blow both to hydropathy and its advocates. Cold-water cures were at once universally abandoned. A century later, Charmis, under Nero, recommended the system of Musa ; he met with the same success and awakened the same enthusiasm ; cold baths again became the fashion and were taken at all hours of the day. Nero was in the habit of adding snow to the water of his baths, and the system really deserved its name of hydropathy, the baths being often preceded by violent perspiration. "We went to the baths," says Petronius, "and there, with bodies all in a perspiration, we plunged into cold water."

Charmis, like Musa, prescribed cold water internally as well as externally, and that in large doses. It was needful, according to Pliny, to drink before you sat down to the table, during the repast, and again before going to sleep ; it was even necessary sometimes to be roused in order to drink again, (*et si libeat somnos interrumpere.*) The temperature of water could never be too low. The impulse given by Charmis continued long after his death. Celsus, who survived him, and the successors of Celsus, frequently prescribed cold water, and we see in their writings the happy use they made of it in the treatment of their patients. History does not tell us whether hydropathy found a second Marcellus. All we do know is that little by little warm baths superseded cold baths, so much so that in our own day the latter had been entirely abandoned, when suddenly their use received a new impulse from

Priessnitz, the German reformer, from whom, in fact, hydropathy must be dated. (Dr. C. James.)

He was a simple peasant of Silesia, a province of Prussia, when in 1816 he was, on his return from the fields, thrown from his horse; the runaway animal injured his face severely with his hoofs, and broke two of his ribs. The little village of Freiwalden, where he lived, could not boast of a physician, and Priessnitz had to cure himself as well as he could. He gradually forced his ribs back to their natural position, by pressing his chest continually against the side of a chair; in place of bandages he employed wet linen; he drank large quantities of cold water, and was soon able to resume his work.

This cure made a great sensation, and Priessnitz recommending the same treatment to others, was, ere long, consulted in all cases of sickness—he invariably applied his cold water system—and being of an observing turn of mind, he tried to supply by observation what he lacked of scientific knowledge. Soon he went from village to village, healing all who applied to him for help, and acquiring a name which gradually became famous. A few years only elapsed and the peasant Priessnitz had founded a vast establishment, resorted to by crowds of invalids from all parts of the world, seeking from empiricism the recovery refused to them by science.

Hydropathy was very tardily received abroad; and a steady opposition to it was maintained for a long time, especially in France; nevertheless little by little men grew accustomed to cold water—and cold baths, cold water effusions and iced compresses now hold their place on the list of medicaments employed by our doctors. In the United States the method—perhaps owing to its simple practical character—became soon eminently popular. A German, Dr. Wesselhoeft, established the first large establishment of the kind at Brattleboro, Vt., and now similar "Water Cures," as they are briefly called, may be found in almost all of the Northern States.

The method of Priessnitz consists in the drinking of cold water, moist wrappings, rubbing with wet cloths, cold douches, cold sit baths and cold foot baths; such were the only prescriptions of the old Silesian peasant. These remedies are, no doubt, excellent in certain cases, and hydropathy is without doubt one of the important branches of the healing art. But the new method has been injured by over-zealous advocates, who have absurdly praised it at the expense of all other systems. What necessity is there to despise all the recognized systems, or to reject all commonly employed medicaments for the sake of this one beverage—cold water? We ought to leave such extravagances to the famous doctor, immortalized by Le Sage.

ARTIFICIAL MINERAL WATERS.

The idea of replacing the mineral waters of nature by similar waters artificially produced, is not new; on the contrary, several of Galen's contemporaries already attempted to prepare beverages which should rival the waters of the most famous springs. But in the opinion of Herodotus no beverage of this description equalled the water from which it derived its name, and numerous attempts have proved that Herodotus was not mistaken. Many kinds of purgative and sulphur water of incontestable efficacy have indeed been manufactured, but there is no comparison between these medicaments and those which nature produces in the bosom of the globe. The Seidlitz water of chemists has nothing in common with the German spring of that name, save the label; and the ordinary Seltzer water, drank at meals, does not in any way resemble that which is supplied by the celebrated spring in the Duchy of Nassau. It is, however, a very wholesome and refreshing beverage, and so universally held in repute that it may be well to describe its preparation.

Seltzer water is simply common water charged with carbonic acid by high pressure, and is prepared on a large scale by means of the apparatus which is represented on the opposite page. The carbonic acid gas, produced in a metal cylinder, under the action of sulphuric acid poured upon carbonate of lime (chalk, marble, etc.,) passes through three purifying vessels and then enters a gasometer; a pump drives it back into the spherical receiver, furnished with a pressure-gauge, and a leaden tube finally takes it to a syphon, which it enters under a pressure of ten or twelve atmospheres.

OZOUF APPARATUS FOR MANUFACTURE OF SELTZER WATER.

CHAPTER VI.

PUBLIC HYGIENE.

"Notwithstanding the abundance with which water is spread over the surface of the earth, it is often lacking in certain spots where it would be of the utmost utility, and there is not a single city the salubrity of which might not be greatly increased by it."—J. DUPUIT.

DRINKING WATER.

TERRIBLE were the punishments suffered by the guilty dwellers in Tartarus; but the greatest of all seemed, even to the ancients, the anguish endured by a monarch whom the gods had once loved as companion, and now in their fury exposed to incredible torture. He had eaten their bread and drank of their nectar—what wonder that earthly food pleased his fastidious palate no longer? The red wine of Phrygia, his own kingdom, could no longer make merry his heart, and his soul longed for the precious drink of the gods on Olympus. In an evil hour he forgot himself, and carried some with him to his earthly home. The indignant masters of heaven and earth condemned him for such grievous misdeed to suffer everlasting thirst in the dark regions where Pluto reigned supreme, and the souls of the wicked met their reward. There the unfortunate king stood, day after day, in the midst of sweet swelling waters, that ever rose playfully, temptingly up to his parched lips, and ever fell back in bitter mockery at the very instant when relief seemed at hand, and torturing thirst about to be quenched. Could human ingenuity devise a more fearful infliction of ceaseless pain, adding to all the horrors of fiercest bodily suffering the soul's unutterable, ever-new anguish?

And yet men daily endure like sufferings now on the earth. The weary wanderer through the desert, and the bold mariner in the seas of the arctic, the becalmed sailor in the tropics, and the lost emigrant crossing the vast dry plains of the Far West—all succumb to the same dread enemy, Thirst, or, if they escape by the mercy of God, remember ever after the days of their torture with shuddering horror. For "even the youths shall be faint and weary," and painful beyond words is that feeling when the "heart sinks," and the soul longeth to part from the earth-born body. A fierce tyrant is Hunger, and grimly it gnaws at our strength, until even the strong are "burnt with hunger and devoured." But the most cruel of all mere bodily wants, that try the soul of man as in a furnace, is Thirst. It breaks the tower of man's fortitude, it loosens even the silver chords of the strongest of earthly affections, the love of a mother: "And the water was spent in the bottle, and Hagar cast the child under one of the shrubs; and she went and set her down over against him a good way off, as it were a bowshot, for she said, Let me not see the death of the child. And she sat over against him, and lifted up her voice and wept."

Water, so indispensable for the economy of nature, is not less necessary for the existence of man. Every part of our body, our bones included, contains water; our food of every kind is mixed up with water, and only thus becomes nutritious, and even certain higher functions can only be performed by its aid, as sight is possible only by the liquid behind the pupil. This alone would require a constant supply of water for our existence. But as our body needs, besides, certain organic substances, like iron, salts, lime, etc., to build up its more solid parts, and to maintain certain organs in activity, water is needed to bring these elements and to introduce them into the system. It is altogether indispensable for the process of digestion, not only by dissolving and distributing our food, but also by keeping up the circulation of the blood and all other fluid parts of the system.

Spring water, containing, as we have seen, a slight admixture of carbonic acid, has thus a cooling power which may increase to slight intoxication. Water cools us when we drink it, bathe in it, or pour it on wounds, because it does not easily heat, and thus withdraws a certain amount of caloric from the body. Hence the soothing and curative effects which water has in cases of sickness. For these combined purposes man consumes, under ordinary circumstances, from three to four pints of water per day; a less quantity would cause real physical suffering. It may be imagined, therefore, what a great influence the salts which water holds in solution, even in small quantities, must exercise over the animal economy. Nor is it sufficient to drink these three or four pints of water a day; the water must be wholesome and of good quality. Opinion in every age has attributed to the action of bad water certain accidental pathological effects, certain endemic diseases, and although these popular impressions have no doubt been often exaggerated, and these theories occasionally rest on false premises, it is none the less true that some waters are highly deleterious and dangerous. It is easy to understand, on the same principle, how waters containing salts favorable to our system and the development of the organs, and holding in solution these gaseous products, which are best calculated to facilitate digestion, become through daily use the surest, most valuable, and most rational of hygienic agents.

Fresh water may be divided into rain-water, spring-water, the water of rivers, of lakes, of ponds, and of wells.

Rain-water, when just collected, is not indeed absolutely pure, but is the purest to be found in nature. It has, however, the defect of not holding any calcareous matter in solution, of not being nutritious, and of not containing sufficient air in solution; hence it is insipid and of a sickly-sweet taste. The water of ponds and pools, rich in decomposed organic matter, has an odor so disagreeable as to unfit it for table use. Springs, lakes, rivers, wells or cisterns, are the only reservoirs of drinkable water; but the ingredients of the water they contain are so different that it is a serious question to which of them the preference ought to be given.

Water may be considered good when it is fresh, limpid, inodorous, not inclined to become turbid when boiled; when it leaves but little sediment after evaporation; when its taste is sweet and pleasant, and neither salt nor insipid; when it holds air in solution; when it melts soap easily without forming clots, and when it boils vegetables well.

Cistern-water, employed in countries which are deficient in springs and rivers, does not answer these requirements, for the rain which trickles down from the roofs of houses carries along with it organic and mineral substances; it is true that this matter sinks to the bottom, and the water becomes pure after resting a few days; but it may be changed again by the decomposition of the organic matter, which takes up and carries away the oxygen it contains, and this leaves only an insipid, disagreeable and highly deleterious liquid.

"Except in rare cases, water which holds in solution a perceptible proportion of organic matter, becomes soon putrid, and acquires qualities which are deleterious. It is evident that diarrhœa, dysentery, and other acute or chronic affections have been induced endemically by the continued use of water holding organic matter in large proportions, either in solution or in suspension. It is admitted as the result of universal observation, that the less organic matter is held by the water we drink, the more wholesome it is."*

To these remarks we may add that in certain towns, such as Cadiz, in Spain, where each house possesses a cistern, care is taken to let off by taps the first rain which falls from the sky, and only when the impurities of the air, of roofs, and of canals, have thus been carried off, is the rain which the clouds continue to pour upon the city, carefully collected.

Well and spring water, also, is rarely pure; for the pure water of the heavens is itself one of the most eager of drinkers. If there be impure gases in the air through which it falls, it will absorb them. If there be earthy or mineral salts in the earth through which it soaks, it will absorb these also. According to the nature of the soil, therefore, will be the nature of the spring or the stream. If the water fall upon granite, slate, or like formations, upon which it can lie, dissolving nothing, it remains pure. A chemist or an engineer fairly versed in analyses, can hence tell from examination of the water of a district what its geology is; or, if he knows its geology, he can describe its water. Even the layman need not long doubt. Regions of granite and clay slate are usually covered with moss, peat, or heath, and the soft rainwater, that is so ready to dissolve anything soluble, will give a dark tinge to streams flowing from rocks clothed with this kind of vegetation. Rain falling upon the new red sand-

* Boutron and Boudet, Annual of French Waters, 1851.

stone, chalk or oolites, will yield water containing lime, magnesia, iron, sulphur, and thereby made heavier, harder, and less fit for use. Generally speaking, the deeper the water sinks, the more earthy matter it holds in solution; deep well water, therefore, is apt to be hard. Hot springs, we have seen, are exceptional, for they may rise through inverted syphon-veins and fissures, from a depth of thousands of feet, while the usual limit to which water can soak, is found to be about 900 or 1,000 feet.

It is astonishing how much rock the springs and rivers carry on their light waves, and even more wonderful how much rock goes into the stomachs of those who drink such waters. In Thames water, and most of the waters supplying London, lime is found to the amount of nearly 16 grains to the gallon. A million of gallons hold, therefore, a ton of lime, and as the great city drinks about 160,000,000 of gallons, 60,000 tons of lime are pumped into London with its year's supply of water—a mountain of lime that would make mortar enough to build a large suburb!

Lime injures the coats of the stomach when taken in the water we drink; when we wash with such water, it curdles soap and takes away the beauty of the skin. Ladies know that pure soft water is the truest beauty wash, and that there is no cosmetic that will counteract the bad effect of hard water on the complexion. Grooms and trainers take good care to give good soft water to their horses, and where a supply cannot be had, large tanks are formed in which to store rain water for their use. Among the Alpine oolites and limestones, on the contrary, pale faces, wens, and cretinism abound. Vegetables are of the same mind with animals as to the wholesome sort of drinking water.

A glass of pure spring water is an article turned out by sea, sky, and earth, and worked upon their grandest scale under the eye of the sun. The less it is of the earth, earthy, the better for those who require more of it than mere eye-service.

The soft water of rivers is the impurest of all, save only the briny floods of the ocean. They betray, as we have seen, even to the eye, their impurities in bright colors. The glaciers of Iceland and the slopes of the Andes send milk-white rivers, filled with white soils, into the sterile plains at their feet. Streams that pass these boggy lakes or peaty regions emerge as brown as they are bitter, and rocks of red marl will burden their rivers with brilliant oxide of iron. Man, however, has not only become accustomed to these solid additions to his daily beverage, but seems to reward himself after a while by a special delight in the taste of muddy waters. The dusky fluid of the Nile is sweet to the palate, and the children of Egypt long and yearn for its waters as the Swiss does for his beloved home in the mountains. The sacred Ganges rewards the faithful who carry its waters to the most distant provinces, with abstract blessings and with a genuine sensual enjoyment. Our own Mississippi water, so repugnant to the traveller at first sight, is a favorite with those who dwell on the river, and often liked because of its peculiar color, and for its admixture. Generally, however, the water of rivers is clarified for use; that of the Ganges by rubbing certain nuts on the edges of the vessel in which it is kept; that of the Nile by a similar use of bitter almonds. Thus we are taught by the Great Master that the bitter waters of Marah were made sweet by the use of a tree which the Lord showed Moses.

DOMESTIC AND INDUSTRIAL USES.

The consumption of water for external use,—that is to say, for the purposes of health and cleanliness,—may be estimated, in towns like Paris, as averaging two gallons to each inhabitant, including only the ordinary citizen who rents the whole or part of a house, and does not exercise any branch of industry which requires a large supply of water, such as that of a dyer, or brewer, or keeper of public baths and wash-houses, and who has neither domestic animals to be taken care of, horses to be watered, a carriage to be cleaned, nor a garden to be watered. Including these exceptional causes of demand for water we reach an estimate of about ten gallons to each inhabitant.

Besides such domestic and industrial uses, water has to be provided for watering the roads when the heat of the summer changes streets and public walks into so many sandy deserts; for cleaning gutters and sewers, to obviate the dangers of standing water; for sewerage and for cooling the air, by means of fountains in open squares and pleasure gardens.

All these supplies of water are imperiously demanded by public hygiene; but it need not be added that in all these cases the quality of water signifies but little; whether it be impregnated with gypsum or limestone, whether it be tepid or cold, it will, for all that, accomplish its cleaning mission.

It is not so, however, with water used for drink, and for cooking and washing purposes; it is not so, even with water used for feeding steam coppers and boilers.

Calcareous waters leave an abundant deposit, which encrusts coppers and boilers, and forms a hard and resistant coating, or stone lining, that covers and seriously injures the metal of the boiler.

This coating keeps the heat from communicating with the liquid within; and if the metal of the boiler becomes red-hot, while the water, held as it were in its coating of stone, is in ebullition, the calcareous deposit is apt to crack, the water comes in contact with the red-hot metallic sides of the boiler, and suddenly changes into steam. The mass of steam thus suddenly set free in a space which has become too narrow, develops instantly an enormous expansive force, the boiler bursts, and woe to the workmen who are near it! Water which contains nitrate of magnesia or chloride of magnesium presents, also, grave inconveniences; for these salts decompose under the influence of heat, and deposit nitric acid and chlorohydric acid, which soon corrode the metal of the boiler and all the metal pipes which they traverse.

These inconveniences are sometimes remedied by purifying the waters first by chemical processes. Thus, to prevent the incrustation of coppers, the waters are mixed with a certain kind of clay. This mixture also soon forms a deposit, but instead of furnishing a hard and brittle coating it appears in the shape of a fine dust, which can be easily removed. Industry has, moreover, discovered other methods by which water may be freed of its organic and earthy matters, and employs a great variety of filtering systems.

Finally, the following are the conditions which public health imperatively demands :

Pure and fresh water in abundance, for the inhabitants of every city.

Water of ordinary quality, in great abundance, for washing the streets, cleaning sewers, watering roads, supplying public and private fountains,—in short, for all the exigencies of domestic and industrial uses.

CHAPTER VII.

THE WATER OF PARIS.—A GLANCE AT THE PAST.

'The aqueducts of Rome are veritable monuments of the past; the Romans, in order to establish them, pierced mountains, levelled valleys, and formed canals, which they suspended in places where there was no ground for them to rest upon. They have long rows of arches, which bear a river, and, sometimes, one or two rivers one above another, at a prodigious height."

PLINY. *Translated by Bezorry.*

THE first inhabitants of Paris drew the waters which served for their alimentation directly from the Seine. At a later period the Romans constructed the aqueduct of Arcueil, and the remains of their labor are still to be seen in the Emperor Julian's Palais des Thermes. This aqueduct perished with the Roman empire, and it was not until the eighteenth century that the monks procured water from the springs of Belleville and Près St. Gervais. This impure and selenitic water would now be rejected by all, and yet Paris knew no other water during more than four centuries, (from 1200 to 1608), until the time when the pump of the Samaritan woman was established on the Pont Neuf.

During the whole of the Middle Ages and the Renaissance period the sovereigns of France, never very solicitous for the wants and the welfare of the people, granted large monopolies to the nobles and the monasteries. The abuse became such that many portions of Paris were on the point of being abandoned for want of water in the public fountains. Notwithstanding the famous edict of Charles VI. (Oct. 1392); notwithstanding the noble initiative taken by a Provost of the Merchants, who, in 1457, caused the aqueduct of Belleville to be rebuilt, favoritism still continued to triumph, and the people continued to be without water.

In 1553 Paris only received a quantity of water equivalent to about a pint and a half to each inhabitant. This quantity would have scarcely sufficed for a city a hundred times less populous.

When the evil had become flagrant, when the complaints of the inhabitants, timid as they still were, reached the ear of the government, when the dearth of water had become too threatening, when the fountains no longer dropped anything but tears, an ordinance of the police delivered by the Provost of the Merchants, commanded every monopolist to present his title. This ordinance was issued in bad faith; it was a hollow form, a shameful mockery and delusion which always ends in some new monopoly, and re-established things in a state more deplorable than before. There was neither order nor responsibility, but everywhere injustice and iniquity. In connection with water as with everything else, it was always the same sad story of the rich being fattened at the expense of the poor; it was the great lord draining, on his own authority, the conduits of the town before the eyes of the people, from their own humble dwellings, to his mansion, where he wanted a new fountain, perhaps merely for ornament; or it was a community of monks who only consulted their own selfish interests, and watered their lands with the most revolting prodigality, unmindful of the thirst of the honest burgher, the laborer and the artisan.

It was reserved for a great king to remedy the evil by energetic measures. Henry IV. at length succeeded in getting his edicts obeyed. All the pipes which conveyed water to the Abbey lands and the palaces of the rich, were cut off without mercy; a minute revision of the titles of monopoly was carried out with unusual care and impartiality, and the number of the monopolists reduced to fourteen. For the first time money was paid for these monopolies, and Martin Langlois, Provost of the Merchants, was the first to pay to the city a rent of 35 livres 10 sous, for the right of getting water from the fountain of Barre-du-Bec.*

Abuses, like weeds, grow up in proportion as you try to tear them up, and so great an evil could not be so promptly abolished. In 1608 the want of water again made itself felt. Henry IV. again reduced the number of monopolies and set a noble example by submitting himself to considerable curtailment. The fountain of the Samaritan woman was erected on the Pont Neuf, and the same year saw the inauguration of an admirable project—the reconstruction of the aqueduct of Arcueil. But this work,

* *Registers of the City, vol. xiv., fol. 640.*

arrested in its progress by the death of the king, was not completed until much later under Mary de Medicis. Yet all things considered the reign of Henry IV. is a page in the history of Paris, which can be perused with satisfaction. It was then that for the first time hydraulic pumps were made use of, for the first time also money was paid to the town for the privilege of holding monopolies, and all these improvements are gems in the diadem which decorate the memory of one of the greatest kings. Under the next sovereigns, however, the abuses reappeared with new and scandalous energy, and several unhealthy quarters of the city were on the eve of being abandoned. All the fountains became dry while Louis Quatorze was spending millions of money wrung from his people in forming the famous water-works at Versailles for the delectation of his court. In 1671, however, a new pump, that of Notre Dame, was constructed, but notwithstanding this highly beneficial work, Paris still continued to receive only about five pints to each inhabitant. At the commencement of the eighteenth century, numerous papers published on the subject of the Water Supply of Paris showed that public attention was turning to that great question, but a few unimportant improvements were the sole result of long and unproductive discussions. De Parcieux, somewhat later, suggested a plan for supplying the capital from the waters of the Yvette, a little river which falls into the Seine above Long Jumeau. This plan was eagerly discussed, and public opinion then, as at the present day, hesitated between plans for obtaining water from a distance, and others for raising the level of the Seine water by means of engines. In 1767 the Chevalier d'Auxiron, advocating a system of raising the water of the Seine by new engines, replied to de Parcieux. The two adversaries became involved in warm and eager discussions, and while they were engaged in a mighty war of words, and the public took sides with eagerness, no water came. In 1771 the plan of obtaining water from a distance and carrying it into Paris by aqueducts found a powerful supporter in the illustrious Lavoisier, who lent to his project all the weight of his mighty genius.

At length appeared two able men, both merchants, who cut the Gordian knot of these difficulties. The brothers Périer proposed to the city to establish, at their own expense, a system of machinery on the Seine, consisting of a number of fire engines, by the aid of which 150 metres of water could be raised daily. The citizens of Paris were about to see at work, under their own eyes, steam engines which had been constructed in the workshop of Watt; they were about to drink water raised by the apparatus which was then exciting so justly universal admiration, and public opinion was quite ready to declare in favor of the Périers' system. On February the 7th, 1777, the Parliament authorized the brothers Périer, by letters patent, to establish at their expense, in localities designated by the Provost of the Merchants, fire engines, which were to carry the waters of the Seine into the capital. The new company was organized forthwith, but unfortunately began operations by a serious blunder; the first steam pump being erected at Chaillot, near the mouths of the city sewers.

Delays, unlooked-for obstacles, unforeseen disappointments, put a stop, for some time, to the work, and, unfortunately, public capital was led into a different channel. The appearance of the ill-fated financier, Law, the creation of his ruinous system, and the commencement of stock jobbing, turned the heads of the money-making public, and caused the water system, like so many others, to burst like a bubble.

The company indeed gave water in 1782, but the promises it had given were so badly kept, its most solemn engagements so little respected, that government saw itself compelled to interfere, and the undertaking was put a stop to altogether. A famous lawsuit, indeed, was carried on for some time on the subject, in which two illustrious names were engaged. Beaumarchais defended the company, and Mirabeau was his adversary. The author of "Le Mariage de Figaro," however, proved incapable of parrying the blows of the matchless orator; his accustomed genius deserted him, and the arms of the pleader fell from his hands. Truth lost its charms to the public eye, and the sonorous voice, the clear, precise statements of Count Mirabeau crushed the Water Supply Company to atoms, and threw it into the most complete disrepute.

The eighteenth century was, nevertheless, in this as in other respects, one of progress. At the time when the French Revolution broke out, Paris received enough water daily to furnish each one of its 547,755 inhabitants about twenty pints per head in 24 hours. This volume of water would barely suffice for a population seven times less numerous, consequently the progress due to the eighteenth century is not of much interest; but an age that listened to Voltaire and Rousseau had but little time to bestow upon problems of this description.

During a long series of years, the sad political troubles and terrible convulsions of France diverted the minds of men from questions purely administrative; capital, moreover, left the country, and financial speculations on the subject of water were not much in favor. It was only in the year 1797 that once more a bold enterprise was started,—the construction of the canal of Ourcq. After long debates and protracted discussions, and after having passed through most unexpected phases, this project appeared likely to be actually carried out, under the auspices of the first Napoleon. On the 29th Floréal, of the year X., the Legislative Assembly passed a decree, ordaining that "a canal should be opened to turn the river Ourcq, and that this river should be conveyed to Paris, into a basin near La Villette." The first works were commenced in 1801, and, on the 15th of September of the following year, M. Girard assumed the direction.

Carried on with activity till 1812, suspended by national disasters, and again recommenced at a much more recent period, this work was completed in 1837. After the completion of the canal of Ourcq, after the establishment of eighteen steam engines, which drew water from the Seine, and the boring of the Artesian wells of Grenelle and Passy, the city of Paris received, in the year 1864, 195,000 cubic metres of water a day.

This water, if analyzed, will be found to be in the following proportions:

Water from the Ourcq,................	105,000
Water from the Seine,................	80,000
Water from the Artesian wells,........	10,000
Total,	195,000

A calculation which would establish a mean of three gallons to each inhabitant in 24 hours, a quantity very inferior to that which is received by other great cities, as may be seen by the following table:

GALLONS TO EACH INHABITANT EVERY TWENTY-FOUR HOURS.

Modern Rome,..........................	207
New York,.............................	124½
Carcassonne,..........................	87½
Marseilles,...........................	40½
Genoa,................................	30½
Glasgow, ...	22
London,...............................	20
Philadelphia,.........................	20
Geneva,...............................	16
Edinburgh,............................	11

In almost every country and city of the world, where any attention is paid to the well-being of the citizens, the important question of water is prominent. Few of the great capitals of Europe are without more or less magnificent works, supplying an abundant quantity; but they are even surpassed by the lavish prodigality of our own cities. That eminently wise and practical statesman, Benjamin Franklin, suggested, as far back as 1764, after a visitation of yellow fever, the importance of furnishing Philadelphia with a copious supply of pure, fresh water, and in his will urged the matter upon the authorities of the city. Before the end of the

View of the Schuylkill near Philadelphia.

century measures were taken to carry out the suggestion, and the famous water works of the city, drawing an inexhaustible supply from the Schuylkill, and enlarged from time to time with the increase of the demand and the growth of the city, are now able to furnish over forty million gallons a day, besides providing numerous steam engines and manufactories with the water they require.

On the summit of an eminence, known as the Mount, and towering more than 60 feet above the most elevated part of the city, the falls and the river below, an area of nearly 30 acres holds the supply of water for a large portion of the city. The whole is divided into four separate reservoirs, capable of containing over 27,000,000 gallons, and one of these is again divided into three sections for the purpose filtration. Like every other part of these famous Fairmount Water-works, as they are appropriately called, this reservoir also is beautifully kept, and surrounded by a gravelled walk from which a superb view of the city and the adjoining country may be obtained. The four reservoirs are twèlve feet deep, lined with stone and paved with brick, laid in a bed of clay, in strong cement, and made water-tight. The river not having sufficient head to fill the basins, the water has to be raised by forcing pumps from a place where the Schuylkill is dammed across. These pumps are ingeniously made to be moved by the current of the river itself, and thus the water may be said to rise, after all, by its own force. This dam is 1,600 feet long, and the races cut in solid rock, upward of 400 feet long and 90 wide; each one of the eight pumps employed in the well-houses, als › built of solid stone, is capable of raising one and a half million gallons an hour. Thus the four reservoirs of Fairmount and another large reservoir, capable of holding 37,000,000 gallons, are easily supplied. Nevertheless this amount only suffices for ten wards of the city, others being furnished by the Schuylkill Water-works, above Fairmount and 124 feet above high water, by the Delaware Water-works, on the river of that name, capable of furnishing nine million gallons, and by the 24th Ward Water-works on the Schuylkill, opposite Fairmount, having no reservoir, but a stand-pipe in the shape of a beautiful tower, which is an ornament to the city, and from which a superb view may be obtained. The highest portions of the city are supplied by a new large basin at George's Hill, an eighty acre plot of land, the most picturesque part of Fairmount Park, and so called from Mr. and Mrs. George, who presented this valuable property to the city.

Baltimore has been signally favored by nature in having an almost inexhaustible supply of fresh, pure water in the immediate neighborhood, and being so situated that by the simple use of the existing slope which extends down to the waters of Chesapeake Bay, the precious element may be easily and cheaply brought to every portion of the city. Set upon hills and surrounded by heights pierced on every side by numbers of living springs, it has, besides, its brooks and creeks, Jones' Falls, Gwynn's Falls, Gunpowder Falls, and countless other runs, which by their very name suggest their impetuous character, and the great danger they bring in times of high water. No other city can boast of such a wealth of falls and dams, and the water-power that is placed at its disposal has been stated as being sufficient to work a million looms. Hence, Baltimore is able to do more for the health, comfort and safety of her

FAIRMOUNT WATER WORKS, PHILADELPHIA.

citizens by bestowing upon them a more lavish supply of excellent water than any other city of our land. Her lakes, reservoirs and conduits are far beyond all competition. Thus, Swan Lake, at the head of the Jones' Falls, and about eight miles from the city, extends over 116 acres, and has, since 1861, furnished easily a supply of 500,000,000 gallons. A dam 60 feet thick and 40 feet high, raises the water to the proper height, and an oval conduit of brick and cement carries it thence, a distance of five miles, to the receiving reservoir at Hampden, passing on the way through a tunnel a mile long. This reservoir, 217 feet above the tide, holds nearly 50,000,000 gallons. Mount Royal Reservoir, fed by large pipes laid across the falls and alongside the Northern Central Railway, serves as a base of distribution to the lower parts of the city; it is a beautiful circular basin, five acres in surface and holding 30,000,000 gallons. But even this ample supply was not deemed sufficient, and a new lake has recently been formed on grounds adjoining the south side of Druid Hill Park and purchased by the city authorities. Here a natural basin, vast and convenient, offered an admirable opportunity for beautifying the park with a large lake, and for furnishing at the same time the city with a still greater abundance of water. Druid Lake, as it is called, covers a surface of 55 acres, is at the mouth of the drain-pipe 92 feet deep, and holds 600,000,000 gallons, at a height of 217 feet above the tide. As the daily consumption of water has never been estimated at more than ten million gallons, the total capacity of the new lake alone will suffice for a sixty days' supply, and Baltimore may justly boast of being the best provided with water, of any city in the Union, perhaps in the world.

The city of New York is furnished with its supply of water by what is known as the Croton Aqueduct. This superb structure, a little over forty miles long, from Croton Dam to the receiving reservoir, is, beyond comparison, the most important of all similar modern constructions in extent and magnificence. A dam constructed across the river raises its waters forty feet high, and forms a lake, covering over 400 acres, and containing, with a depth of six feet, 500,000,000 gallons. Hence, without any new supply from the river source, the quantity of water actually at hand could furnish eight million gallons a day for more than two months. Nevertheless the increasing size of the Empire City has made even such a supply inadequate to the demand, and new reservoirs have been added since 1842, when the aqueduct went first into operation. Large storage reservoirs and lakes have also been constructed in Putnam County, at the head waters of Croton River, insuring ample supply for all future wants.

From the dam to Harlem River, a distance of about 33 miles, the aqueduct is built of stone, brick, and cement, carrying over sixty million gallons at the rate of about a mile and a half an hour; it has an inclination of a little over a foot to the mile. When the gigantic structure reaches Harlem River, it changes into what is popularly known as

High Bridge, one of the most magnificent triumphs of engineering skill to be found in this country. Originally the water was conveyed in a three-foot pipe down one bank of the river and up the other: this arrangement, however, was said to interfere with the navigation of the river, and the State Legislature was induced to pass laws which imposed serious restrictions. Thus it became necessary to carry the water over a lofty granite bridge across the river, and the entire valley, from cliff to cliff, at a point where the distance amounts to more than a quarter of a mile. It consists of eight principal arches, eighty feet wide, and with an elevation which gives a hundred feet clear of the river from the lower side. At both ends, however, an additional number of arches with an average span of forty-five feet each, extends the bridge to a total length of 1,460 feet. The whole height of the bridge at high water is 114 feet, and at this enormous elevation the water is carried across in immense iron pipes, of such a diameter that a tall man can conveniently stand upright in them; and over all is a pathway for pedestrians, thus earning for the noble structure a just claim to the title of High Bridge. From thence to the receiving reservoir the pipes pass in an inverted siphon across Manhattan Valley, descending on one side 109 feet, and rising on the opposite bank to within three feet of their previous level.

The receiving reservoir covers an area of over 35 acres, and is capable of containing 150,000,000 gallons of water. Iron pipes of smaller size carry it then a distance of over two miles to the distributing reservoir, the capacity of which is twenty million gallons. It is a superb stone structure, 45 feet above the streets of the city, and covering a little more than four acres; from thence pipes extending to a length of 134 miles convey the water to all the lower parts of the city. As there was some difficulty in supplying the upper parts as well, a new immense reservoir has been constructed on the lofty bank at the southern end of the High Bridge, which will be elevated enough to furnish water to the highest portions of the city. For this purpose a number of powerful engines are employed, and from this point a most extended and beautiful view may be obtained of the city, the bay, and all parts of Westchester County.

The city of Brooklyn, the third in size in the United States, is supplied with excellent water, drawn from natural and artificial ponds, fifteen to twenty miles distant, on Long Island. The water is brought in conduits, or aqueducts of masonry, to East New York, near the city line, where it flows into an immense well. Over this well is an engine house, containing three powerful steam engines, each connected with an enormous pump, capable of raising a thousand gallons (more than thirty-two barrels) of water to a height of 163 feet at every stroke, and of making ten strokes per minute. Two of these pumps are kept in operation the greater part of the time, lifting this water into an immense reservoir on Ridgewood Hill, having a capacity of 150,000,000 gallons, which is also connected with another within the city limits on Prospect Hill, having a capacity of about 20,000,000 gallons. From these two reservoirs, the water is carried to all parts of the city, through 260 miles of iron pipe. The amount of water consumed daily in the year 1870, was 18,013,000 gallons, or an average of about fifty gallons daily for each inhabitant. The cost of raising this water into the reservoirs, was a little more than two cents for each thousand gallons.

The city of Boston draws its supply of water from a sheet of water, once modestly called Long Pond, but since more pretentiously known as Lake Cochituate, at a distance of about 20 miles from the beautiful fountain on Boston Common, and nearly 24 miles from the great reservoir in East Boston. The water is of unusual purity and freshness, and furnished at the rate of seven and a quarter million gallons a day. As this was not deemed ample enough for an increasing population, additional water rights were secured by the provident city, and especially Jamaica Pond, a sheet of water which can furnish, according to the stage of the water, from 28 to 112 million gallons. Cochituate Lake is confined at the outlet by a massive granite dam, and in this is constructed a flume, designed to hold water, eight feet deep. Under a gate-house of hammered granite the aqueduct itself begins and is carried on for 14 miles as a conduit of brick masonry; then it crosses Charles River in a line of iron mains, and finally passes by means of two tunnels through the towns of Newtown and Brookline. The whole line is carried over the country at such a depth as nowhere to interfere with rural occupations, being covered by at least four feet of earth throughout its length, except the culverts in crossing Charles River, and a bridge over a valley in Needham. The two tunnels are especially beautiful works, piercing through porphyritic rock of unusual hardness, and exposed to such influx of water, that seven powerful steam engines had to be kept constantly pumping during the construction. With a descent of only four feet in 14 miles, and a depth of three feet ten inches, the aqueduct nevertheless conveys over 10,000,000 gallons a day. It thus supplies first Brookline Reservoir, a structure covering 38 acres, with a water surface of over 22 acres, and a capacity of 200,000,000 gallons. This was originally a natural depression in the surface, and has only been improved and perfected by engineering skill. Then there are distributing reservoirs at Beacon Hill, back of the State House, built of solid granite; at Chestnut Hill, of recent construction and a favorite popular resort, and on Mount Washington at South Boston—a place formerly known as Dorchester Heights, from which Washington compelled the evacuation of Bosten by the British. Ten public fountains and quite a number of others, provided by the munificence of private citizens, adorn different parts of the city and are supplied by the Cochituate Aqueduct.

A new plan has been pursued by the city of Chicago, which has built, at an expense of nearly half a million, an immense tunnel under the level of Lake Michigan, and thus obtains its daily supply of water. It is raised by pumps in a manner similar to that of Brook-

WATER CARRIERS.

1. Water Carrier of Malaga.
2. Pongo.
3. Water Carrier of Mexico.
4. Water Carrier of Guaymas.
5. French Water Carrier.
6. Arabian Woman at the Fountain.

lyn, and in amount and extent of distributing pipe, is about the same.

What an immense gain this is in comparison with the old-fashioned way of paying water carriers, who sell the precious liquid by the tumbler, in the streets, or carry it, by the pailful, to the top of lofty houses, as is still the custom in Spain and other countries! Even now, many a city in the Old World, possessing no water of its own, that is fit for use, has to fetch it from a great distance; and several cities of Holland, to this day, distribute large quantities of the precious element, in vessels specially built for the purpose. It is a strange sight there, to see boats gliding down the canals, which intersect the towns in all directions, filled with water, which is eagerly sought for by all the citizens, although those who enjoy the blessing of fresh, cool water would not be able to appreciate the insipid beverage, which has been carried about for hours, and often for days.

The engraving opposite shows the different modes of carrying water in different parts of the world. It is probable that these types will soon die out; the best method of supplying water being, beyond all doubt, the construction of an immense aqueduct, which, by means of pipes, brings to all the dwellings—rich and poor—a pure and cold water, instead of a polluted liquid, offered you in a leather bottle, or heated in open buckets.

SEWERS.

In the town, as in the field, drainage is necessary. When once the water has fulfilled its purifying mission, when it has swept the gutters, given drink to the citizens, and brightened up the gardens, it is no longer pure, it has been changed—has grown turbid; it is loaded with putrid matter, and must be removed as speedily as possible, or it will produce disease and death.

There was a time when large portions of England were as dreary as our own Dismal Swamp; the inhabitants built their houses on rising grounds, which were islands when the waters rose, and they scarcely knew what health was. Ague was in every house; and almost the only produce of these fens was water-fowl, an abundance of eels, and leeches enough for all Great Britain. Subsequently, millions of acres were scientifically drained, and hailed as a great triumph of knowledge and skill. Then discoveries followed each other rapidly. It was found out that any superabundance of water is injurious to the soil; its temperature is fatally lowered by the presence of water, and when the roots of plants lodge in stagnant water they become diseased, and can give no vigor to the stem above ground. The structure of the soil is injured by the wet, which causes it to crack and to exclude the air, which roots need as much as water. From such discoveries grew up the practice of agricultural drainage. Now there is no country which carries on agriculture to advantage without its system of arterial drainage, and every valley saved from inundation, every river restored to its natural course, every farm or village made healthy, is so much gain, and for the cost, it is invariably and speedily repaid by the increased value of land and houses, and the improved security of produce.

The sewerage of cities is, at least, of equal importance. The waste liquids and the offal of large towns must not be allowed to accumulate within their walls, or they will inevitably bring disease and death. And yet how little here, also, has yet been done to obey this simple law!

Paris and its system of sewers had formerly but three main outlets,—the Seine, which flowed through it, and two natural drains, one on each bank of the river,—the river Bièvre, and the brook of Ménilmontant, which, after having followed the outer boulevards, joined the Seine at Chaillot. The first covered sewer dates from 1343. At a later period Francis I., being desirous of freeing his palace of Tournelles of the odorous vicinity of a drain, proposed to move towards the market the polluted stream, the offensive odor of which had mounted to the royal nostrils. But the Provost of the Merchants stoutly resisted the will of his Majesty, and absolutely refused to infect the markets and the Rue St. Denis, then inhabited, as he expressed it, by "the flower of the ancient burghers of the aforesaid city."

The Provost was a man of energetic will, who managed to get the better of royalty. Francis not being able to prevent the unsavory emanations from spoiling his court festivals, resolved to shift his quarters, and accordingly began the palace of the Tuileries.

In 1610 Marie de Medicis, feeling anxious lest the health of her subjects should suffer through the contagious maladies which threatened to result from the stagnant, foul contents of the sewers, charged the treasurer of France with the duty of seeing to their cleaning. But notwithstanding the wise recommendations of the queen, no cleaning of the sewers took place save that which heaven accomplished by means of rain, and the evil grew greater and greater each day. There was no water to drink, much less for sweeping the streets and cleaning out the gutters, and the sewers became choked with the offal of the city.

Towards the middle of the eighteenth century the great minister, Turgot, caused the little creek of Ménilmontant, which gave out the most disagreeable and unwholesome exhalations, to be cleared out and bricked up. At the commencement of the present century the sewers were once more all cleared, but the want of water prevented such efforts from being effective. In fact it was not so long ago, that the subterranean arrangements of Paris were still a real source of danger to the public health, a fact proved by a work published in 1824, by Parent Duchâlet on the subject, stating the inconvenience resulting from the then existing system. The author distinguishes in the sewers six different varieties of emanation which are prejudicial to health, betraying themselves severally by their distinct and noisome odors.

The least disagreeable, which is peculiar to the better kind of sewers, is a faint odor, which, though not so disgusting as some of the others, yet enervates and turns the stomach. He next specifies an *ammoniacal odor*, which produces ophthalmia; then a still more dangerous escape of *sulphuretted hydrogen*, which strikes those who venture too near with a sort of asphyxia, known among French workmen by the name of *plomb*. We need not enter into particulars respecting the others, the putrid odor of which suggests reminiscences of a dissecting room, *the smell of soap and water*, which is considered the worst of all, and one which is induced by the number of cattle kept in the metropolis. We may leave to the reader's imagination the injurious effects to health produced by sewers with such abominable odors. In the year 1830 a decided improvement in the sewerage of Paris took place, resulting from the regular cleaning out of the drains by means of the waters of the Ourcq. But this incontestable progress was marred by an evil which still exists. The impure streams which cross in all directions under the city, discharged their horrible load, in the heart of the town, into the Seine itself, where black torrents pollute the banks of the river and poison the air of the neighborhood.

This odious and uncivilized system, worthy only of nations far behind in the march of progress, is at last to disappear. The sewers are in future to discharge their contents into a large reservoir, which will carry the drainage water of Paris down stream, below the bridge of Asnières, after having passed in a tunnel through the subsoil of Clichy.

This work will be the most remarkable, the greatest and the latest of any of the same kind which have been undertaken by any nation.

The *Cloaca Maxima* of ancient Rome, which has hitherto been considered justly the masterpiece of sewerage works, is smaller in its dimensions. The form of the Asnières drain is oval, and its breadth and height exceed fifteen feet.

In a few years' time the numerous ramifications of the subterranean hydraulic system of Paris will all be constructed on the model of a sewer, which now forms a vast tunnel under the Macadamized road of the Boulevard de Sebastopol. During the whole course of this subterranean artery the odor is so slight, that the visitor is able to distinguish the smell which emanates from a neighboring perfumery establishment. An agreeable journey can be made through this subterranean way, either in a boat or by train, and the sense of smell is nowhere subjected to very severe trials. Underneath every house a lower court will be placed in communication with the drain, and the cleaning of sinks and cesspools will be managed underground by means of wagons propelled on iron rails.

These subterranean conduits will also receive the telegraph wires, the water pipes, and perhaps the gas pipes of Paris, and travel will thus never be interrupted when the latter have to be introduced or repaired.

In 1853 Paris and the suburbs counted nearly 120 miles of sewers, which, placed end to end the whole length of the Lyons railway, would have reached the town of Tonnerre. In a few years they will form an immense canal, which, drawn out in a straight line in the direction of Berlin, would enable the Parisians, were they so minded, to invade the Prussian capital underground, to return the unpleasant visit paid by the latter to Paris above ground.

Notwithstanding all these improvements, there is much to be done yet to perfect this vast network of subterranean highways. The impure waters which circulate in their bosom do not, it is true, any longer flow into the Seine in the heart of Paris, but they poison the river below Asnières to the very natural annoyance of those who live on its banks. In the second place, the sewage of the capital, disagreeable and injurious as it is to man, is highly beneficial to plants; it is a source of nourishment, nay, of life for cereals, vegetables, fruits, and all the products of the earth. It is thus a mine of gold, which now is thrown into the sea, and consequently a dead loss to the country from which it comes.

Let us hope that our descendants, carrying to perfection these works which their forefathers commenced, will be able to profit by this now neglected source of wealth—that they will give to the soil the liquid distilled in the veins of our cities and pay these cities back by the cultivation of a new source of prosperity. It is well known that this has long been done near London and the several large cities of England, where the productiveness of land has been increased to an almost fabulous extent by the judicious application of the contents of sewers.

CHAPTER VIII.

ARTESIAN WELLS—SUBTERRANEAN RESERVOIRS.

"It appears to me that a *torsière* (a twist drill) would easily pierce through certain soft stones, and that by that means we might be able to reach a soil of marl, nay even water, and thereby to open wells, which might often rise higher than the level where the point of the drill found them. And this may be the case, provided they come from a higher place than the hole which we have made."—BERNARD DE PALISSY.

IT is not merely from rivers that man can draw the liquid which is so indispensable to his social existence. The ground on which our cities stand, conceals subterranean aquatic treasures, which are ample enough to water entire countries and to quench the thirst of the most densely populated towns; but these Titanic cisterns are protected by rocky layers, which seem to play the part of the dragons of ancient fable. What a persistent warfare, what untiring labor it requires to obtain these treasures, which Nature seems to hide so jealously from our view! The art of discovering these precious liquid veins, of unveiling these sources of latent vitality, has for a long period exercised the fancy of the superstitious, and led to the grossest credulity, having always had a special fascination for the untaught mind. What scores of mediæval magicians and wizards have vainly shaken their mystical divining-rod over an arid and sterile soil, in the hope of finding water! How many a warlock and enchanter has implored without success the aid of those nymphs and genii, who hid from their view the wealth-giving waters of concealed springs! Mankind was then ignorant of the fact that the epidermis of the globe contained inexhaustible sheets of water, precious treasures of water-courses everywhere. No one suspected that by merely digging into the soil he would be brought into contact with immense reservoirs, from whence he might draw both riches and fertility.

Antiquity was fully alive to the vast importance of this great problem, and the sacred prophet is represented in Holy Writ as appearing in the fullness of his power and majesty, when smiting the rock to let the living waters gush forth.

For fountains and springs have, from time immemorial, been cherished and almost revered by all nations of the earth. In the vast steppes of the East the few wells are the centres around which cluster whole tribes of nomads; in the desert, the life of entire caravans depends upon their reaching the long looked-for well before they are utterly exhausted. Bloody battles have been fought, age after age, for the possession of wells, from the time of Jacob's well, near Shechem, to our own day. Where the blessed water hides in the ground, grass springs up, the palm and the tamarisk flourish, man settles down, changes his tent into a permanent hut, and becomes the founder of a town or a kingdom. In the Pusztas of Hungary, the huge crank that brings the brimming bucket from the deep well is welcomed with loud cheers by the thirsty shepherd and the weary wanderer; in every village and town of the Old World the public fountain is the gathering-place of young and old, who sit and lean around in picturesque groups, and chat and sing, while the restless purling of the water enlivens the silent moonlight night. Persia and China would be forsaken deserts but for their wells, and the Sahara of Africa, as the wastes of our Southwest, owe to the newly sunk wells the only life they possess.

Hence, from time immemorial, also, men have ever sought diligently after the precious element, and, where nature denied them the living spring, they have formed spacious cisterns in the ground, or even excavated rock into vast basins, to contain the waters of the sky. Such artificial storehouses of water are still in use in many a dry country, generally little more than deep pits, lined with wood or stone, and carefully protected against the rays of the sun. In ancient fortresses, as in some of our own forts on the coast, these wells are made bomb-proof, and often fed by the rain or snow from the house-roofs, which is led into them by numerous pipes. In the Old World even the highways offer, at regular distances, fountains of fresh water to the weary traveller and his thirsty cattle, while with us the large cities begin to be adorned with public fountains, the gifts of benevolent persons, among which one in Cincinnati stands pre-eminent, as its water is artificially cooled in summer by passing through many miles of pipes packed in ice, so that it never rises above 40°.

But after all, the occult sciences, the history of pretended miracles, the literature of legends, all offer nothing more imposing than the spectacle of Arago, who, after waiting for years, with unexampled perseverance, for the realization of his theories, at length beheld water rising in the well of Grenelle, bearing witness at once to his genius, and to the accuracy of his predictions.

All the great masses of water which lie upon the surface of the globe meet at different distances from the level of the sea. The waters of some lakes, like that of Lake Pavin, in Auvergne, and of Œschi, in Switzerland, are, as it were, suspended at great elevations, in natural basins, hollowed out of the mountains. The illustration on the next page shows the relative height of various bodies of water, and indicates the enormous difference between their respective levels. We may suppose that these lofty reservoirs possibly penetrate, by their subterranean channels, into the bowels of the earth, and by that means extend to a great distance from the point where they started first. If there be an opening in the soil, above the level of such subterranean sheets of water, the liquid, obedient to the laws of hydrostatics, will rise by the path thus opened for it, and finally reach the level of the reservoir whence it escaped. If the level of the reservoir, on the other hand, be above that of the soil, in which the Artesian well has been bored, the liquid gushes up like an immense jet, and its waters overflow in all directions.

Artificial water-works are, in fact, merely varieties of Artesian wells. Those of the Tuileries, for instance, draw their water from the hills of Chaillot, and rise to a considerable height, merely following the invariable law, which compels water to regain

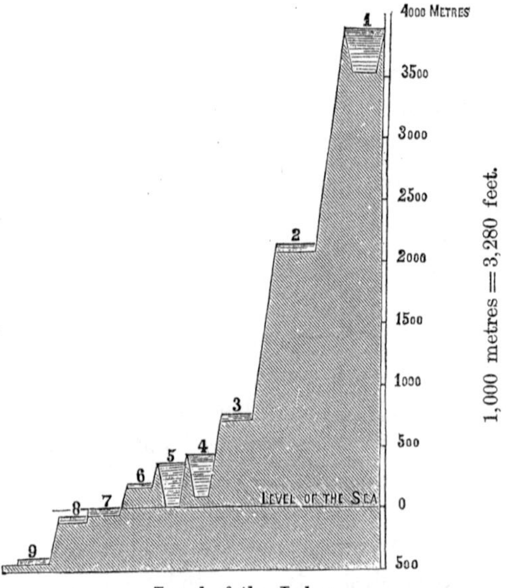

Level of the Lakes.

1, Lake Titicaca. 2, Lake Truball in Switzerland. 3, Lake Walchen. 4, Lake Constance. 5, Lake of Geneva. 6, Lake Superior. 7, Caspian Sea. 8, Lake of Tiberias. 9, The Dead Sea.

the level of its source. If we take a tube, in the shape of the letter U, and pour water or any liquid into one of its branches, we find that the liquid in the other branch has risen to a level exactly equal

—the level of the two liquid columns being always upon exactly the same horizontal plane.

This simple principle has always been regarded as applicable to Artesian wells. In 1761, Cassini said, speaking of the fountains of Modena: "Possibly these waters have travelled by subterranean channels from the heights of the Apennines, a distance of ten miles off."

But all the water situated in the depths of the soil does not rise thus above the surface. There are certain pools which remain inactive in the earthy crust, and which are generally to be found at a slight depth. Woe to the workmen who should stop at these unwholesome and stagnant sheets of water! They would furnish nothing but an impure fluid, incapable of rising to the level of the bore, and are often adulterated with the fetid infiltrations of cities. But let them not lose heart; let them work their way through this muddy water, let them dig unweariyingly; let them force their way far down into the soil, and they are sure to be rewarded in the end, by overcoming all the obstacles which at first it seemed impossible to surmount; and, having penetrated into the bowels of the earth, they will reach pure and transparent streams which the sages of India call "the breasts of the world."

We need not be astonished to meet here the names of the prophets of Brahma; for these sages understood the art of digging wells; and in China there exists to this day an artificial excavation which is well nigh as ancient as the world, and which was originally made for the purpose of finding rock salt. It has a depth of nearly 2,000 feet. The Chinese, our predecessors in so many valuable and useful discoveries, have long understood the art of boring Artesian wells,—works which will certainly attract the admiration of those who refuse to praise anything new, and reserve all their enthusiasm for antiquities and things of olden times.

Artesian wells have been dug in France ever since 1126. The first was excavated in Artois, and

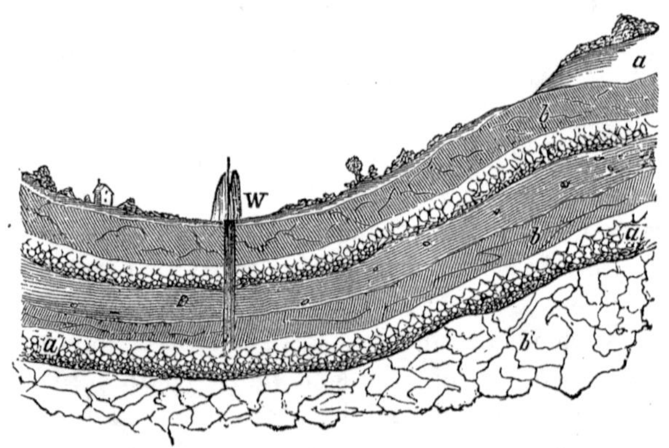

Artesian Well.

W, mouth of the well; *a, b, c*, different strata of the earth's crust through which the well passes.

hence the name of that province has been bestowed on these artificial springs. In the 17th century Cassini caused an Artesian well to be constructed at Fort Urbain, which threw up its water to a height of fifteen feet above the level of the ground. Bernard de Palissy, whose vast intellect left no scientific problem ungrappled with, who may be looked upon as the father of geology, since he was the first to recognize that fossils are neither freaks of nature nor the result of blind chance, but vestiges of annihilated worlds,—this Bernard de Palissy had, as the note at the head of this chapter testifies, also conceived the idea of the Artesian well.

After the well of Artois and that of Cassini, other wells were dug in other localities, in which the water was not far below the soil. The most remarkable results which have been obtained in France have been at Tours, at St. Ouen, at Elbeuf and at Perpignan—nor have England or Germany been slow to imitate the example of France in fetching the precious liquid from the bowels of the earth, while Algeria and parts of Northern Africa begin, by the aid of Artesian wells, to verify the ancient prediction that " the desert shall bloom as the rose."

THE WELL OF GRENELLE.

Five years after the Revolution of July, (1830,) Arago having proved that the sub-soil of Paris was so formed as to collect the subterranean waters which were gathered here from all the surrounding country, and that nature herself seemed to have adopted the system of centralization for the waves also, which travel through the interior of the earth, induced the municipal council to provide for the welfare of the metropolis by having certain wells sunk. Sheets of subterranean water existed beneath the level of the brilliant capital—so Arago and other geologists maintained firmly. But at what depth was the water to be found?

That was a point which no one could decide, and the result of the diggings afterwards proved that these subterranean reservoirs were protected by a formidable stratum, the dimensions of which were worthy of one of the great capitals of the civilized world.

It was soon discovered that the subterranean mass of water having already been utilized for the purpose of feeding countless wells in the neighborhood, no longer possessed sufficient upward power to rise to the level of Paris. Arago, noways disconcerted by this discovery, boldly proposed to dig below this liquid layer, to pierce the deposit of soil formed by the cretaceous ocean, and to reach the green sands, deposits of which appeared on the surface of the soil in the neighborhood of Troyes. The ministers in council were hesitating and perplexed, but Arago assured them of success, and in due time received a commission authorizing him to carry out his bold enterprise.

On the 7th of November, 1833, the machinery which was to achieve one of the noblest works of excavation which have ever perhaps been executed, was erected at Grenelle. The auger was first set in motion by a crane worked by several men, but these were soon replaced by horses, and the direction of the work was confided to M. Mulot, who displayed through the whole undertaking, the most admirable perseverance. What mortifications, what cruel disappointments he had to endure! But he had faith in his scheme, and, certain of ultimate success, he was able without presumption to count on victory.

The first portion of the work was completed without obstacle, but in undertakings of this description it must be borne in mind, that the proverb, "*Il n'y a que le premier pas qui coûte,*" has to be reversed, for here the difficulties increase in proportion as the work advances. Many times during the progress of this long work, which was commenced in 1833, the borer broke and was lost in the well. Imagine a steel implement so heavy that it has to be set in motion by a ram weighing nearly nine tons, falling 1,200 feet to the bottom of a hole less in diameter than a man's body! What a perplexity to the machinist, who has not only lost his tool, but finds the road which he ought to open into the ground blocked up by an enormous mass of steel! How is he ever to recover through a dark hole full of mud and full of water fragments of iron, firmly fixed in stone? The only thing to be done is to throw into this gulf hooks or spoons, instruments which after all, work by chance only, for they are hundreds of feet away from the hand that directs them.

To appreciate the difficulties fully, we ought to hear Arago himself relate the thousand hindrances which he found in his work, and the varied emotions to which they gave occasion.* On the 30th of November, 1834, the screw broke in seven pieces, and could only be gotten out again three months later. Again, four years after the commencement of the

---

See Arago's Works. Artesian Wells.

work, in 1837, the auger fell for the third time, a cable having snapped off suddenly. This time the work was delayed for the space of 14 months. Nothing yet announced that it was approaching completion. The funds were nearly exhausted and still no water had been discovered. Those who were hostile to the undertaking, Arago's own enemies and almost the entire press, did not cease to heap sarcasm and ridicule upon the poor workers. It looked, indeed, as if this deplorable accident would certainly put an end to the whole undertaking. But Arago, fertile in resources and possessed of a persuasive eloquence, succeeded in reviving the confidence of those on whose aid he depended for the carrying out of his work, and in spite of new difficulties constantly arising, the work went on. Daily they came nearer and nearer to the precious and longed for liquid.

At length this admirable enterprise reached the wished-for termination.

They had reached a depth of 1,740 feet, when on the 25th of February, 1841, the borer brought up a green sand very wet and clayey, which somewhat revived their hopes. Consequently at the early hour of six the next morning, masters and men were promptly at their posts.

The following day the borer went down easily to the length of 18 inches. It was a good omen. Suddenly the horses which were used in the work experienced a violent shock which shook the whole machinery, and then they turned the crane without making an effort. The director of the work at once cried out, "The auger is broken and we have reached water!" Presently a sharp whistling sound was heard and the water gushed up forcibly high above the spring-work.

Some hours later, Arago, who was attending a sitting of the Chambers, received the following note:

> "MONSIEUR ARAGO,
>
> "We have reached water.
>
> "MULOT."

This was on the 26th of February, 1841, at 32 minutes past two.

The work had been begun on the 4th of November, 1833!

Artesian wells have since been dug in almost every part of the world, some far surpassing in depth and costliness those we have mentioned. These efforts are, however, always slow, difficult and very expensive, and can, therefore, generally only be undertaken where the nature of the soil is well known beforehand and a reasonable certainty exists, that at a given depth water will surely be reached. More than one such enterprise in this country also, has had to be abandoned because the cost exceeded the possible benefits derived even in the most favorable contingency.

UTILIZATION OF THE GENERAL HEAT OF THE GLOBE BY MEANS OF ARTESIAN WELLS.

If we only looked at the estimates which have been made of the expense occasioned by Artesian wells, we should doubtless find much subject for regret; but if we study this great work from the standpoints of experimental science we are obliged to acknowledge that all has turned out as well as could reasonably be expected, on this best of all possible worlds.

For many centuries there has been no end of travellers, who have traversed the earth from one end to the other, and given us descriptions of lands hitherto unknown. As these explorations increase they bring us nearer to the time when we shall accurately know the whole superficial extent of the globe. But it is otherwise with subterranean geography. What mysteries are concealed beneath the terrestrial epidermis? The depths of the earth are as little understood as the depths of the firmament, and we hardly know any more of the constitution of our own planet than of that of the most remote star. And yet how deeply interesting, as well as useful, are these subterranean explorations, and what a grand result it would be could we ever learn to utilize the central heat of our planet!

Volcanoes, hot springs, and Artesian wells, all prove that excessive heat reigns at a certain depth. Enormous expenses are incurred in bringing to the surface of the earth the coal necessary to supply us with heat; would it not be better to bring the heat itself instead of the combustibles which produce it? Is there anything impossible in the idea of sending into the bowels of the earth water which should come back boiling to the surface of the soil, and would supply us with all the steam necessary for our machinery? All things may be accomplished by means of heat. Human labor is replaced by that of a few ounces of coal. By means of fire the inclemencies of the seasons and the inconveniencies of the climate may be warded off; food may be prepared, the growth of vegetables may be aided, new varieties may be raised, and bodies may be decomposed and re-composed.

What we have to do, therefore, is to obtain from the jealous grasp of the earth this precious element, which it possesses in such great abundance, and to remember that Prometheus, when he bestowed fire on man, gave him the empire of the world. The earth is a vast mine of heat which ought not to be left unemployed. We are not here speaking of the well of Maupertuis—that famous well of which Voltaire writes—which was to pierce the globe from one side to the other, in order that we might have the pleasure, when standing upon its edge, of seeing our antipodes, as at the bottom of a vast telescope. We have only to pierce to a depth of four leagues at the most, and then we shall have attained a temperature of boiling water. We are merely adding our weak voice to that of Elie de Beaumont, of Walferdin, and of Babinet, who have more than once invited public attention to this question, without, however, succeeding in their efforts. Will this vast enterprise ever be realized? We cannot tell; nevertheless we cannot but hope that one day another Arago will accomplish this task—gigantic, if we compare it with man's stature, but small indeed, relatively to the diameter of our terrestrial sphere. A great number of geologists and other men of science have already thrown out the idea which we are here reproducing, but the day is perhaps still distant which will enable us to draw from the interior of the earth an inexhaustible supply of boiling water and of motive force.

The clearest truths require to be often repeated, in order to be understood, and the wisest schemes are by no means those that are soonest realized. Yet we have abundant experience of the past, that, by dint of constant asking, we are pretty sure finally to succeed in obtaining what we need, and that, by dint of steadily pursuing an end, we reach it sooner or later. The elder Cato, with his "*Delenda est Carthago,*" is an example to the point.

CHAPTER IX.

THE OASIS IN THE DESERT.

"The water begins to gush....A blessed river has been forced out of the mysterious depths of the earth."—GENERAL DESVAUX.

IF countries endowed with rivers and cool water-courses offer to us the gladdening spectacle of an abundant vegetation and a luxuriant nature, full of exuberant life, with all its enjoyments, arid and dry countries, on the contrary, present nothing to our sight but endless wastes of sand, entirely devoid of verdure, and suggesting no images save those of melancholy and desolation.

But if in the midst of these burning deserts, dried up as they are by the rays of the sun, water comes bursting from the bowels of the earth, these sands no longer remain sterile, but impart life to plants, which rapidly grow up beneath the influence of a beneficent moisture, and that desert-land is speedily covered with a verdure which, spreading its dominions daily, further and further, finally supports numbers of animals, who will make it their abode. This dying, barren, and desolate landscape is changed into a rich and animated scene, full of life, and smiling with the charms of a perennial and generous vegetation. Flowers, fruits, and seeds will be infinitely multiplied, and laughing meadows and rich pastures will take the place of uncultivated deserts and arid plains--of these tracts, which nature seemed to have abandoned, since she had forgotten to fertilize their soil by a single stream.

To give life to the deserts, to break, by the beauty of turf and foliage, the melancholy monotony of naked soil, to people with life these mournful and silent sands,—this is the work which can be effected by means of Artesian wells.

The vast desert of the Sahara has not always been a plain of sand, and the numerous remnants of mollusks, which are to be met with there, teach us plainly that its site was once covered by the sea. On some of its hills we can even discern traces of the action of the waves, and the sand is usually impregnated with salt. Here and there, indeed, salt lakes still spread forth their waters, like the last drops which adhere to the bottom of a vessel which has been emptied.

It is possible that the ocean, which formerly covered the desert, dried up slowly, and, probably rose gradually, drop by drop, in the form of vapor. Rain is very rare in these burning zones; the few mountains found there are but seldom covered with a diadem of snow, and the skies refuse to these regions the water of which they are so prodigal in other countries. The water distilled by the sun is never replaced, and thus, in time, this great inland sea was dried up. A sea of sand replaced the liquid ocean, and the eye of the traveller who crosses these deserts reaches a distant horizon without perceiving aught but an infinitely prolonged plain—a vast sheet, of a yellowish hue, without boundary and without limit.

But beneath the sand of this desert lies a sheet of water which man can utilize; and, for many years, modes for digging Artesian wells have been known to the native tribes who inhabit the borders of the Sahara. Tools of the rudest character suffice them; armed with the most indomitable patience, they slowly dig into the ground, little by little, till they make their way deeper, scooping away and throwing upon the edge of the hole the soil they dig out, and, thanks to their marvellous perseverance, they often reach a depth of 100 or 200 fathoms. After having successively pierced layers of sand, gravel, and clay, they attain a schistous crust, not unlike slate. This last envelope covers the precious liquid,—the Bahr-el-Tahani (*sea below the earth*): they have only to dig through one layer more—the last effort of these indefatigable workers—and the water bursts forth with such upward force, that the diggers, taken by surprise at the last moment, sometimes lose their lives in their final effort.

But if they frequently risk their lives, they have the consolation of seeing themselves the objects of absolute veneration on the part of their countrymen. They form a corporation known under the name of the "R'tass," and the severest labor is for them the object of a noble ambition. They are deterred by no obstacle, and the work which is commenced in ground perfectly dry, frequently has to be done in the end under the pressure of a column of water 180 feet in thickness, due to the waters of infiltration which it is impossible to avoid.

If we picture to ourselves these unhappy natives compelled to plunge into the liquid and remain in it four or five minutes, to labor in muddy water and to bring up the few handfuls of sand which they have extracted, hoisting themselves up by means of a rope, we are struck with admiration for a perseverance so indomitable and so marvellous in a trying climate.

When their task is rendered difficult in this manner, they are unable to accomplish in one day more than two or three descents, and hence the work proceeds with discouraging slowness. The work of several years is often not sufficient to enable them to reach the wished-for goal, and to snatch from the sand of the desert the water with which it seems loth to part.

"Sometimes," says Mr. Charles Laurent, "it happens that a well-digger is suffocated, either before he reaches the bottom or during his work, or whilst he is reascending to the light of day. One of his companions, who holds alternately the cord which serves at the same time for direction and for signal, being warned by its shaking that his companion is in danger, hastens to his assistance, whilst another replaces him at his post of observation, which he in turn has to quit at a new signal calling him down to rescue both of his comrades."

Very different, indeed, is this rude and elementary process from the scientific method of digging wells;

different, indeed, these handfuls of sand extracted with so much difficulty from the masses of rock, which occasionally break our most formidable drills and require strong steel spoons for the recovery of the mere fragments. Nothing can resist our powerful implements, whereas a somewhat harder layer of stone is to the native engineers an insurmountable barrier.

The well once dug, the walls are strengthened by a few planks to prevent their falling in, notwithstanding which precaution these wells are not long lived, being quite ephemeral in their nature. In a very short time the moist soil caves in, and the blessed spring is closed up forever, its opening having become obstructed. Near the fountain a husbandman has been enabled to live, finding there the subsistence needful for his existence; a few palm trees having protected by their foliage the first growths of the desert. But the well is choked up, the oasis is destroyed. The burning wind of the desert will soon destroy these scant traces of human industry, and verdure and cultivation once more disappear. The sand will cover with a thick mantle these remains and ruins which are the only evidence now of marvellous persevering efforts.

Two French engineers, Messrs. Fournel and Dubocq, were the first who determined upon substituting our methods of boring for the simple and primitive process of the Arabs. General Desvaux gave them a cordial and powerful support. "Chance,' says this officer in a report addressed to the governor of Africa, "led me to the summit of a sand-hill, which overlooks the entire oasis. It would be totally impossible for me to describe to you the impression made upon me by the sight of this oasis. On my right were verdant palm trees, cultivated gardens, in a word, life; while on my left were sterility, desolation, death. I sent for the Sheik and the inhabitants, and was informed by them that the reason of this difference consisted in the northern well being choked up by sand, while waste waters prevented their digging new wells. In a few days the whole population was to scatter, forsaking their houses and the graveyards where their fathers slept. I saw in a moment what valuable results would accrue to this country from Artesian wells, and thanks to you, who have so kindly received and encouraged my suggestions, life will be restored to many of the oases of the Oued-Rir, and the future is pregnant with hopes of a most cheering character."

In 1855 Mr. Charles Laurent was directed to explore the land for the purpose of studying Artesian borings, and it was not long before an expedition for boring was equipped. M. Jus, a civil engineer, took charge of the works for the well at Philippeville. The implements which this work required, were under great difficulties transported to the Oasis of Tamerna, but at length everything was in train, and on the first of May, the first blow was struck upon the soil of the Sahara. Five weeks later they had reached a depth of 60 metres, when suddenly a terrible noise was heard and an immense torrent burst forth from the bowels of the earth, a torrent so abundant as to furnish 3,500 quarts per second—1,050 more than is discharged by the well of Grenelle!

The workmen thus received an ample reward for their labors, which for more than a month had never been suspended, in spite of the rays of the sun, which raised the mercury to a temperature of 115° in the shade.

The inhabitants of Tamerna and its neighborhood were immediately informed of the good news, and rushed in a body to the spot. Every one wished to be present at the miracle and to see with his own eyes this water which the French had been able to obtain in five weeks, while the natives would have worked as many years and with five times as many laborers. Women and children of all ages rushed towards the gushing spring and drank of it out of the canteens of our soldiers. With frantic delight they embraced one another, and cries of joy broke the silence of the sandy desert.

They did not stop after this happy beginning. This first well set a good example, and in a short time five others were sunk in the desert. The Sahara became enriched with a tribute of over 20,000 gallons per minute, a quantity equivalent to the current of a small river.

At Badna, at Biskara, at Ourlana, new Artesian fountains were dug, and at the present time Eastern Sahara is fertilized by copious springs, which pour upon the arid soil over 300,000 cubic feet of water every 24 hours.

Henceforward, man and civilization will be enabled to invade these immense sandy plains—these vast deserts, which arrest the progress of life in parts of some of the continents—and the human family will spread, thanks to Artesian wells, over regions which have been hitherto held accursed, but which now will be transformed into vast oases. The agency of water will everywhere change the appearance of the hitherto bare soil, and, being judiciously distributed through irrigating canals, it will fertilize the ground that has so long been lying barren.

During the last ten years 550,000 palm trees have sprung up on the soil of the Sahara, rendered fertile by Artesian wells; and these generous trees, by the shade they impart, daily improve the soil, sheltering it from the piercing rays of the burning sun.

Day by day the branches grow larger and spread further, and, in proportion as they do so, cultivation of the ground beneath their shadow becomes easier. Certain parts of Algeria, which formerly suffered from the effects of the simoom, and the silicious soil of which was uniformly covered with utterly sterile sand, are now overspread by a soft envelope of fertile earth, on which apricot trees grow, and from which, even in winter, crops of barley and other grains can be raised.

Too much praise cannot be bestowed on these noble undertakings, which have been crowned with such encouraging success, and the sinking of these wells in the desert may be considered as one of the few lasting and glorious results of the French invasion of Algeria; for this is a purely pacific victory, a hundred times preferable to those which are won at the price of blood. May these works inaugurate a new era, in which the reign of the sword shall give place to battles which are waged solely by industry and agriculture.

The happy results thus obtained in Algeria led the enterprising Khedive of Egypt to order similar efforts to be made in favorable parts of his kingdom, and many a long-abandoned district, once equal to the famous land of Goshen, has once more bloomed forth and produced rich crops, to the infinite relief of the poor Fellahs. But it is not only the immediate profit which rewarded the wise policy of the Viceroy, but the hope of thus being able to oppose a powerful barrier to the daily encroachments of the desert, which, without such energetic means of resistance, threatens to overwhelm, inch by inch, all the fertile lands of the Nile.

We might prolong, *ad infinitum*, our enumeration of the services rendered by water to man, to science, and to industry, and we should never finish, if we had to speak in detail of the multiform uses to which the precious liquid may be applied. Steam, the great motive power, animates those engines which are indispensable now to every branch of industry—steam carries the locomotive along the iron rail; steam drives those enormous vessels through the ocean, which beat the waves with their colossal wheels as with the fins of some formidable marine monster. Thanks to steam, industrious England has multiplied her forces tenfold, so that the work she now accomplishes annually by the aid of steam, is equivalent to that which would be produced by 400,000,000 men!

As a liquid, water turns the mill wheel and grinds our corn. Rivers and canals also assist in effecting communication between provinces and countries. These "moving highways" form the basis of commerce and of the intercourse between nation and nation. Mr. de Lesseps, in cutting the canal across the isthmus of Suez, opens to Europe a highroad to India, and thus uniting the seas which by their union give to civilization a new impulse, he may be considered a worthy representative of modern science.

But all these questions, interesting as they are, must be passed over in silence, lest our picture exceed the prescribed limits of its frame.

Our little book is not, properly speaking, a scientific work, and we have only endeavored to explain a few important facts in the history of one of the most important bodies in nature; we have simply endeavored to sketch the part which it plays in the harmony of the world, the importance of studying it, and the advantage of its employment in industry and hygiene.

Our aim will be accomplished if the reader has without too much fatigue, turned the pages of this little volume, and our utmost hopes are fulfilled if we have been able to inspire him for one instant with admiration for some of the beautiful phenomena of nature, and a few of the leading conquests of science.

Jean Jacques Rousseau pretended that he considered science to have the effect of rendering man guilty and miserable, and avowed his preference for the ignorant man who led a peaceful life, unconcerned about what surrounded him, over the scientific man who interrogated nature. He forgot that it was not in man's own power to resist the noble aspirations which are the prime motives of his life, the desire of knowledge which urges him on, the insatiable craving which will not suffer him to be at rest.

Wherever the waves of the sea strike the shore, the sense of a free and powerful Nature takes hold of us. At the sight of these waves, filled with a world of life, of those seaweeds and fuci which furrow the ocean with a thousand verdant lines, we feel convinced by mysterious intuition, that every thing in the universe obeys eternal and immutable laws. Whenever our eyes gaze upon the face of Nature, our mind abandons itself to sweet reveries, and yielding to the gentle impulse of the thoughts that stir within us, aspires to penetrate into the sphere of the ideal.

The ignorant man may, indeed, enjoy the physical pleasures of material life, but it is not his to enjoy the boundless happiness which Nature reserves for him who comprehends her secrets, and to taste the ineffable joy of the seeker after truth, who succeeds in adding a few lines to the great volume of human knowledge.

Science is an inexhaustible spring, and all men may slake their thirst there ; all may reap ample harvests in her domain; in this spiritual realm there will never be a lack either of fields to reap or of conquests to gain, and the victories of the intellect can never be confined to the narrow limits of a world.

APPENDIX.

Analyses of the Waters of the Principal Mineral Springs of the United States.

ANALYSIS OF CONGRESS SPRING, SARATOGA.

A pint of water contains :	Grains.
Chloride of sodium,	54.30
Hydriodate of soda,	Trace.
Carbonate of soda,	2.00
Bi-carbonate of soda,	Trace.
Carbonate of magnesia,	4.00
Bi-carbonate of magnesia,	Trace.
Carbonate of lime,	18.00
Carbonate of iron,	Trace.
Silica,	Trace.
Hydrobromate of potassa,	Trace.
	78.30

DR. LEWIS C. BECK, *Mineralogy of New York.*

ANALYSIS OF SHARON SPRINGS, SCOHARIE CO., N. Y.

A pint of water contains :	Grains.
Sulphate of magnesia,	2.65
Sulphate of lime,	6.98
Chloride of sodium,	0.14
Chloride of magnesia,	0.15
Hydrosulphuret of sodium, Hydrosulphuret of calcium,	0.14
	10.06

DR. J. R. CHILTON, *New York.*

ANALYSIS OF MAGNESIA SPRING, AT SHARON.

A gallon of water contains:	Grains.
Bi-carbonate of magnesia,	30.5
Sulphate of magnesia,	22.7
Sulphate of lime,	76.0
Hydrosulphates of magnesia and lime	0.5
Chloride of sodium and magnesium	3.0
	132.7

PROF. LAWRENCE REED, *New York.*

ANALYSIS OF AVON NEW SPRING, LIVINGSTON CO., N. Y.

A pint of water contains:	Grains.
Carbonate of lime,	3.37
Sulphate of lime,	0.44
Sulphate of magnesia,	1.01
Sulphate of soda,	4.84
Chloride of sodium,	0.71
	10.37

ANALYSIS OF ROCKBRIDGE ALUM SPRING, ROCKBRIDGE CO., VA.

A gallon of water contains:	Grains.
Sulphate of potash,	1.755
Sulphate of lime,	3.263
Sulphate of magnesia,	1.663
Sulphate of protoxide of iron,	4.863
Alumina,	47.905
Crenate of ammonia,	0.700
Chloride of sodium,	1.008
Silicic acid,	2.840
Free sulphuric acid,	15.224
Carbonic acid,	7.536
	56.876

DR. HAYES, *of New York.*

ANALYSIS OF RED SULPHUR SPRINGS, MONROE CO., VA.

50,000 grains of water contain :	Grains.
Silicious and other earthy matter, ...	6.70
Sulphate of soda, ...	3.55
Sulphate of lime, ...	0.47
Carbonate of lime, ...	4.50
Carbonate of magnesia, ...	4.13
Sulphur compound, ...	7.20
Carbonic acid, ...	2.71
	23.26
Of dissolved gases the same quantity contains :	
Carbonic acid, ...	1.245
Nitrogen, ...	1.497
Oxygen, ...	.260
Hydrosulphuric acid, ...	.086
	3.088

DR. HAYES, *of New York.*

ANALYSIS OF BLUE SULPHUR SPRINGS, GREENBRIER CO., WEST VA.

100 cubic inches contains :	Grains.
Sulphate of lime, ...	20.152
Sulphate of magnesia.	2.760
Sulphate of soda, ...	9.021
Carbonate of lime, ...	2.185
Carbonate of magnesia, ...	0.481
Chloride of magnesium, ...	0.407
Chloride of sodium, ...	1.868
Chloride of calcium, ...	0.005
Peroxide of iron, ...	0.075
Nitrogenized organic matter, ...	3.000
Earthy phosphates, ...	Trace.
Gases in a free state.	Cubic inches.
Sulphuretted hydrogen, ...	0.45
Nitrogen, ...	3.25
Oxygen, ...	0.50
Carbonic acid, ...	2.75

DR. W. B. ROGERS, *of Boston, Mass.*

ANALYSIS OF HARRODSBURG (GREENVILLE) SPRING, KY.

A pint of water contains :	Grains.
Bi-carbonate of magnesia,	2.87
Bi-carbonate of lime,	0.86
Sulphate of magnesia (crystallized)	16.16
Sulphate of lime (crystallized)	11.06
Chloride of sodium,	Trace.
	30.95

ANALYSIS OF SALOON (CHALYBEATE) SPRING, HARRODSBURG, KY.

A pint of water contains :	Grains.
Bi-carbonate of magnesia,	0.43
Bi-carbonate of lime,	4.31
Bi-carbonate of iron,	0.50
Sulphate of magnesia (crystallized),	27.92
Sulphate of lime (crystallized),	20.24
Chloride of sodium,	1.24
	44.60

DR. C. H. RAYMOND, *of Cincinnati, O.*

ANALYSIS OF BLUE LICKS SPRING, KY.

1,000 grains of water contain :	Grains.
Carbonate of lime,	0.3850000
Carbonate of magnesia,	0.0022065
Alumina, phosphate of lime, and ox. iron,	0.0058330
Chloride of sodium,	8.3472930
Chloride of potassium,	0.0226690
Chloride of magnesium,	0.5272000
Bromide of magnesium,	0.0009394
Iodide of magnesium,	0.0007340
Sulphate of lime,	0.5533300
Sulphate of potash,	0.1519190
Silicic acid,	0.2819861

PROFESSOR PETER, *of Louisville, Ky.*

ANALYSIS OF WARM SPRINGS, BUNCOMBE CO., N. C.

Three quarts of water contain :	Grains.
Muriates of lime and magnesia,	4.0
Sulphate of magnesia,	6.0
Sulphate of lime,	14.5
Insoluble residue,	2.5

PROFESSOR E. D. SMITH, *Silliman's Journal.*

ANALYSIS OF BEER SPRING, OREGON.

One quart of water contains :	Grains.
Sulphate of magnesia,	12.10
Sulphate of lime,	2.12
Carbonate of lime,	3.86
Carbonate of magnesia,	3.22
Chloride of calcium,	1.33
Chloride of magnesium,	1.12
Chloride of sodium,	2.24
Vegetable extractive matter,	0.85
	26.84

GENERAL FREMONT'S OFFICIAL REPORT.

ANALYSIS OF BEDFORD (ANDERSON'S) SPRING, BEDFORD CO., PA.

One quart of water contains :	Grains.
Sulphate of magnesia,	20
Sulphate of lime,	3¾
Muriate of soda,	2½
Muriate of lime,	¾
Carbonate of iron,	1¼
Carbonate of lime,	2
	30¼

DR. CHURCH, *of Bedford Springs.*

ANALYSIS OF WHITE SULPHUR SPRINGS, GREENBRIER CO., W. VA.

100 cubic inches of water contain :	Grains.
Sulphate of lime,	31.680
Sulphate of magnesia,	8.241
Sulphate of soda,	4.000
Carbonate of lime,	1.530
Carbonate of magnesia,	0.566
Chloride of magnesium,	0.071
Chloride of calcium,	0.010
Chloride of sodium,	0.226
Protosulphate of iron,	0.069
Sulphate of alumina,	0.012
Earthy phosphates,	Trace.
Nitrogenized organic matter,	5.000

DR. W. B. ROGERS, *of Boston, Mass.*

THE END.

A NEW AND VALUABLE SERIES

For Readers of all Ages and for the School and Family Library.

The Illustrated Library

OF

TRAVEL, EXPLORATION,

AND ADVENTURE.

EDITED BY

BAYARD TAYLOR.

The extraordinary popularity of the ILLUSTRATED LIBRARY OF WONDERS (nearly *one and a half million* copies having been sold in this country and in France) is considered by the publishers a sufficient guarantee of the success of an ILLUSTRATED LIBRARY OF TRAVEL, EXPLORATION, AND ADVENTURE, embracing the same decidedly interesting and permanently valuable features. Upon this new enterprise CHARLES SCRIBNER & Co. will bring to bear all their wide and constantly increasing resources. Neither pains nor expense will be spared in making their new Library not only one of the most elegantly and profusely illustrated works of the day, but at the same time one of the most graphic and fascinating in narrative and description.

Each volume will be complete in itself, and will contain, first, a brief preliminary sketch of the country to which it is devoted; next, such an outline of previous explorations as may be necessary to explain what has been achieved by later ones; and finally, a condensation of one or more of the most important narratives of recent travel, accompanied with illustrations of the scenery, architecture, and life of the races, drawn only from the most authentic sources. An occasional volume will also be introduced in the LIBRARY, detailing the exploits of individual adventurers. The entire series will thus furnish a clear, picturesque, and practical survey of our present knowledge of lands and races as supplied by the accounts of travellers and explorers. The LIBRARY will therefore be both entertaining and instructive to young as well as old, and the publishers intend to make it a necessity in every family of culture and in every private and public library in America. The name of BAYARD TAYLOR as editor is an assurance of the accuracy and high literary character of the publication.

THE INITIAL VOLUME OF

THE ILLUSTRATED LIBRARY OF

TRAVEL, EXPLORATION, AND ADVENTURE

Will be issued about Nov. 15th, and will be devoted to

JAPAN.

It will be Illustrated with a Finely Engraved Map, and more than 30 Beautiful Wood-cuts.

The following volumes are also well advanced, and will be issued at about monthly intervals.

ARABIA, SOUTH AFRICA.

WILD MEN AND WILD BEASTS.

By Lieut.-Col. GORDON CUMMING.

The volumes will be uniform in size (12mo), and also in price ($1.50 each).

☞ *Catalogues, with specimen illustrations, sent on application.*

CHARLES SCRIBNER & CO., 654 Broadway, N. Y.

A NEW SERIES OF

The Illustrated Library of Wonders,

ENLARGED IN SIZE, IN A NEW STYLE OF BINDING, AND EDITED BY PROMINENT AMERICAN AUTHORS.

The extraordinary success of the ILLUSTRATED LIBRARY OF WONDERS has encouraged the publishers to still further efforts to increase the attractions and value of these admirable books. In the new series, which has just been commenced with THE WONDERS OF WATER, the size of the volumes is increased, the style of binding changed, and the successive volumes are edited by distinguished American authors and scientists.

The following volumes will introduce

THE SECOND SERIES OF THE

ILLUSTRATED LIBRARY OF WONDERS.

MOUNTAIN ADVENTURES. (39 Illustrations.) Edited by J. T. HEADLEY.

WONDERS OF ELECTRICITY. Edited by Dr. J. W. ARMSTRONG, President of the State Normal School, Fredonia, N. Y. *In December.*

WONDERS OF VEGETATION. (Over 40 Illustrations.) Edited by Prof. SCHELE DE VERE. *In November.*

WONDERS OF WATER. (64 Illustrations.) Edited by Prof. SCHELE DE VERE. *In November.*

WONDERS OF ENGRAVING. (34 Illustrations.) *Now ready.*

For specimen Illustration, see page 4.

THE FIRST SERIES OF

The Illustrated Library of Wonders

Comprises Twenty Volumes, containing over 1,000 Beautiful Illustrations.

These twenty volumes in cloth, or in half roan, gilt top, are furnished in a black walnut case for $30.00 (the case gratis), or they may be bought singly or in libraries, classified according to their subjects as below, each 1 vol. 12mo. Price per vol. $1.50.

WONDERS OF NATURE.

	No. Illus.
THE HUMAN BODY	43
THE SUBLIME IN NATURE	44
INTELLIGENCE OF ANIMALS	54
THUNDER AND LIGHTNING	39
BOTTOM OF THE SEA	68
THE HEAVENS	48

6 Vols. in a neat box, $9.

WONDERS OF ART.

	No. Illus.
ITALIAN ART	28
EUROPEAN ART	11
ARCHITECTURE	60
GLASS-MAKING	63
WONDERS OF POMPEII	22
EGYPT 3,300 YEARS AGO	40

6 Vols. in a neat box, $9.

WONDERS OF SCIENCE.

	No. Illus.
THE SUN. By Guillemin	58
WONDERS OF HEAT	93
OPTICAL WONDERS	71
WONDERS OF ACOUSTICS	110

4 Vols. in a neat box, $6.

ADVENTURES & EXPLOITS.

	No. Illus.
WONDERFUL ESCAPES	26
BODILY STRENGTH & SKILL	70
BALLOON ASCENTS	30
GREAT HUNTS	22

4 Vols. in a neat box, $6.

☞ Any or all the volumes of the ILLUSTRATED LIBRARY OF WONDERS sent to any address, post or express charges paid, on receipt of the price.

A descriptive Catalogue of the Wonder Library, with specimen illustrations, sent to any address on application.

CHARLES SCRIBNER & CO., 654 Broadway, N. Y

STANDARD WORKS

AT

GREATLY REDUCED PRICES.

	REDUCED FROM	TO
FROUDE'S HISTORY OF ENGLAND. Popular edition. In twelve volumes 12mo. Per vol.	$3 00	$1 25
—— The set in a neat case	36 00	15 00
FROUDE'S SHORT STUDIES ON GREAT SUBJECTS. One volume 12mo	3 00	1 50
MOMMSEN'S HISTORY OF ROME. In four volumes crown 8vo. Per vol	2 50	2 00
—— The set in a neat case	10 00	8 00
DEAN STANLEY'S JEWISH CHURCH. PART I. Maps and Plans. One volume crown 8vo	4 00	2 50
—— PART II. One volume crown 8vo	5 00	2 50
DEAN STANLEY'S EASTERN CHURCH. One vol. crown 8vo.	4 00	2 50
ARCHBISHOP TRENCH'S STUDIES IN THE GOSPELS. One volume large 12mo, cloth	3 00	2 50
LORD DERBY'S TRANSLATION OF HOMER'S ILIAD. Containing all the author's latest revisions and corrections, Two volumes in one	5 00	2 50
FORSYTH'S LIFE OF CICERO. Two volumes in one	5 00	2 50
CONYBEARE & HOWSON'S LIFE AND EPISTLES OF ST. PAUL. Complete and unabridged edition. The two volumes of the London edition in one, with the Text and Notes entire, and the Maps and Illustrations	7 50	3 00
DR. J. ADDISON ALEXANDER'S SERMONS. Two volumes in one, crown 8vo	4 00	2 50
DR. J. W. ALEXANDER'S FAMILIAR LETTERS. Two volumes in one, crown 8vo	4 00	2 50
DR. SCHAFF'S CHRISTIAN CHURCH. Three volumes in two	11 25	7 50
DR. SHEDD'S HISTORY OF CHRISTIAN DOCTRINE. Two volumes 8vo	7 50	5 00
DR. SHEDD'S HOMILETICS. One volume 8vo	3 50	2 50
MAINE'S ANCIENT LAW. One volume crown 8vo	3 00	2 50
BRACE'S RACES OF THE OLD WORLD. One vol. cr. 8vo	2 50	2 00
DR. JNO. LORD'S ANCIENT HISTORY. One volume 12mo	3 00	1 50

These works to be had of all Booksellers, or sent, post-paid, upon receipt of the price, by the publishers,

CHARLES SCRIBNER & CO.,

654 Broadway, New York.

EDINBURGH REVIEW.—"The BEST History of the Roman Republic."

LONDON TIMES.—"BY FAR THE BEST History of the Decline and Fall of the Roman Commonwealth."

NOW READY, VOLUME IV.

OF THE

History of Rome,

FROM THE EARLIEST TIME TO THE PERIOD OF ITS DECLINE.

By Dr. THEODOR MOMMSEN.

Translated, with the author's sanction and additions, by the Rev. W. P. DICKSON, Regius Professor of Biblical Criticism in the University of Glasgow, late Classical Examiner in the University of St. Andrews. With an Introduction by Dr. LEONHARD SCHMITZ, and a copious Index of the whole four volumes, prepared especially for this edition.

REPRINTED FROM THE REVISED LONDON EDITION

Four Volumes crown 8vo. Price per volume, $2.00.

Dr. MOMMSEN has long been known and appreciated through his researches into the languages, laws, and institutions of Ancient Rome and Italy, as the most thoroughly versed scholar now living in these departments of historical investigation. To a wonderfully exact and exhaustive knowledge of these subjects, he unites great powers of generalization, a vigorous, spirited, and exceedingly graphic style and keen analytical powers, which give this history a degree of interest and a permanent value possessed by no other record of the decline and fall of the Roman Commonwealth. "Dr. Mommsen's work," as Dr. Schmitz remarks in the introduction, "though the production of a man of most profound and extensive learning and knowledge of the world, is not as much designed for the professional scholar as for intelligent readers of all classes who take an interest in the history of by-gone ages, and are inclined there to seek information that may guide them safely through the perplexing mazes of modern history."

CRITICAL NOTICES.

"A work of the very highest merit; its learning is exact and profound; its narrative full of genius and skill; its descriptions of men are admirably vivid. We wish to place on record our opinion that Dr. Mommsen's is by far the best history of the Decline and Fall of the Roman Commonwealth."—*London Times.*

"Since the days of Niebuhr, no work on Roman History has appeared that combines so much to attract, instruct, and charm the reader. Its style—a rare quality in a German author—is vigorous, spirited, and animated. Professor Mommsen's work can stand a comparison with the noblest productions of modern history."—*Dr. Schmitz.*

"This is the best history of the Roman Republic, taking the work on the whole—the author's complete mastery of his subject, the variety of his gifts and acquirements, his graphic power in the delineation of national and individual character, and the vivid interest which he inspires in every portion of his book. He is without an equal in his own sphere." —*Edinburgh Review.*

"A book of deepest interest."—*Dean Trench.*

SPECIAL ANNOUNCEMENT.

COMPLETION OF

THE POPULAR EDITION

OF

Froude's History of England,

From the Fall of Wolsey to the Death of Elizabeth.

In Twelve Volumes, 12mo, $1.25 per Volume.

Or the 12 volumes in a neat case for $15. The same in half calf, extra, at $36.

The great merits of this work have secured for it in this handsome but inexpensive form a popular circulation almost without precedent. It is the only history deserving the name of one of the most momentous epochs in English history.

This edition of FROUDE'S HISTORY, containing all the matter of the Library Edition, is a popular one, the price being remarkably low, placing it within the reach of those who are unable to purchase the Library Edition.

It is printed upon good white paper, and the type is large and clear, so that it can be easily read by the weakest of eyes. The binding is substantial and attractive, and the whole work merits the warmest praise.

ALSO NOW READY,

The large paper edition of FROUDE'S HISTORY OF ENGLAND, in twelve volumes. Price per volume, $5.

CRITICAL NOTICES.

"The ease and spirit, the gentleness and force, the grace and energy, the descriptive and passionate power, the unstudied ease, and the consummate art of both imagery and diction which distinguish this remarkable writer, will soon make a place for him among the most interesting and distinguished of those who have attempted to write any portion of the wonderful history of England. Those who have not read any of these volumes can scarcely appreciate, without the trial, how rich a treat is in store for them." — *New York Times.*

"Since Macaulay's first volume, no historical work has appeared which, in brilliance of style as well as in keen analysis of character and events, can compare with the ten volumes of 'Froude's History of England.'" — *New York Independent.*

"The style is excellent,— sound, honest, forcible, singularly perspicuous English; at times, with a sort of picturesque simplicity, pictures dashed off with only a few touches, but perfectly alive. . . . . We have never to read a passage twice. . . . . We see the course of events day by day, not only the more serious and important communications, but the gossip of the hour. . . . . If truth and vivid reality be the perfection of history, much is to be said in favor of this mode of composition." — *London Quarterly.*

THE LIBRARY EDITION OF FROUDE'S HISTORY.

Published in twelve volumes, printed upon heavy tinted paper, and handsomely bound in brown cloth, with gilt side and back, at $3 per volume; in half calf, $5 per volume.

The above volumes sent, post-paid, to any address, by the Publishers, upon receipt of price.

CHARLES SCRIBNER & CO.,

654 Broadway, New York.

THE BIBLE COMMENTARY

(POPULARLY KNOWN IN ENGLAND AS "THE SPEAKER'S COMMENTARY.")

A Plain Explanatory Exposition of the Holy Scriptures for every Bible Reader.

To be published at regular intervals, in royal octavo volumes, at the uniform price of $5.00 *per volume.*

WITH OCCASIONAL ILLUSTRATIONS.

The BIBLE COMMENTARY, the publication of which has just been commenced, by CHARLES SCRIBNER & CO., simultaneously with its appearance in England, had its origin in the widely felt want of a plain explanatory Commentary on the Holy Scriptures, which should be at once more comprehensive and compact than any now published. Projected in 1863, the selection of the scholars to be employed upon it was entrusted to a Committee named by the Speaker of the British House of Commons and the Archbishop of York, and through the agency of this Committee there has been concentrated upon this great work a combination of force such as has not been enlisted in any similar undertaking, in England, since the translation of King James's version of the Bible. Of the THIRTY-SIX DIFFERENT DIVINES who are engaged upon the work, nearly all are widely known in this country as well as in England, for their valuable and extensive contributions to the Literature of the Bible, and in this Commentary they condense their varied learning and their most matured judgments.

The great object of the BIBLE COMMENTARY is to put every general reader and student in full possession of whatever information may be necessary to enable him to understand the Holy Scriptures; to give him, as far as possible, the same advantages as the Scholar, and to supply him with satisfactory answers to objections resting upon misrepresentations or misinterpretations of the text. To secure this end most effectually, the Comment is chiefly explanatory, presenting in a concise and readable form the results of learned investigations carried on during the last half century. When fuller discussions of difficult passages or important subjects are necessary, they are placed at the end of the chapter or volume.

The text is reprinted without alteration, from the Authorized Version of 1611, with marginal references and renderings; but the notes forming this Commentary will embody amended translations of passages proved to be incorrect in that version.

The work will be divided into EIGHT SECTIONS, which it is expected will be comprised in as many volumes, and each volume will be a royal octavo. Typographically, special pains has been taken to adapt the work to the use of older readers and students.

N.B.—The American edition of the Bible Commentary is printed from stereotype plates, duplicated from those upon which the English edition is printed, and it is fully equal to that in every respect.

THE FIRST VOLUME OF

THE BIBLE COMMENTARY

Is now ready. It contains:

THE PENTATEUCH.

The books of which are divided as follows, among the contributors named:

GENESIS	Rt. Rev. E. HAROLD BROWNE, Bishop of Ely, and author of *Exposition of the Thirty-Nine Articles.*
EXODUS	Chap. I-XIX. THE EDITOR.
LEVITICUS	REV. SAMUEL CLARK, M.A.
"	Chap. XX. to the End, and
NUMBERS AND DEUTERONOMY	Rev. T. E. ESPIN, B.D., Warden of Queen's College, Birmingham.

Making one vol. royal 8vo, of nearly 1,000 pages, being the only complete Commentary upon the Pentateuch, in one volume, in the English language. Price in cloth $5.00, less than one-half that of the English edition.

Full prospectuses, with division of sections and names of contributors, sent to any address on application. Single copies sent post-paid, on receipt of price, by

CHARLES SCRIBNER & CO., 654 Broadway, N. Y.

www.ingramcontent.com/pod-product-compliance
Lightning Source LLC
LaVergne TN
LVHW011158110826
845150LV00006B/1255

* 9 7 8 1 4 2 5 5 4 5 5 0 5 *